AF574763

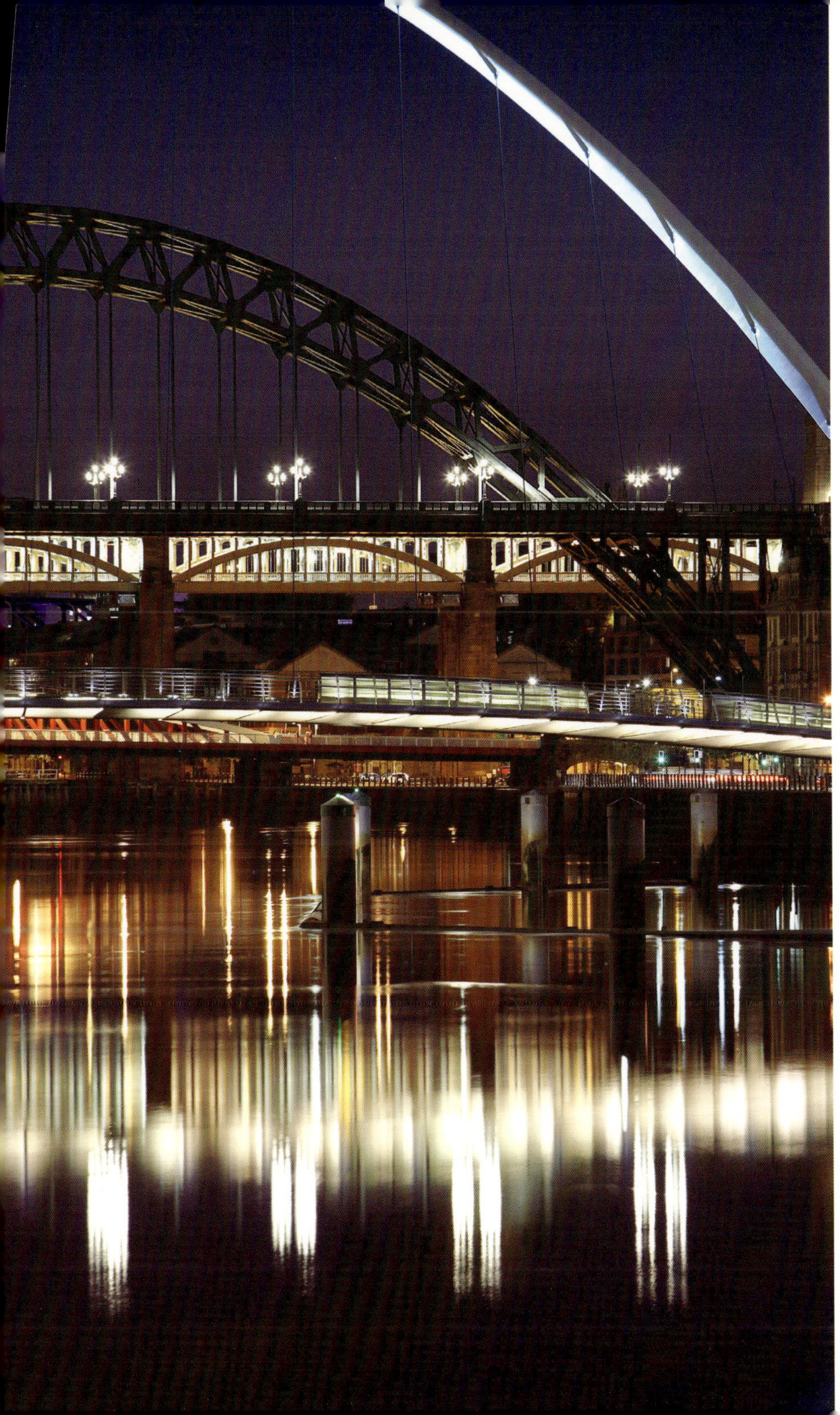

WHILE NEWCASTLE SLEEPS

BY STUART DUNN

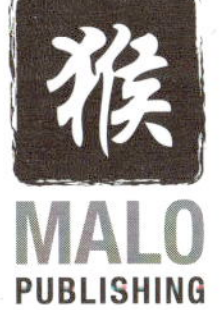

MALO
PUBLISHING

First published in Great Britain in 2012

First Published by
MALO PUBLISHING
19 Beaminster Way, Ouseburn Park, Kenton,
Newcastle upon Tyne, NE3 2QU
www.stuartdunnphotography.com

British Library Cataloguing-in-Publication Data
A CIP record for this title is available from the British Library

ISBN 978-0-9572524-0-0

Publisher, Editor, Author - Stuart Dunn
Designer, Editor - Cristina Dunn
Printed and bound by China Gold Printing Group Limited

INTRODUCTION

Newcastle, a truly captivating city filled with amazing architecture, a vibrant history and the wonderful people that inhabit it. Yet in my opinion to fully appreciate the city in all its glory you have to see it by night.

As the sun sets across the distinctive skyline, shadows elongate, silhouettes emerge creating shapes and reflections that aren't normally apparent. People go home, whilst others come out. The familiar perpetual drone of the city with cars ticking over, buses hissing to a halt, horns beeping, industry moving. Slowly the volume dial is turned down to an almost silent hum. Lights flicker on with an electrical fizz. Colours saturate from the neon and tungsten illuminations and the architecture appears enhanced. An eclectic mix of music reverberates around the city replacing the drone with a vibrant kaleidoscope of sound's, from the back street bars churning out a random array of jazz ridden beats, to the music of the next generation, more repetitive than random, something for everyone. Whilst some people recoil from the night in fear of the unknown, others are drawn to it like a moth to a naked flame.

While Newcastle sleeps the City reveals its true identity, everything that it is during the day is amplified ten fold by night like an alter ego.

I've always loved the City at night, and I've always loved photographing it. Wandering around the city constantly inspired by what I see, the architecture, the variations in light and colour, the people that inhabit it, everything is connected and a sense of romance resides. There appears to be some kind of grand plan or idea, that what looks like a haphazard tapestry of conflicting architecture during the day, somehow makes perfect sense by night. Intentional or not there is something quite special about it.

By Stuart Dunn

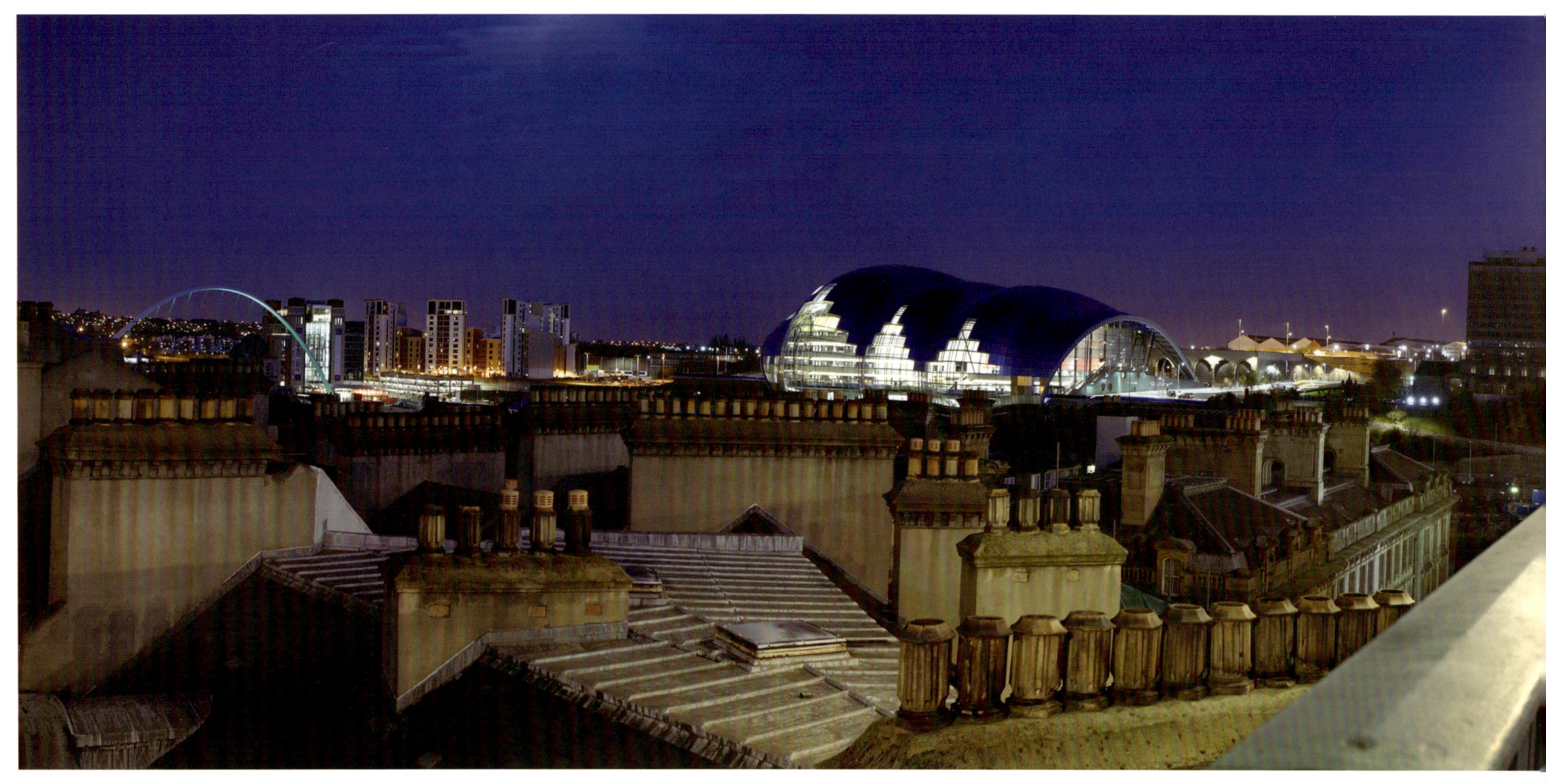

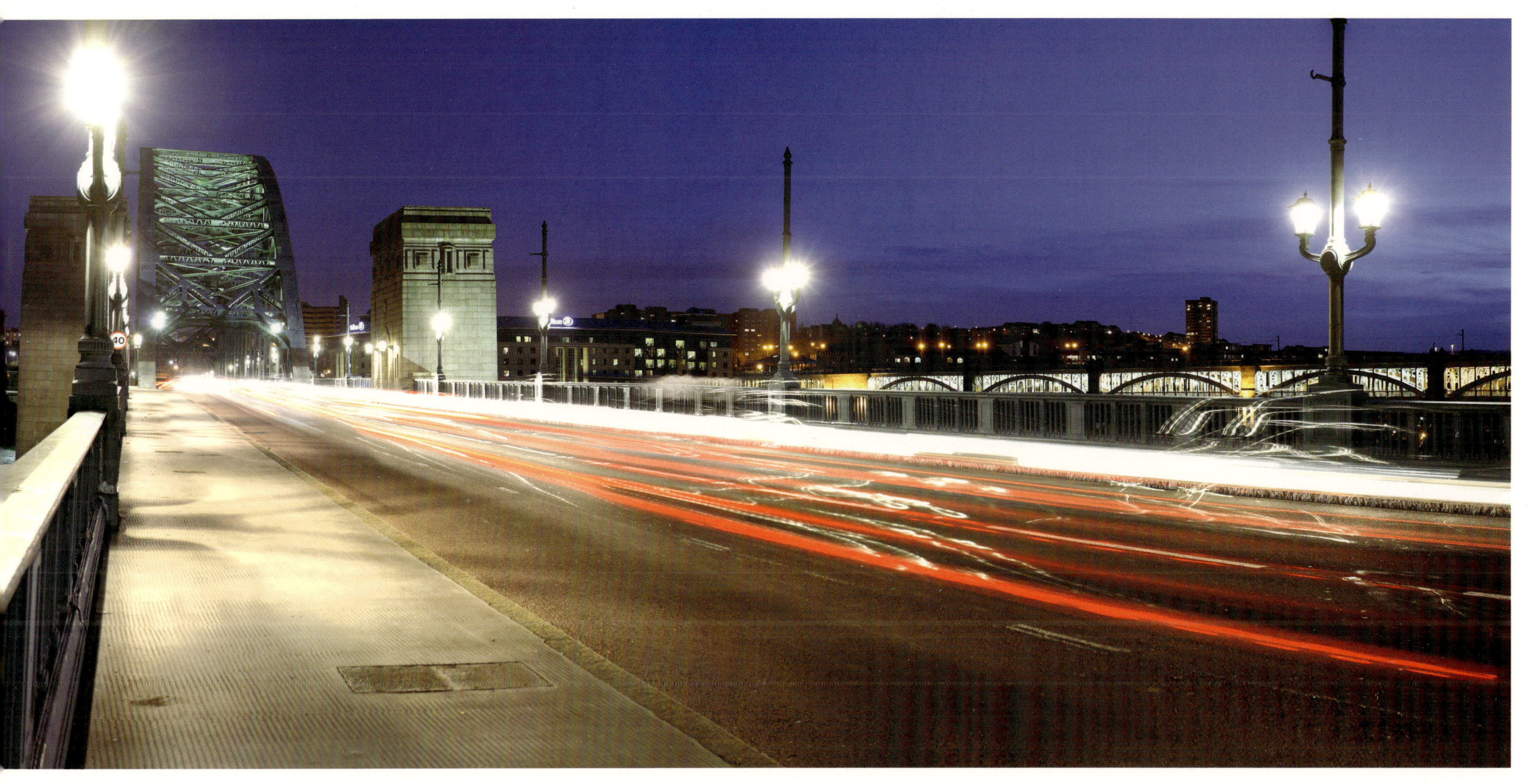
The Tyne Bridge

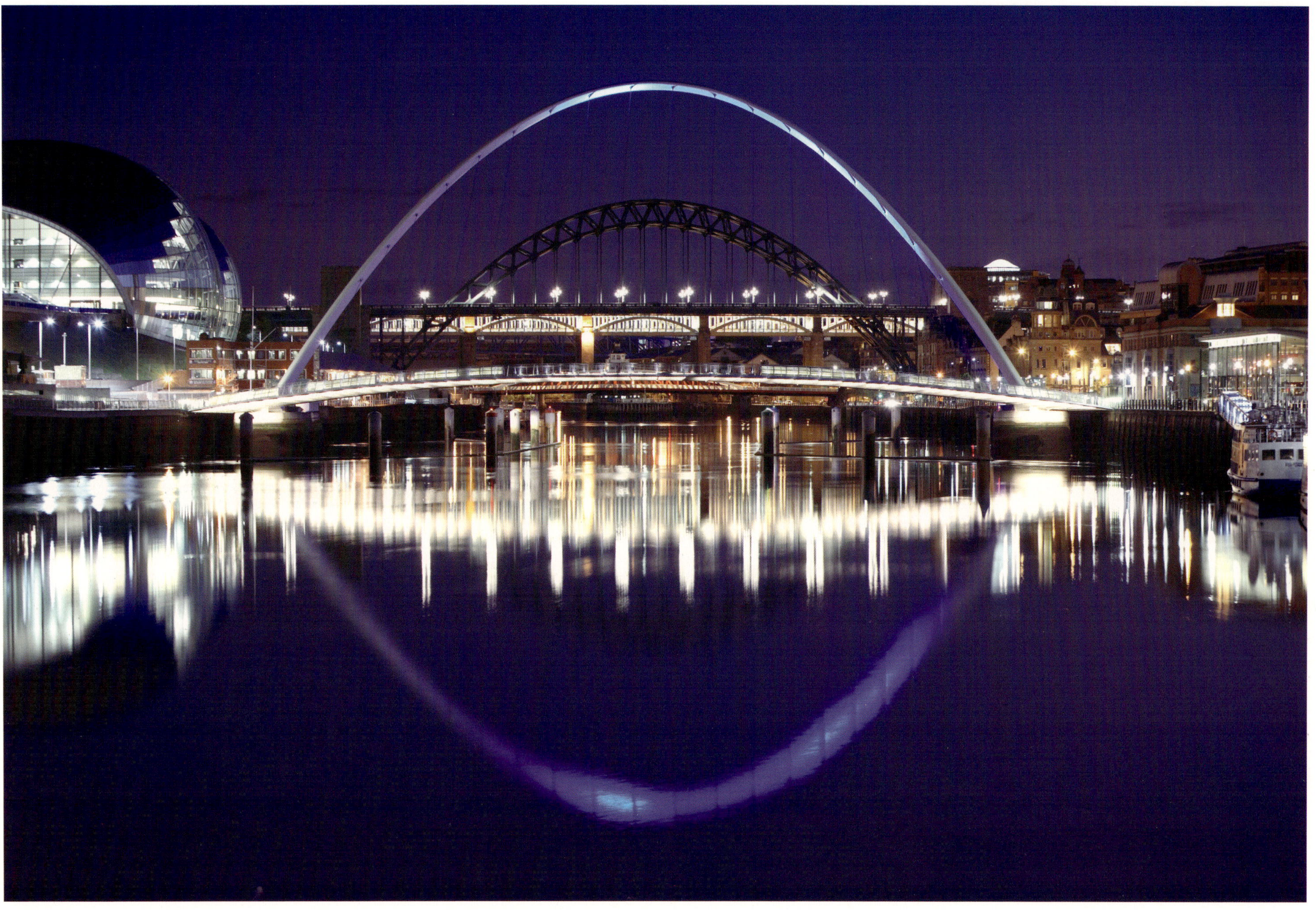

The Tyne

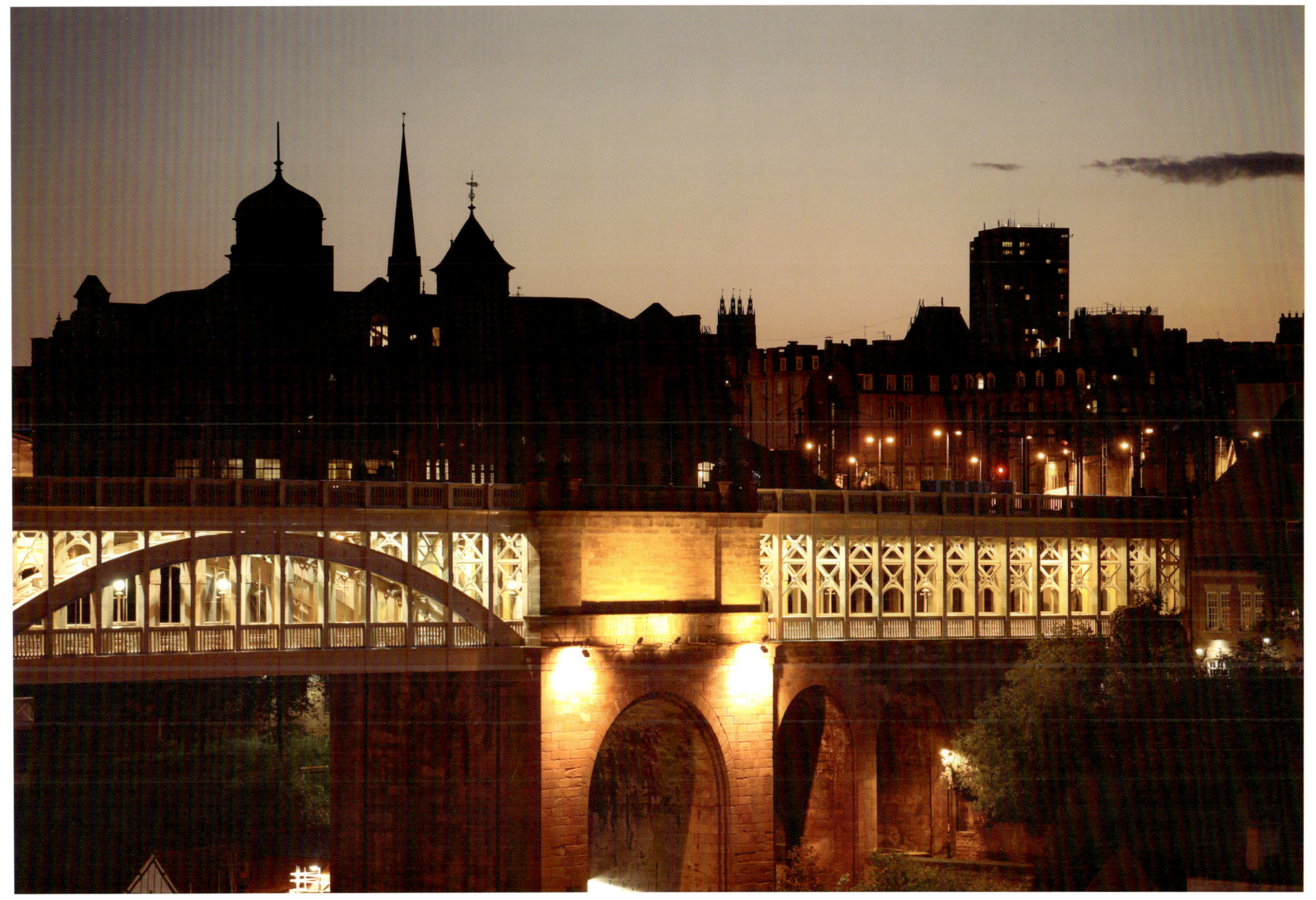

The High Level Bridge

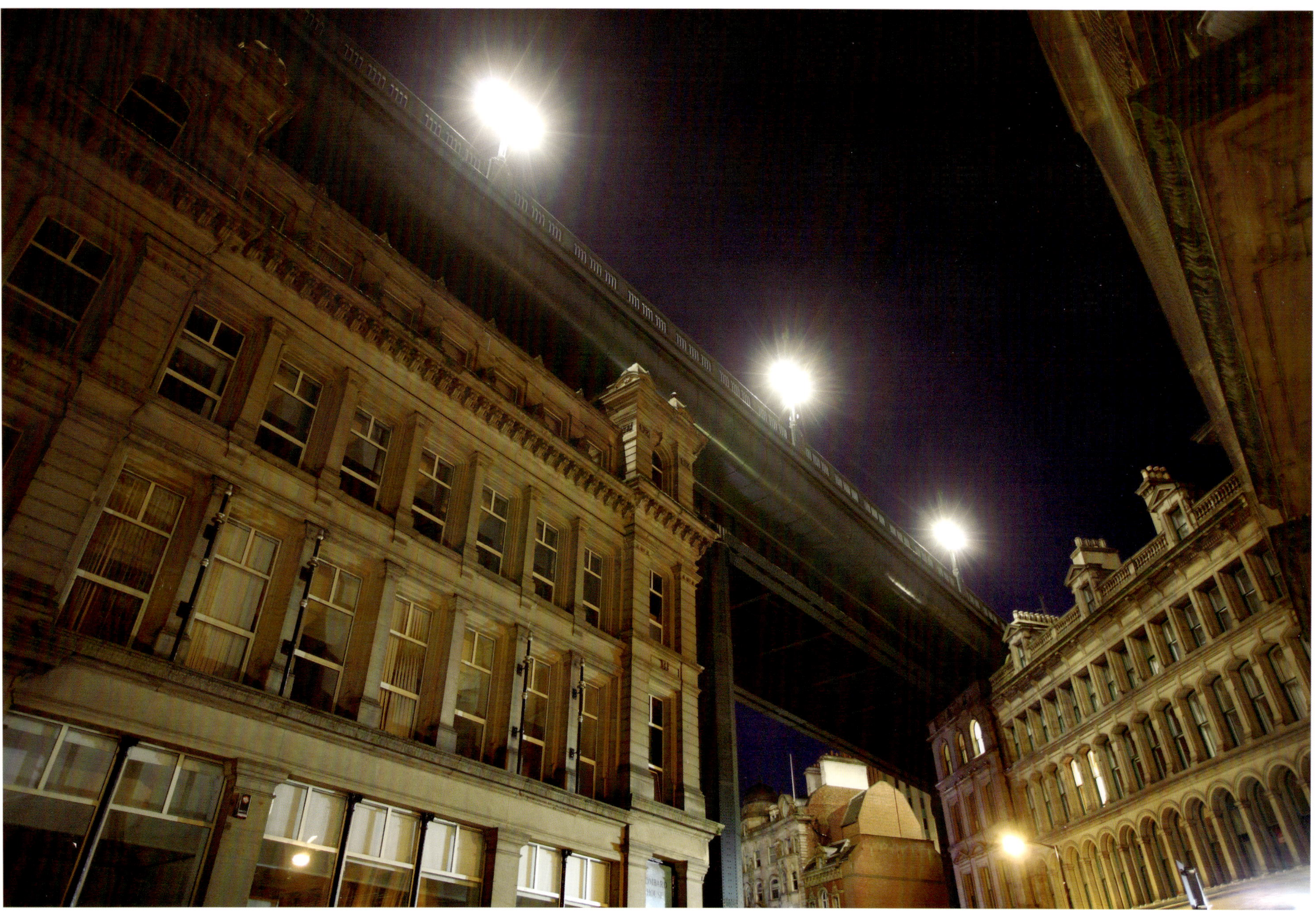

Under the Tyne

Big Wheel at the Hoppings Fair (Town Moor)

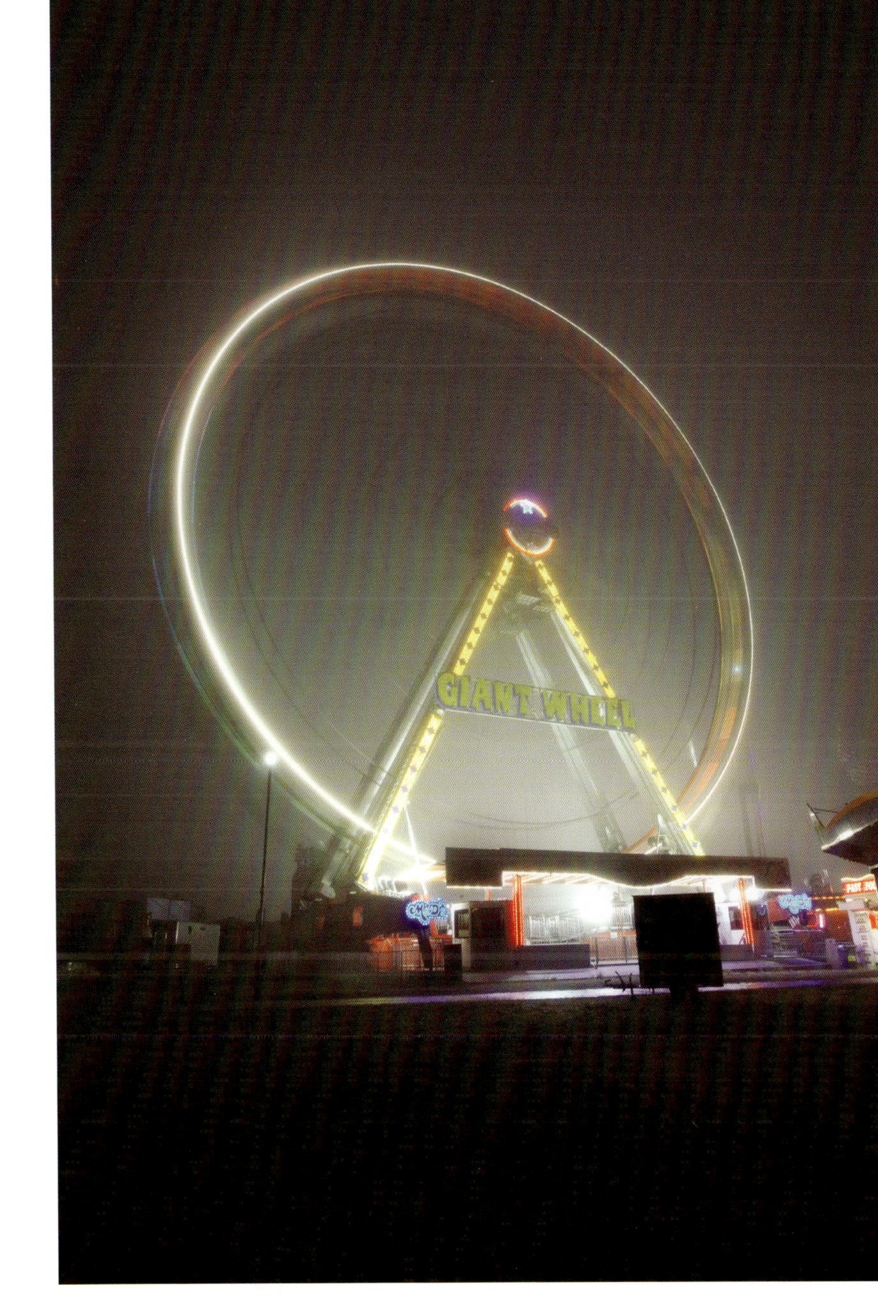

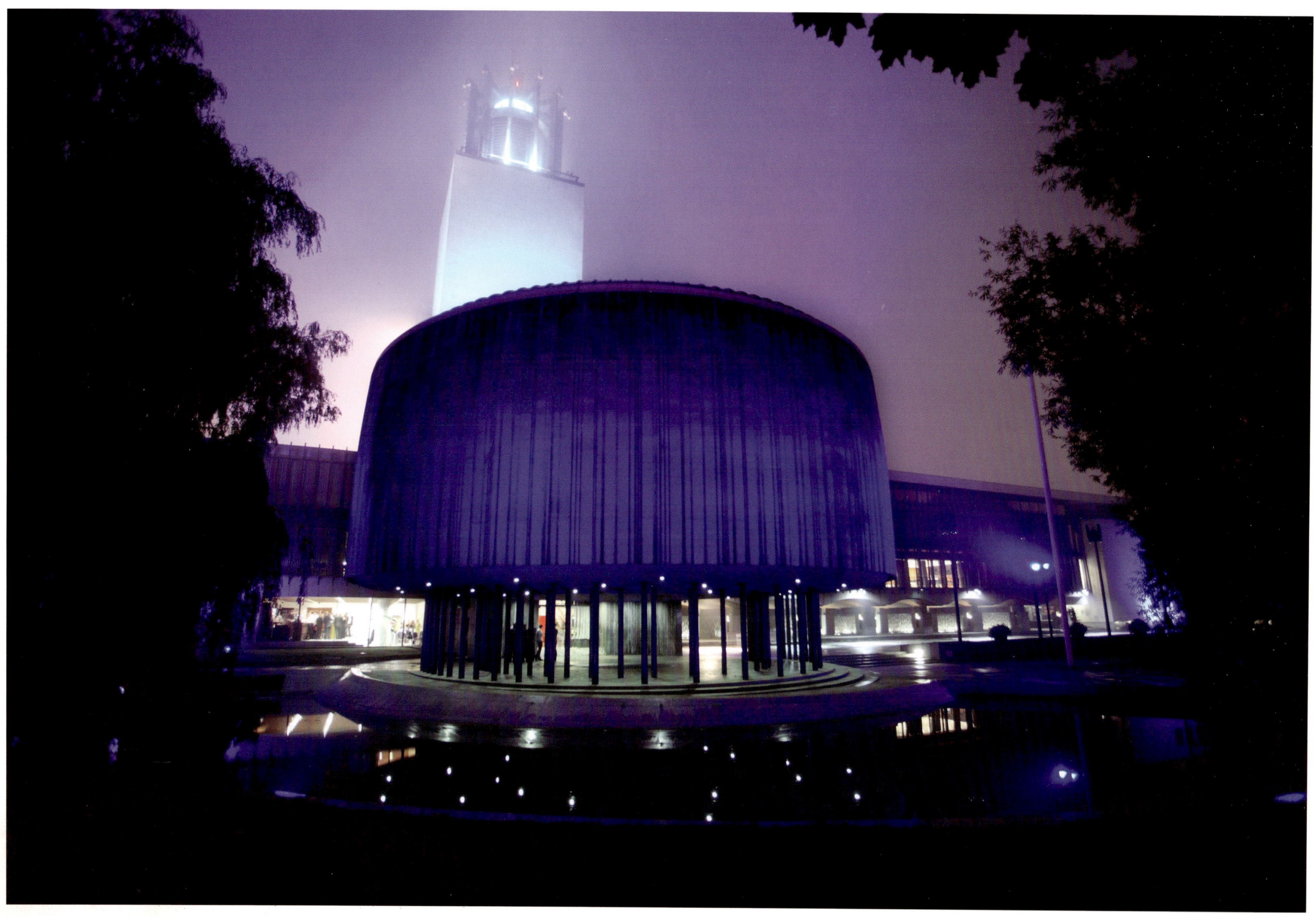

Civic Centre

The Side

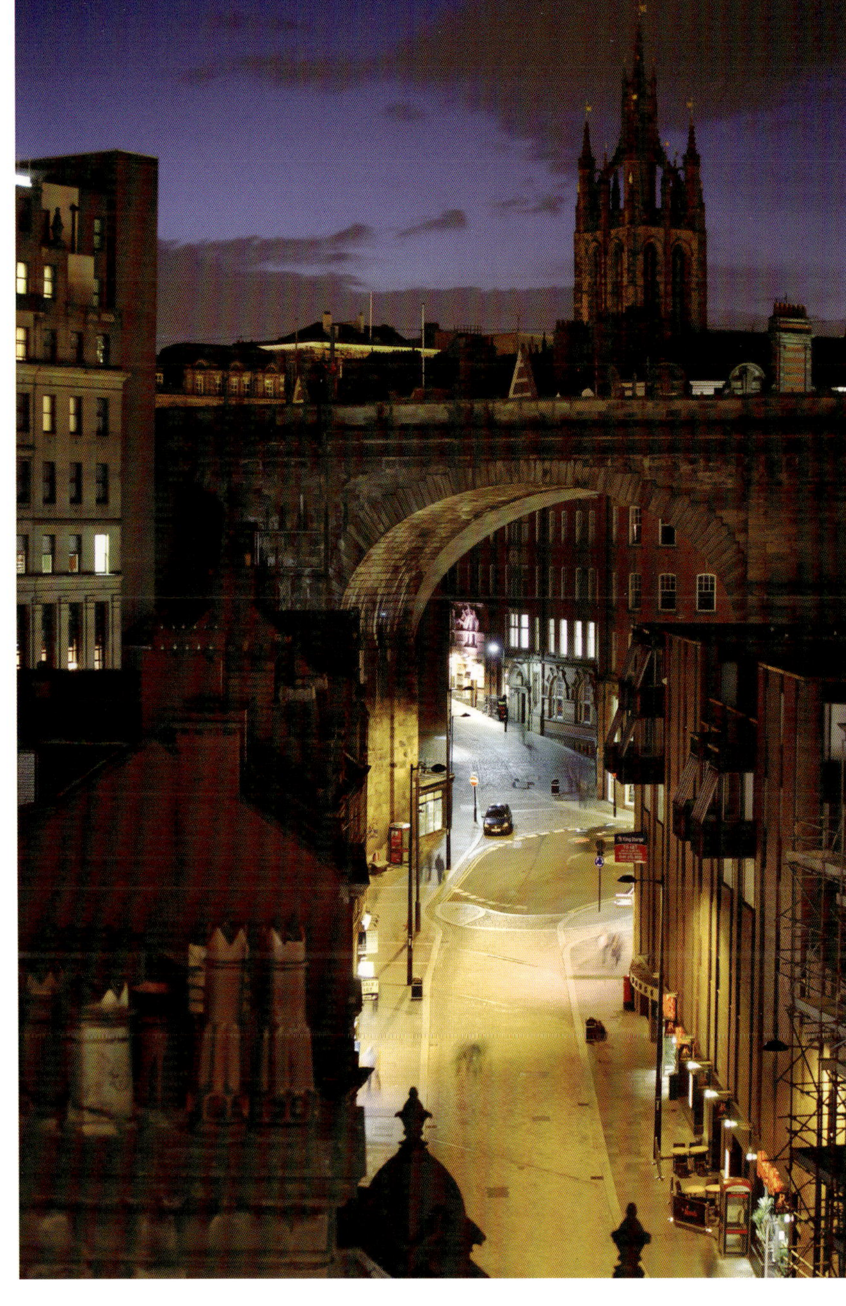

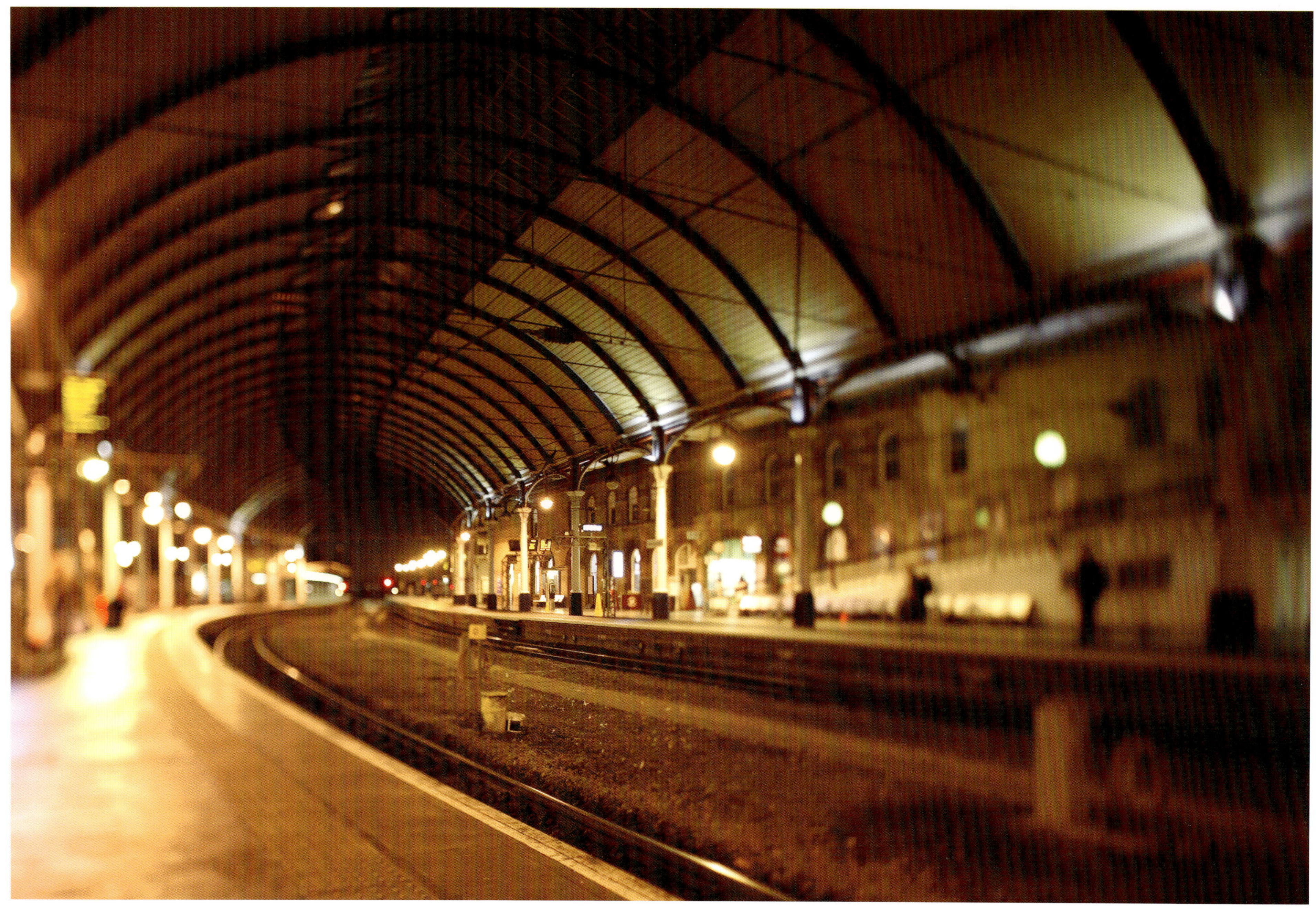

Inside Newcastle Central Station

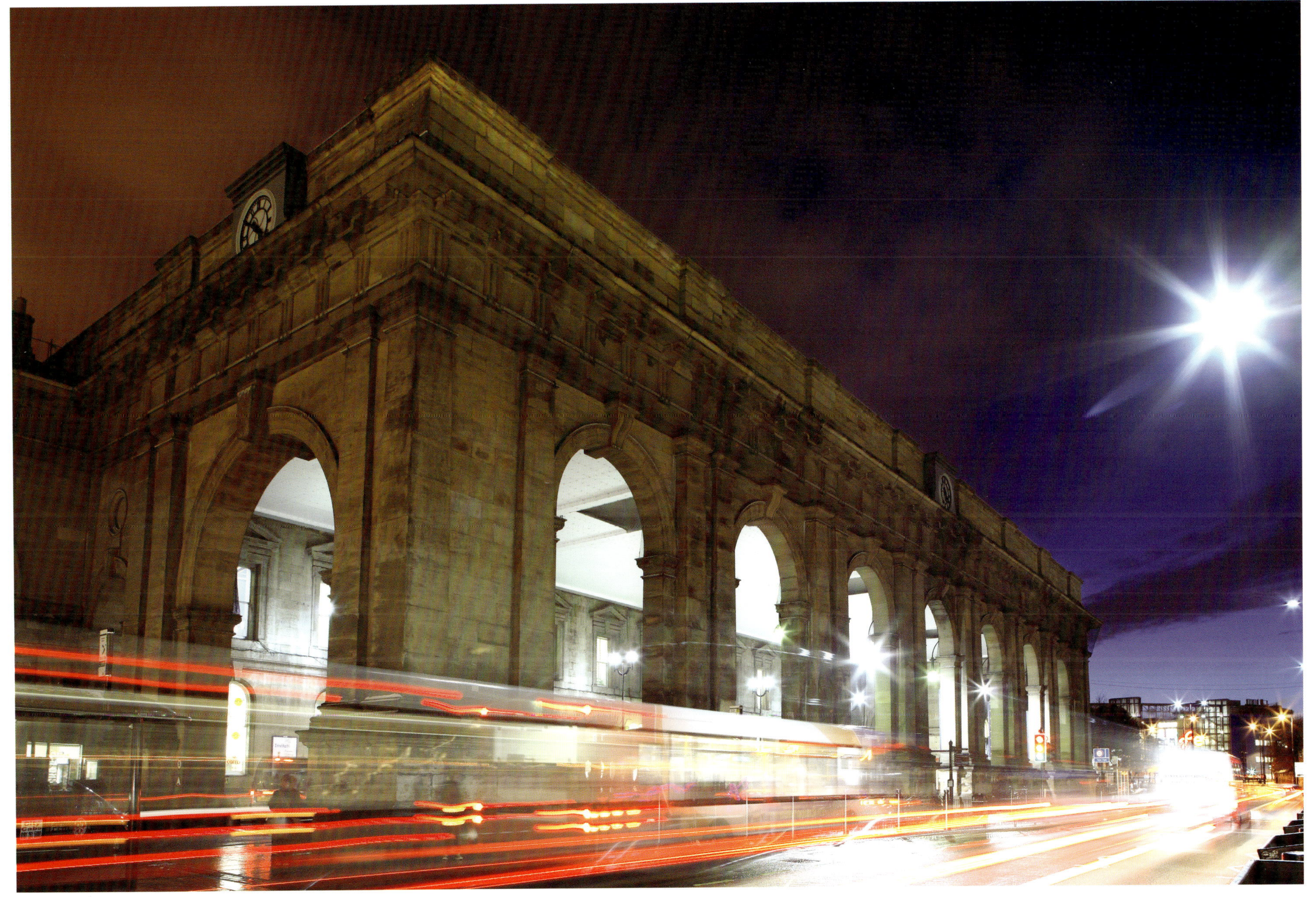

Newcastle Central Station

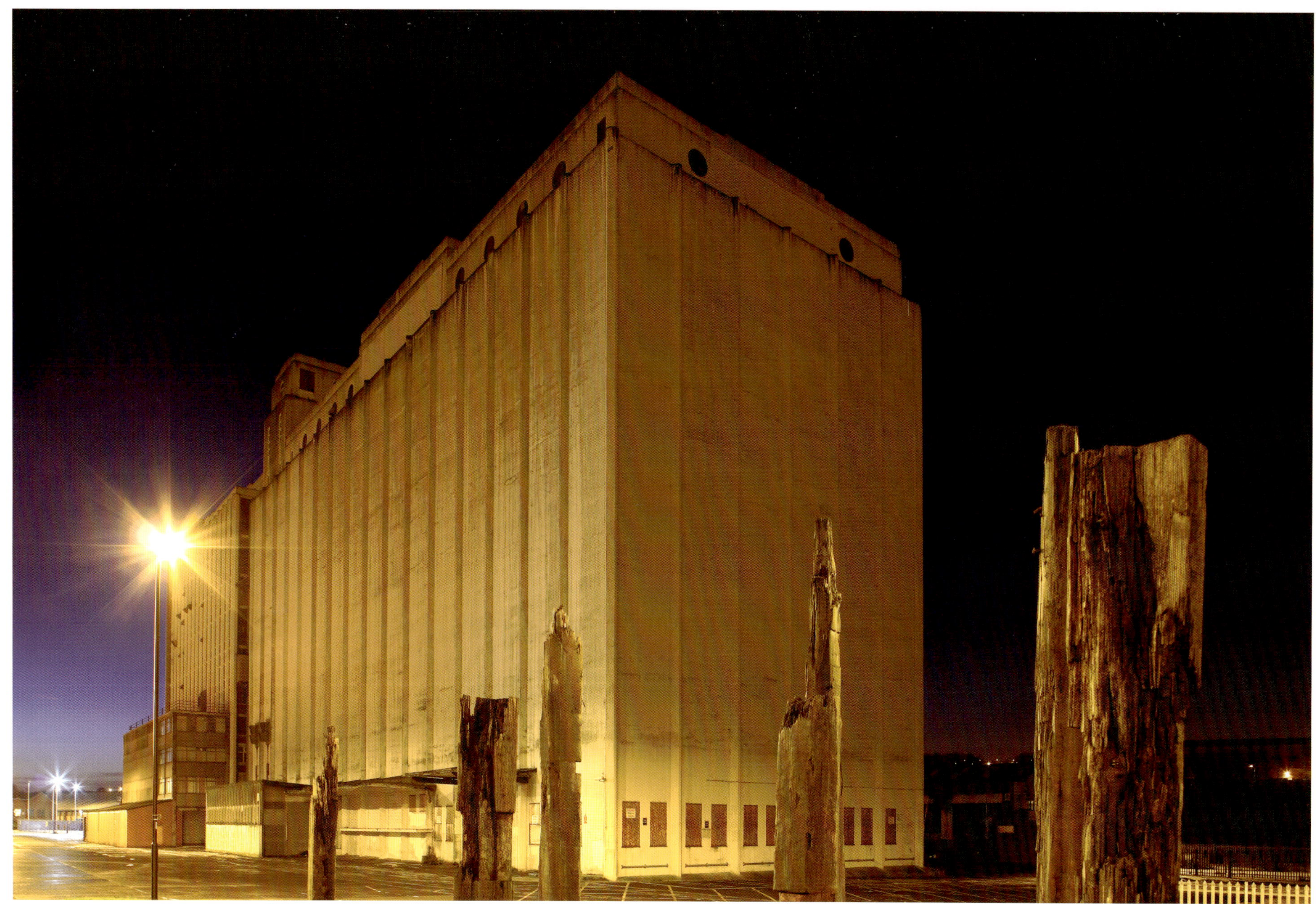

Spillers Tyne Mill

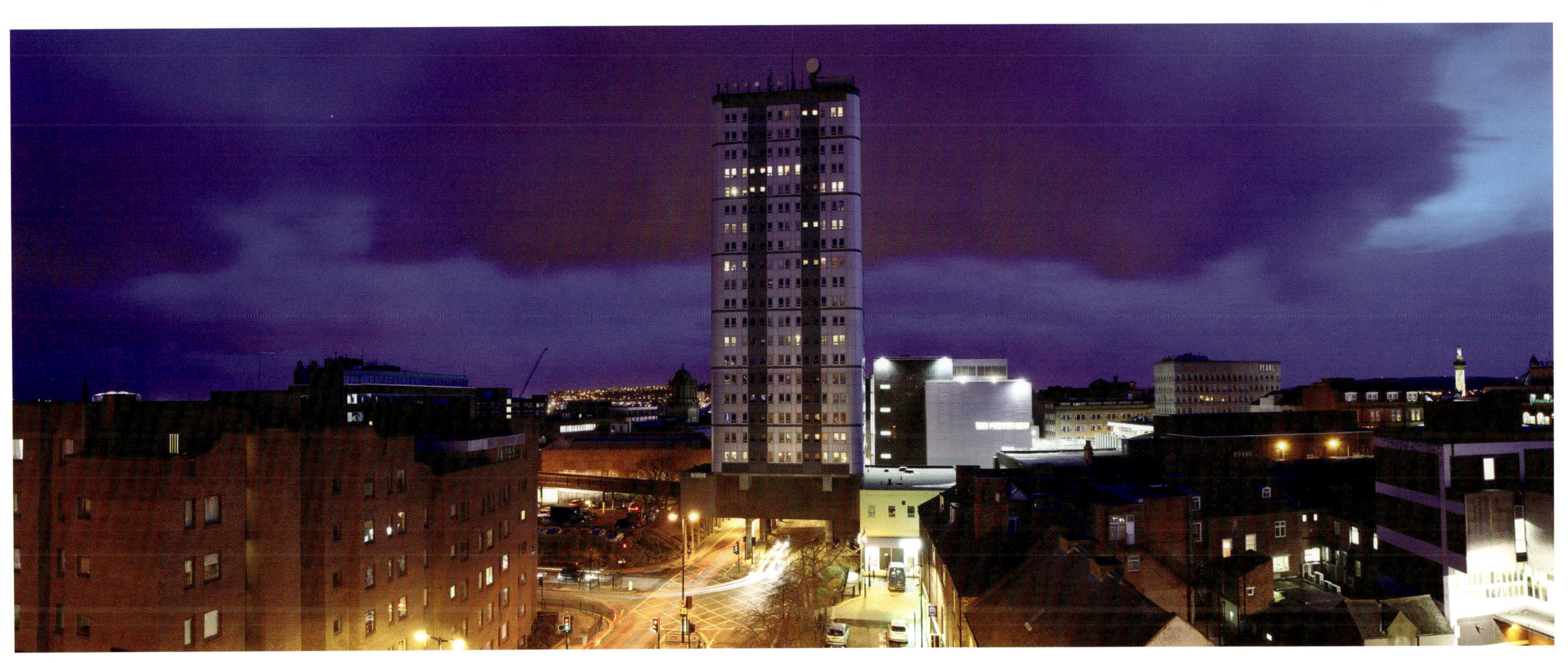

Newcastle Cityscape

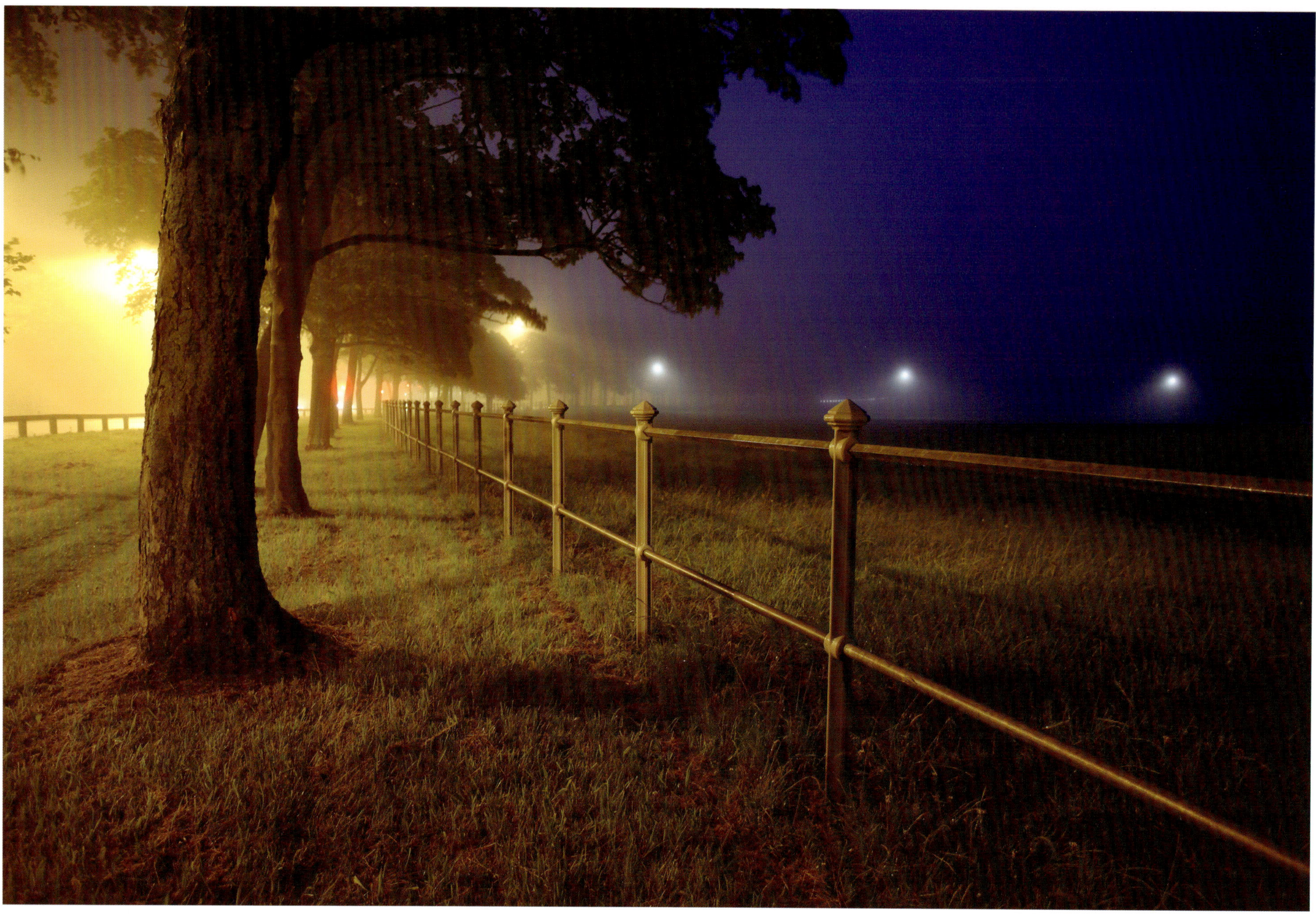

The Town Moor

Unknown Tunnel

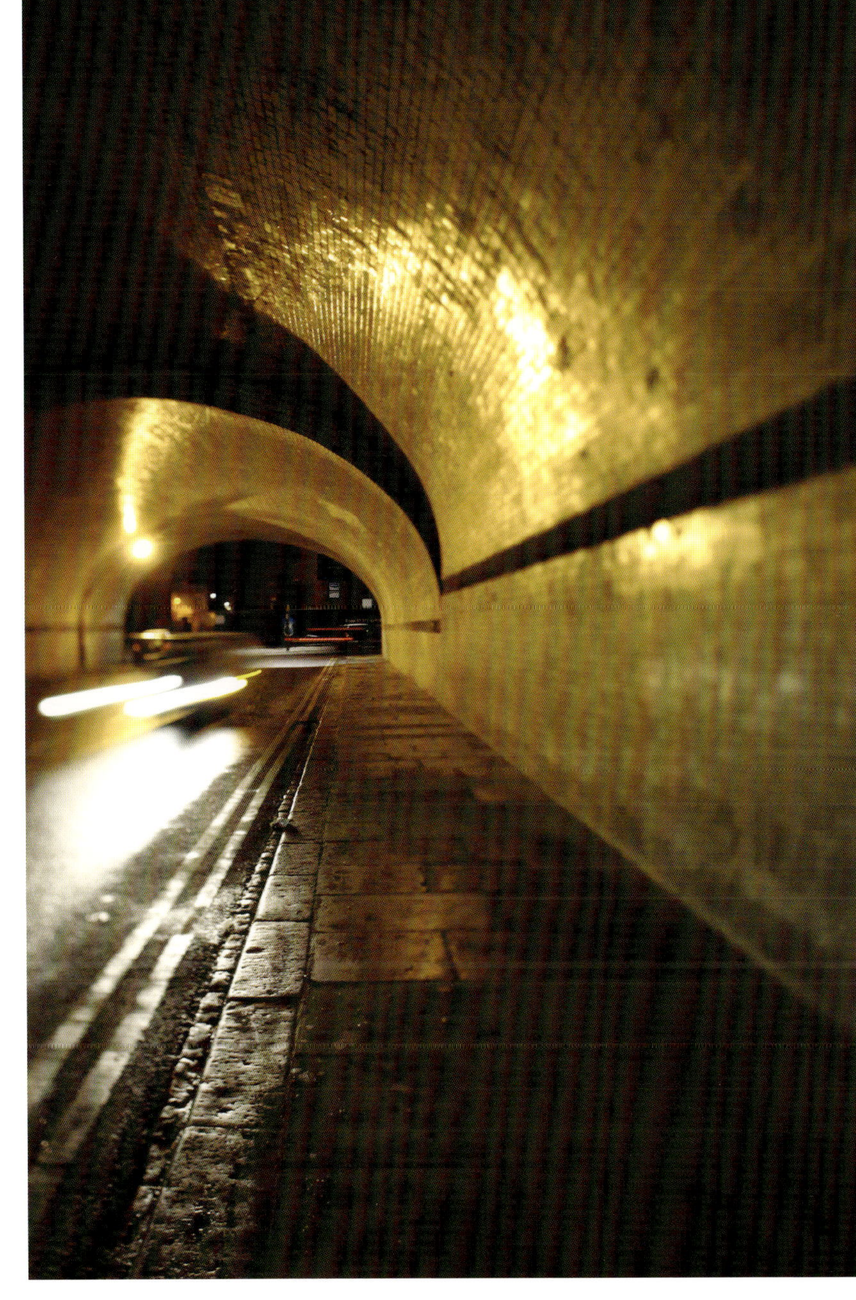

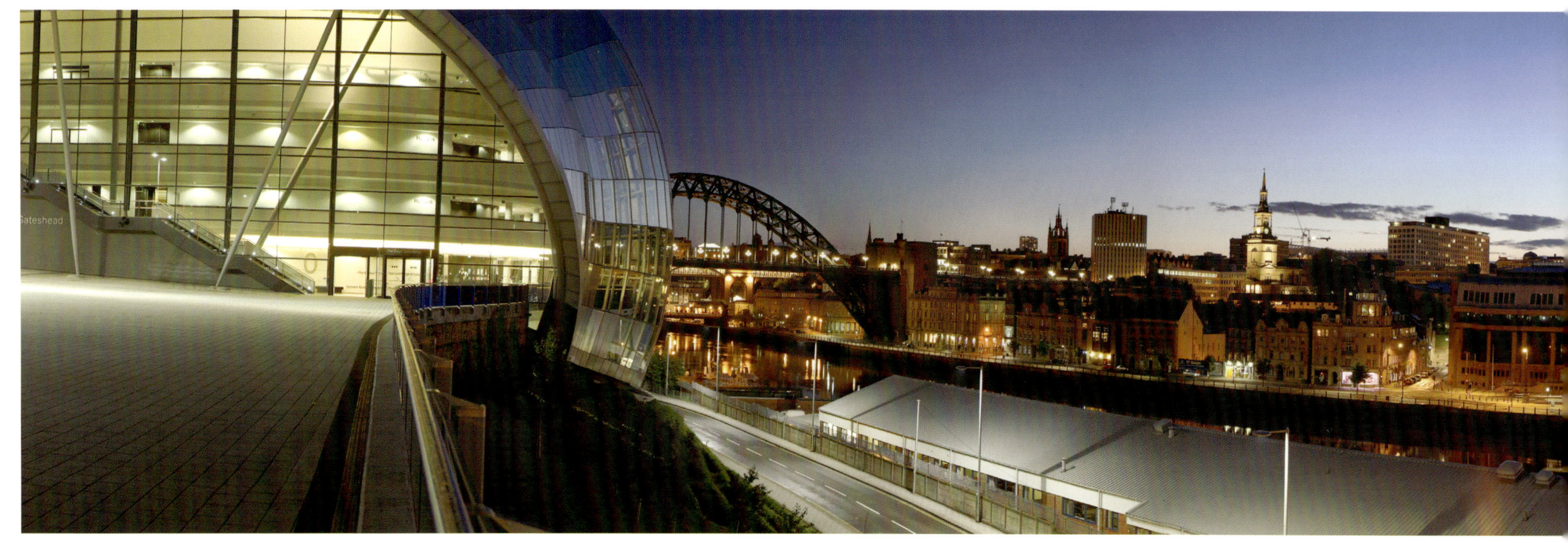

Tyne Panorama

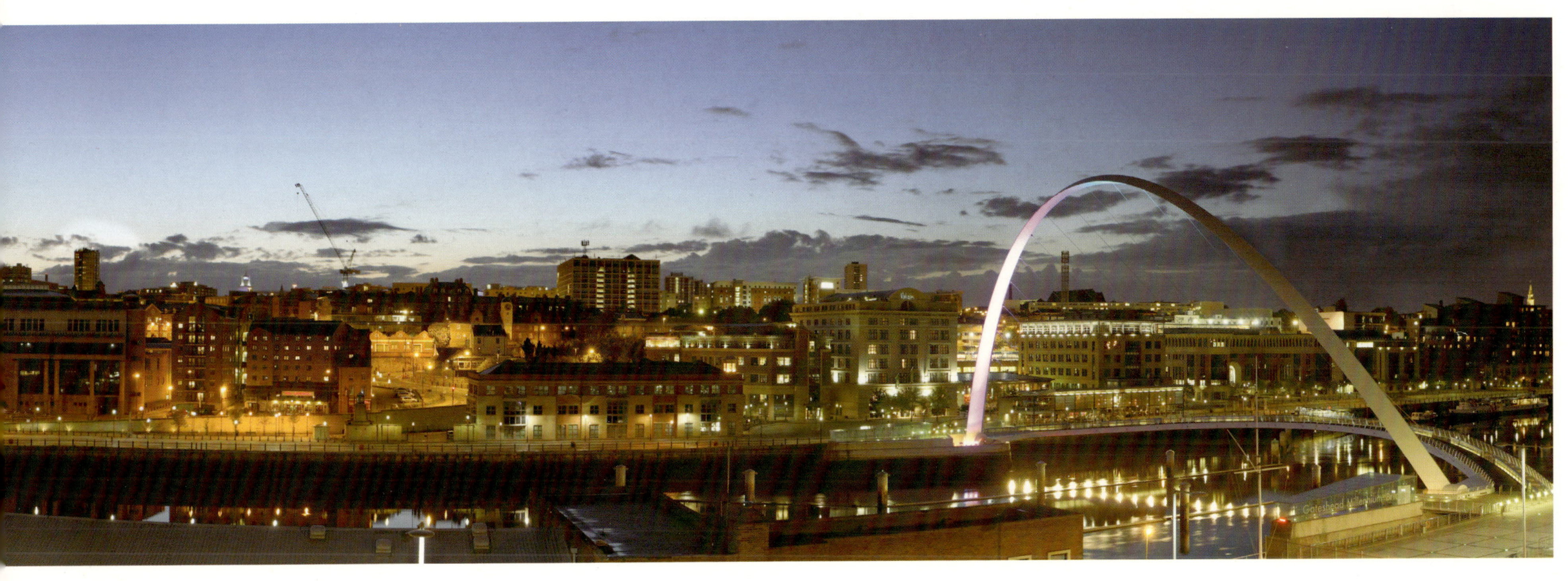
Gateshead

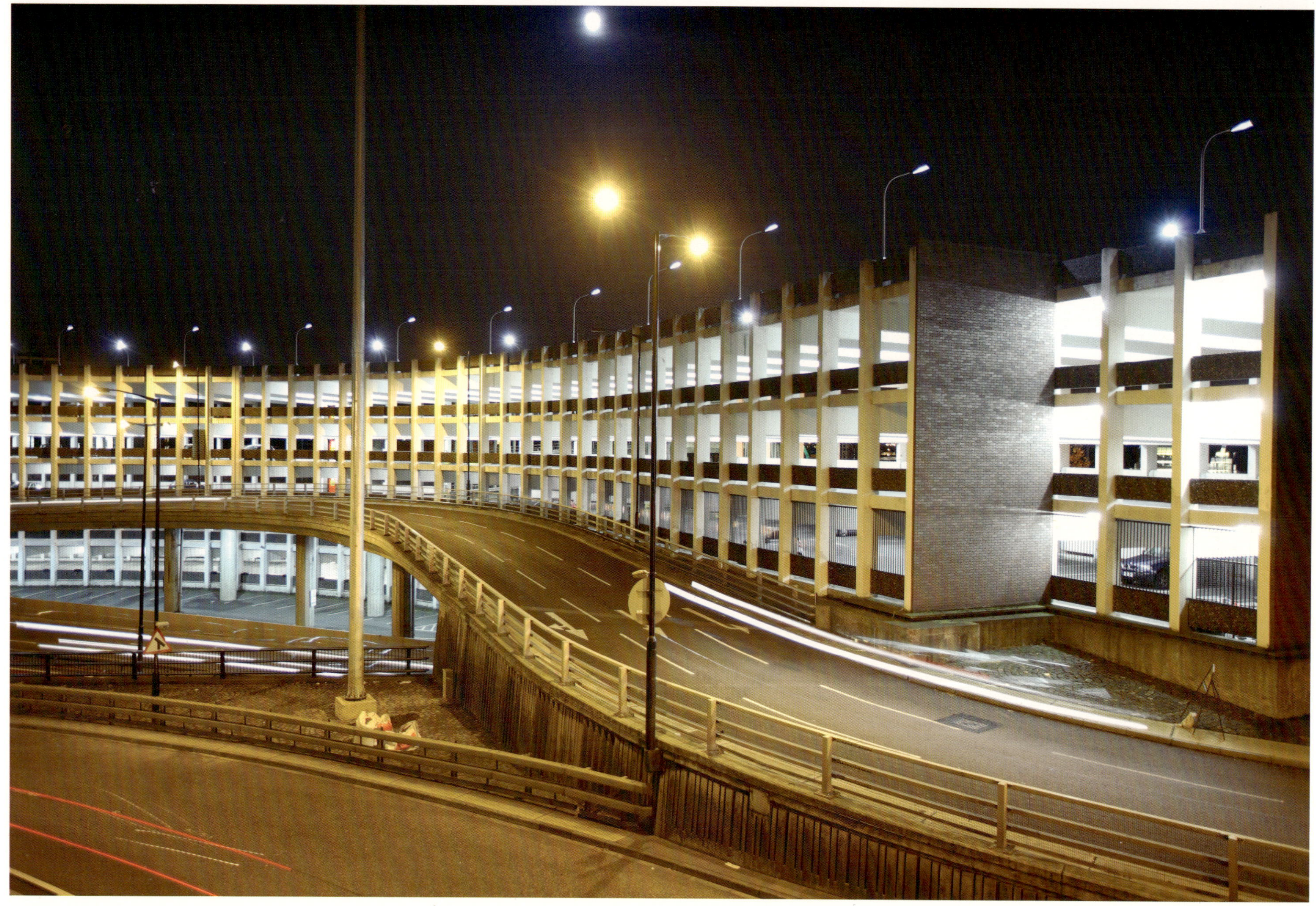

Manors Car Park

Gold Clock on Westgate Road

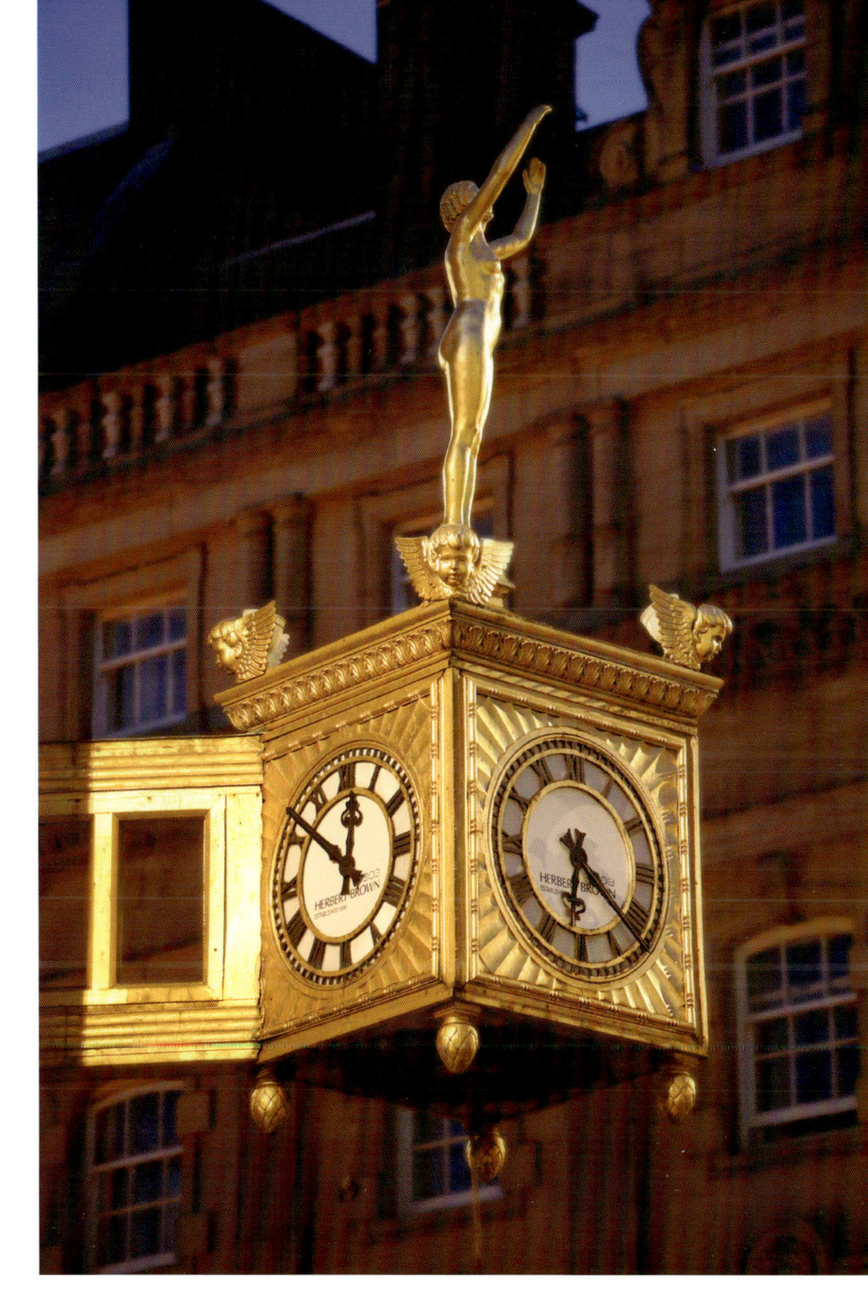

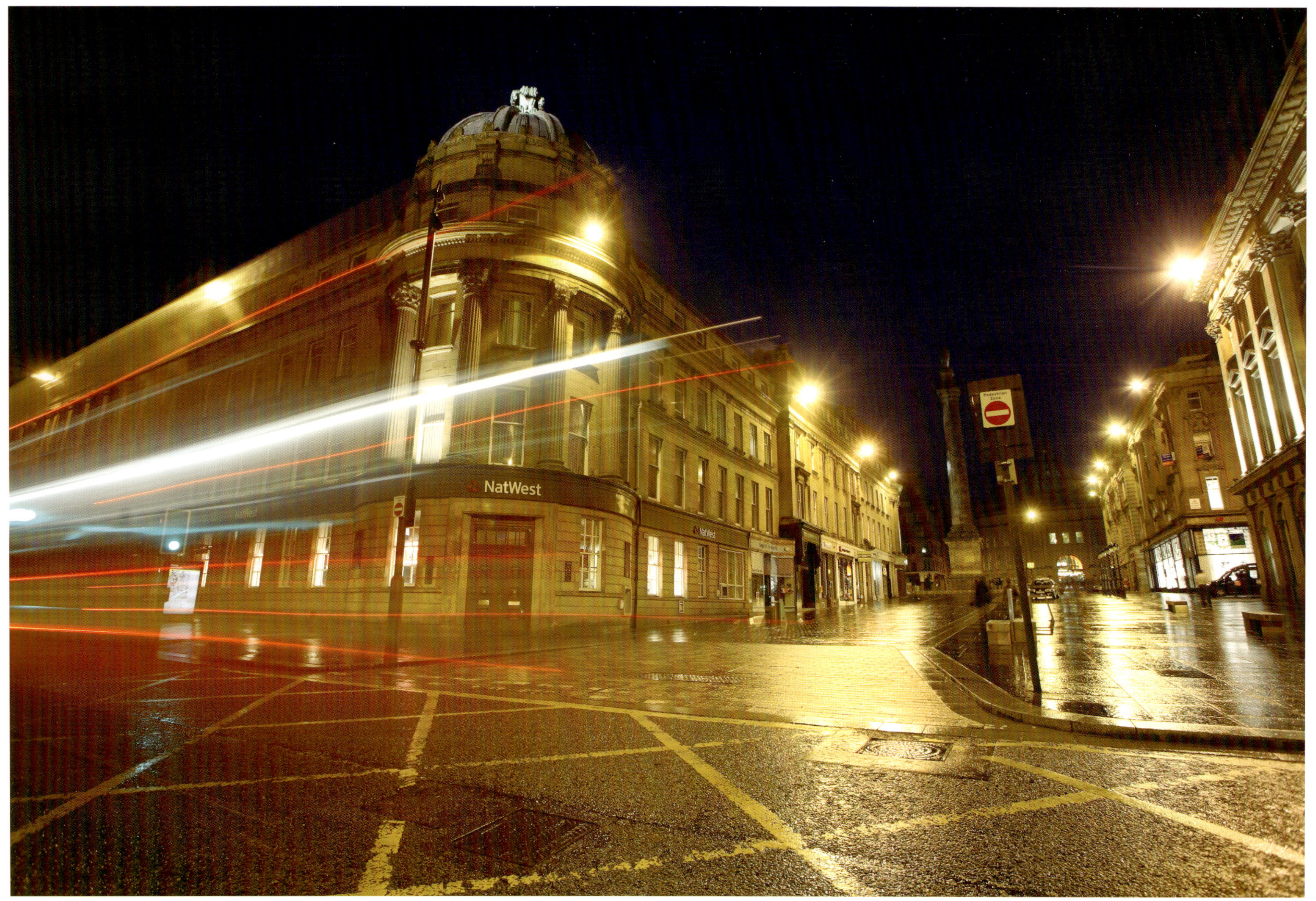

Grey Street

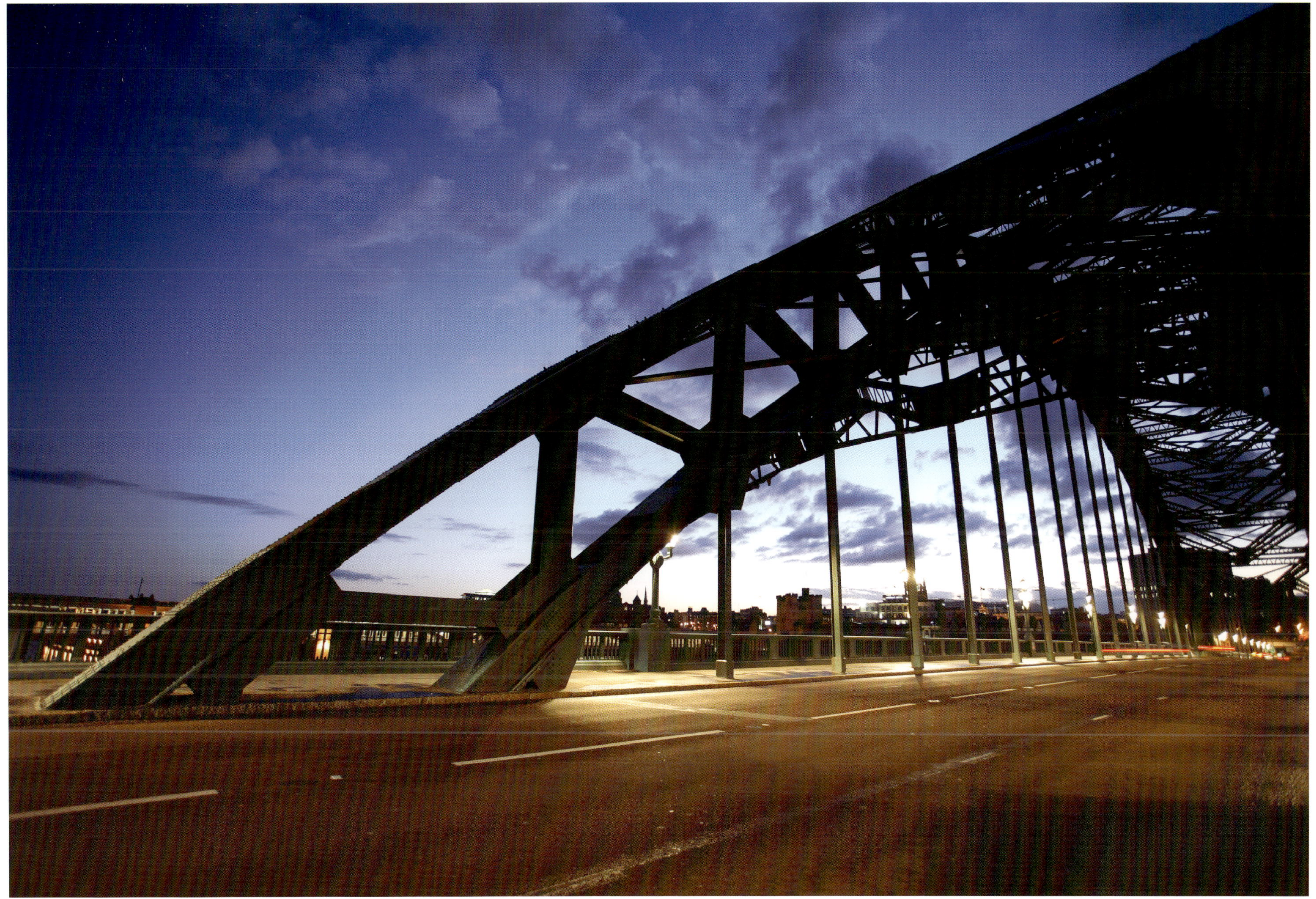

The Tyne Bridge

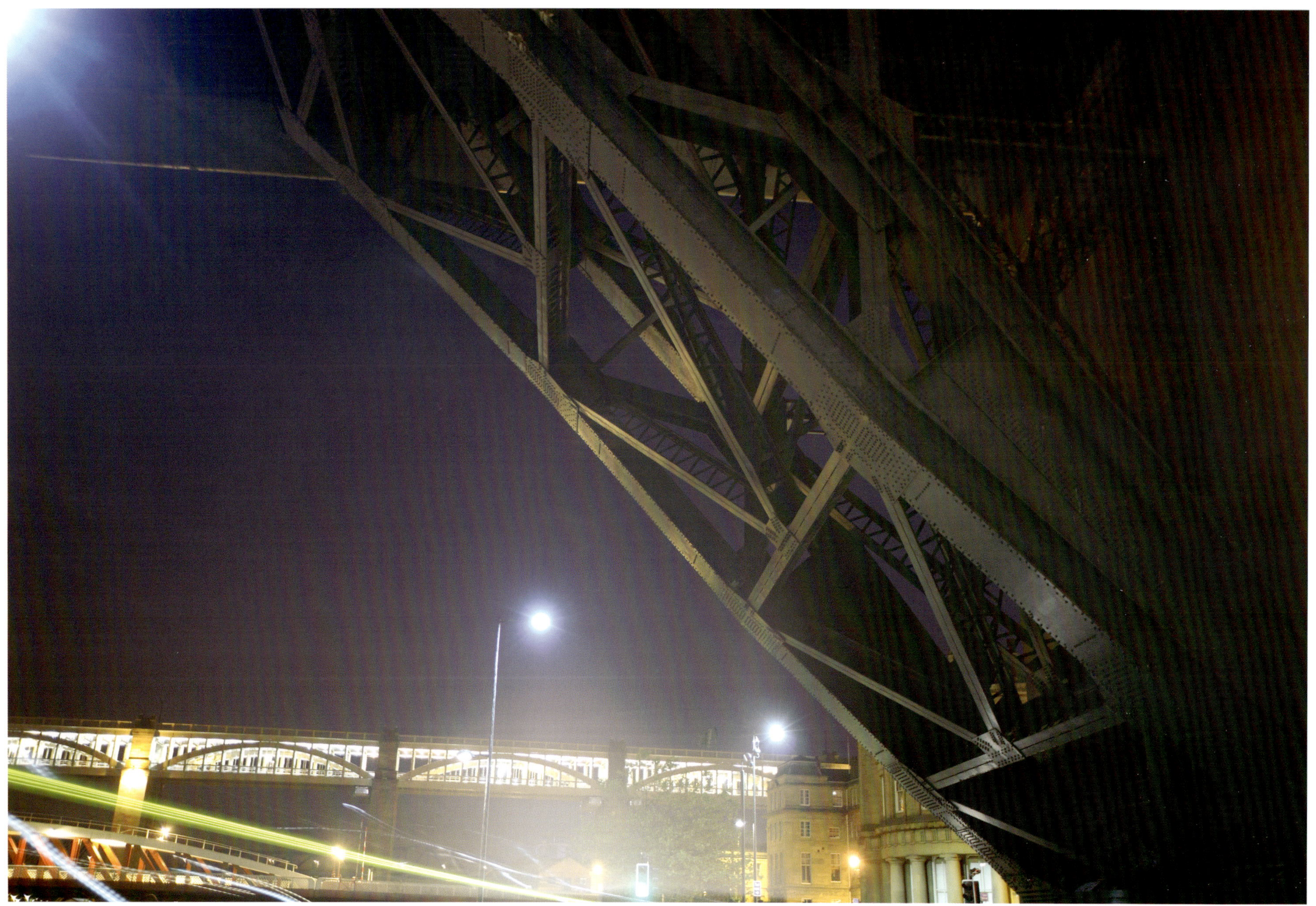

Under the Tyne Bridge

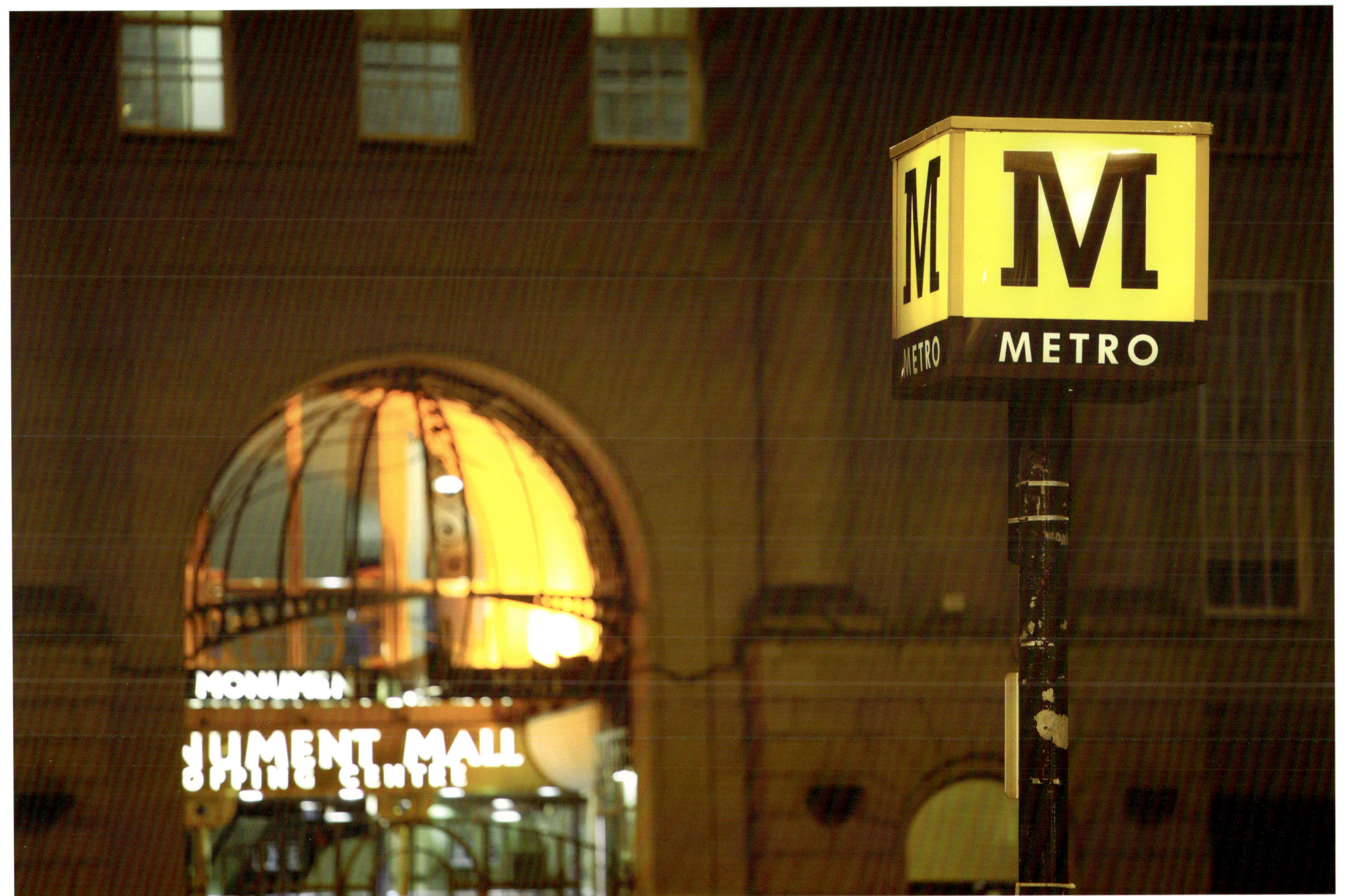

Monument Metro Station

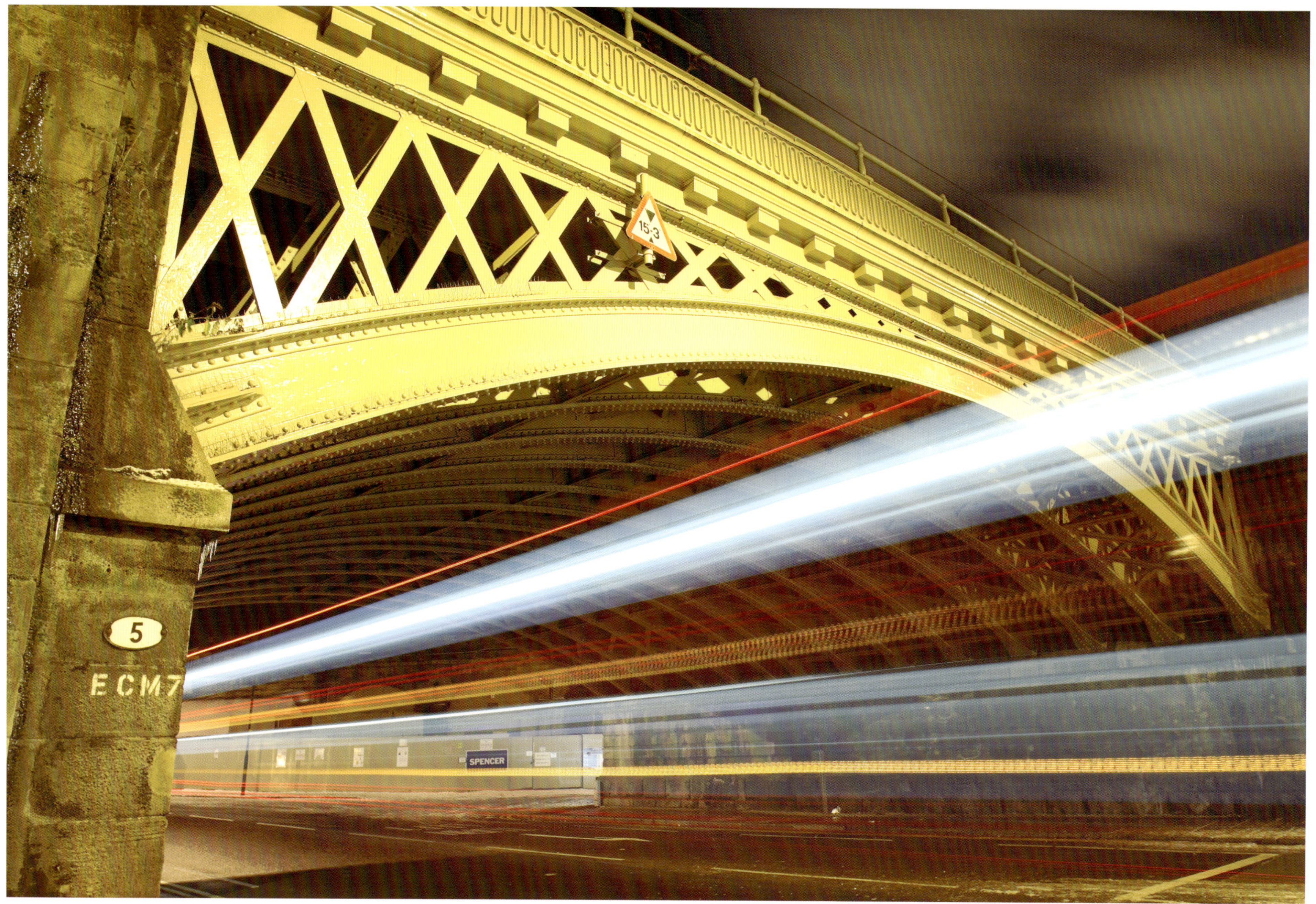

Rail Bridge ECM7

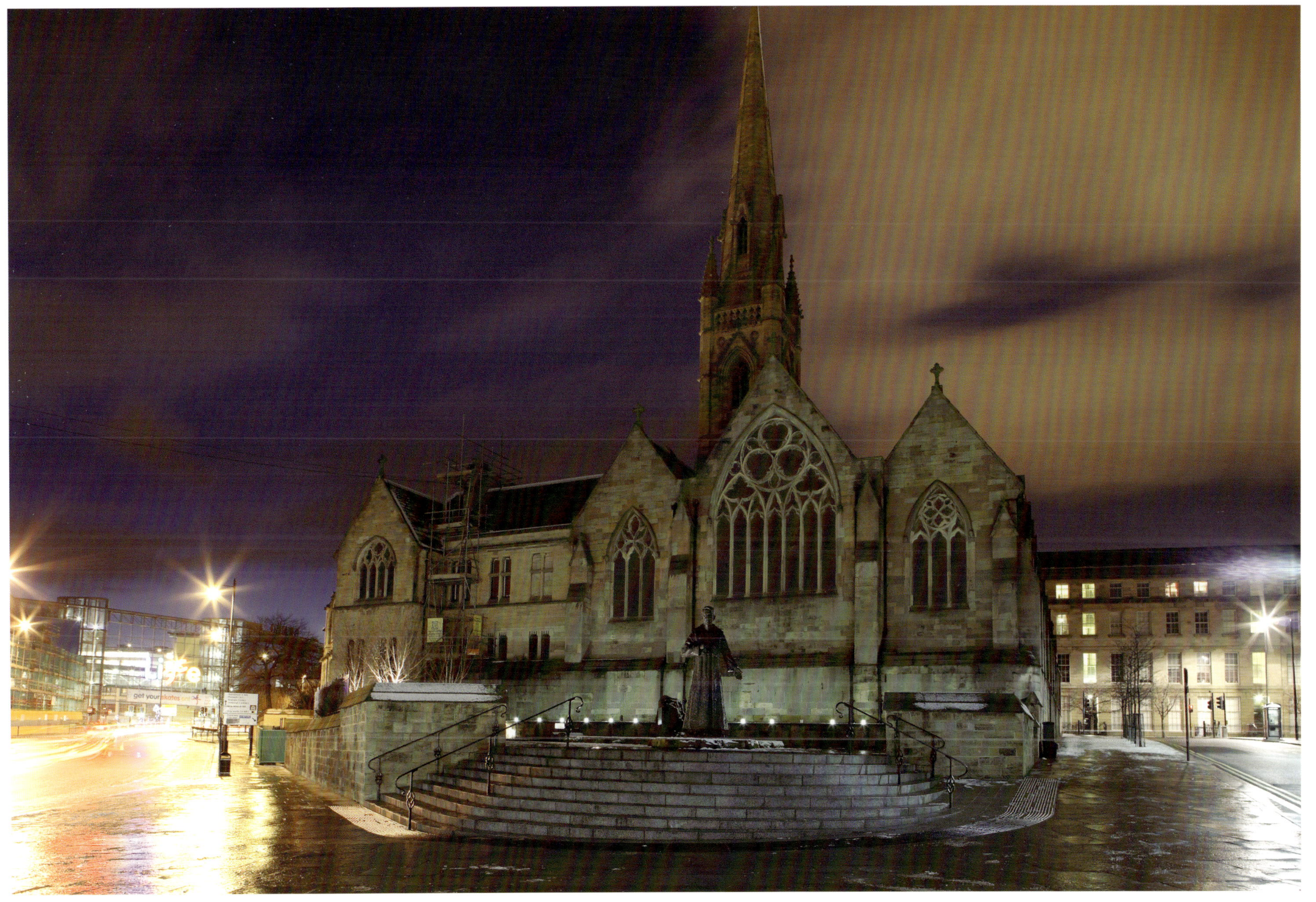

Cathedral Church of St Mary (Clayton Street West)

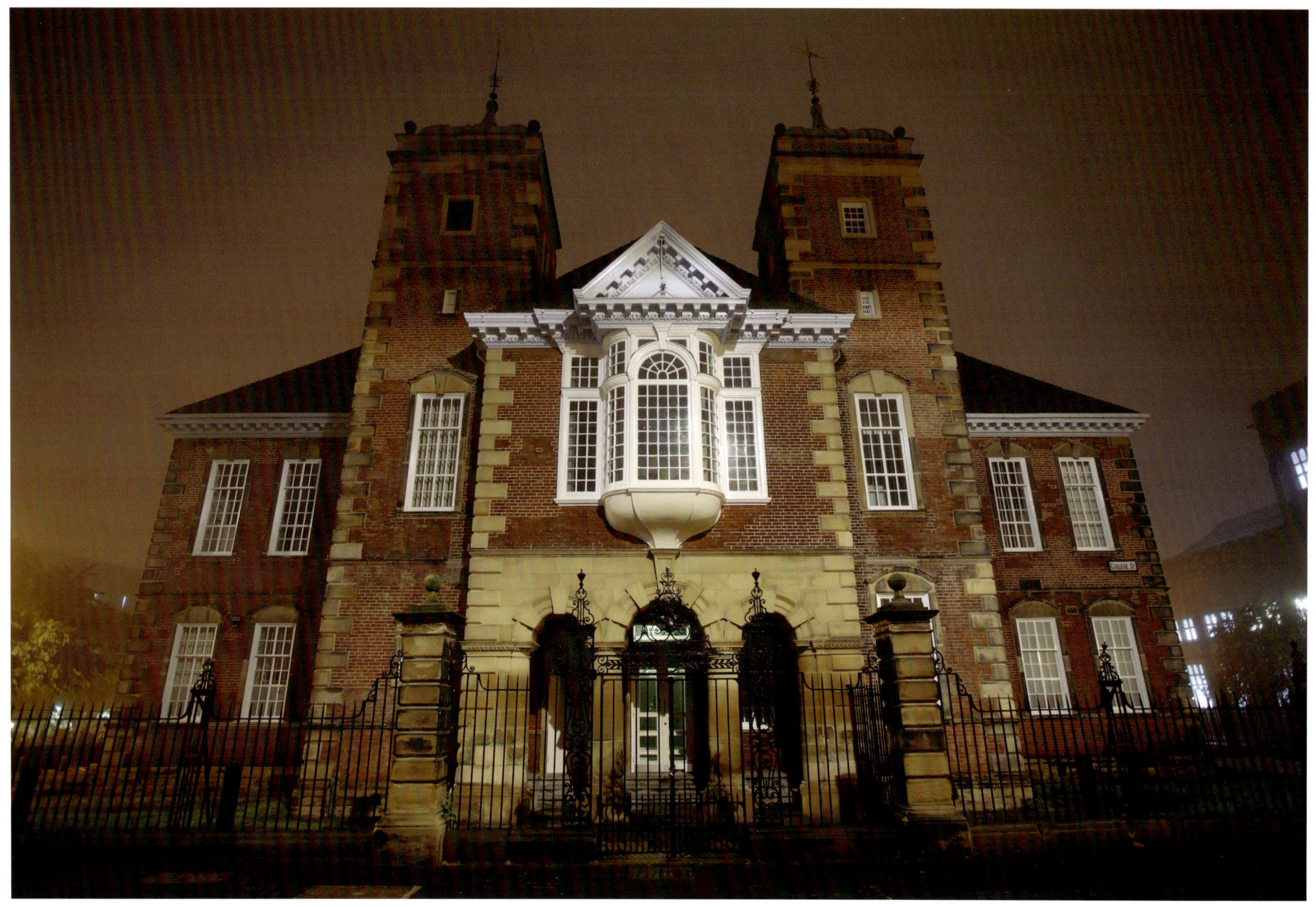

College Street

Back Alley

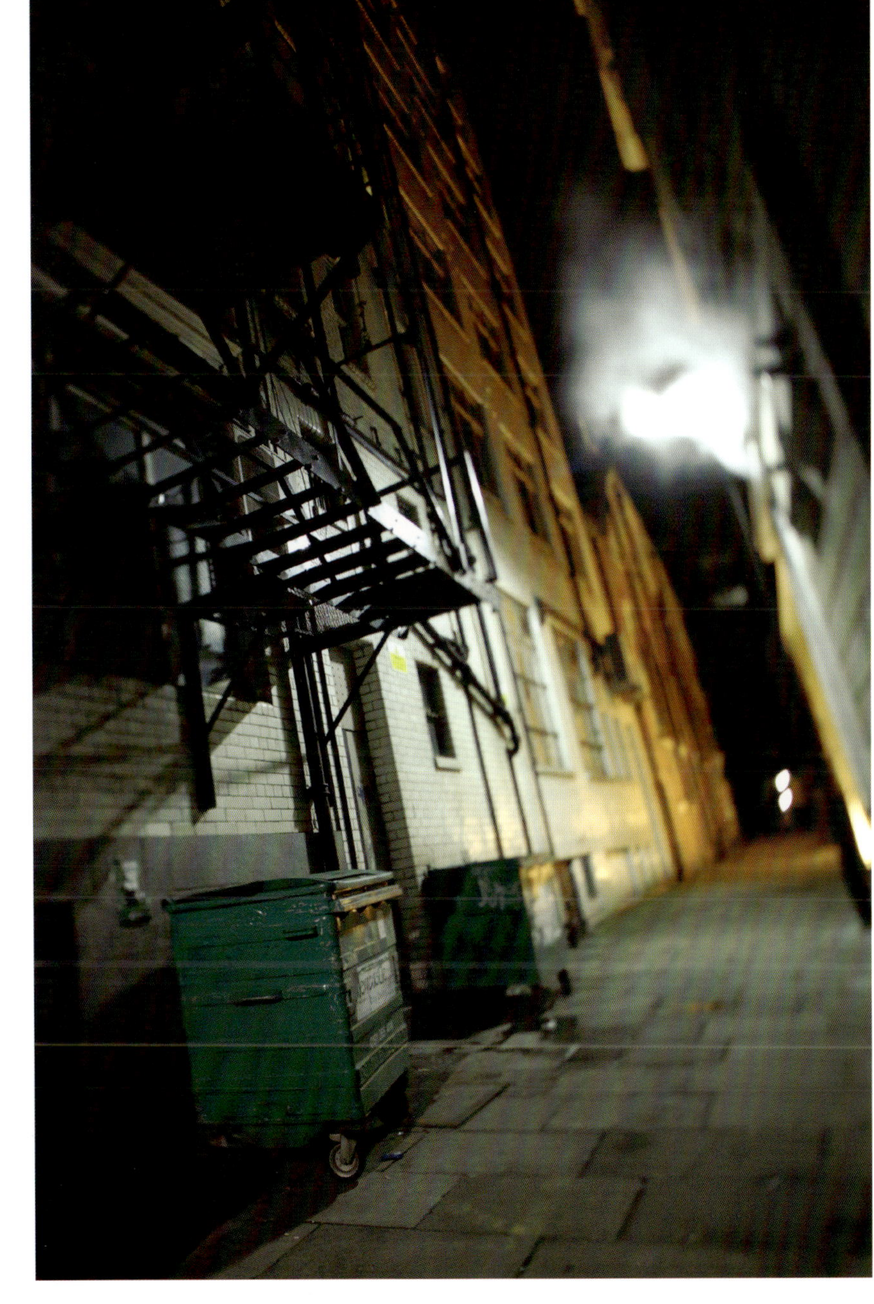

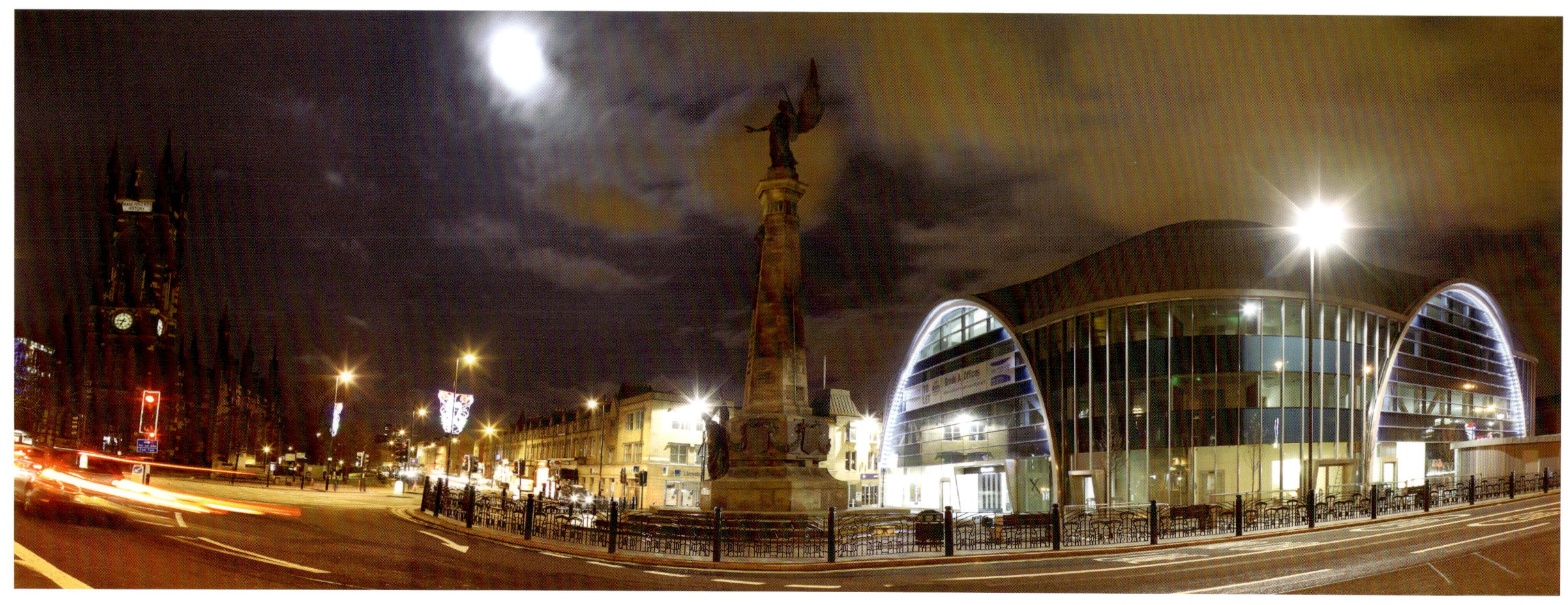

The Haymarket

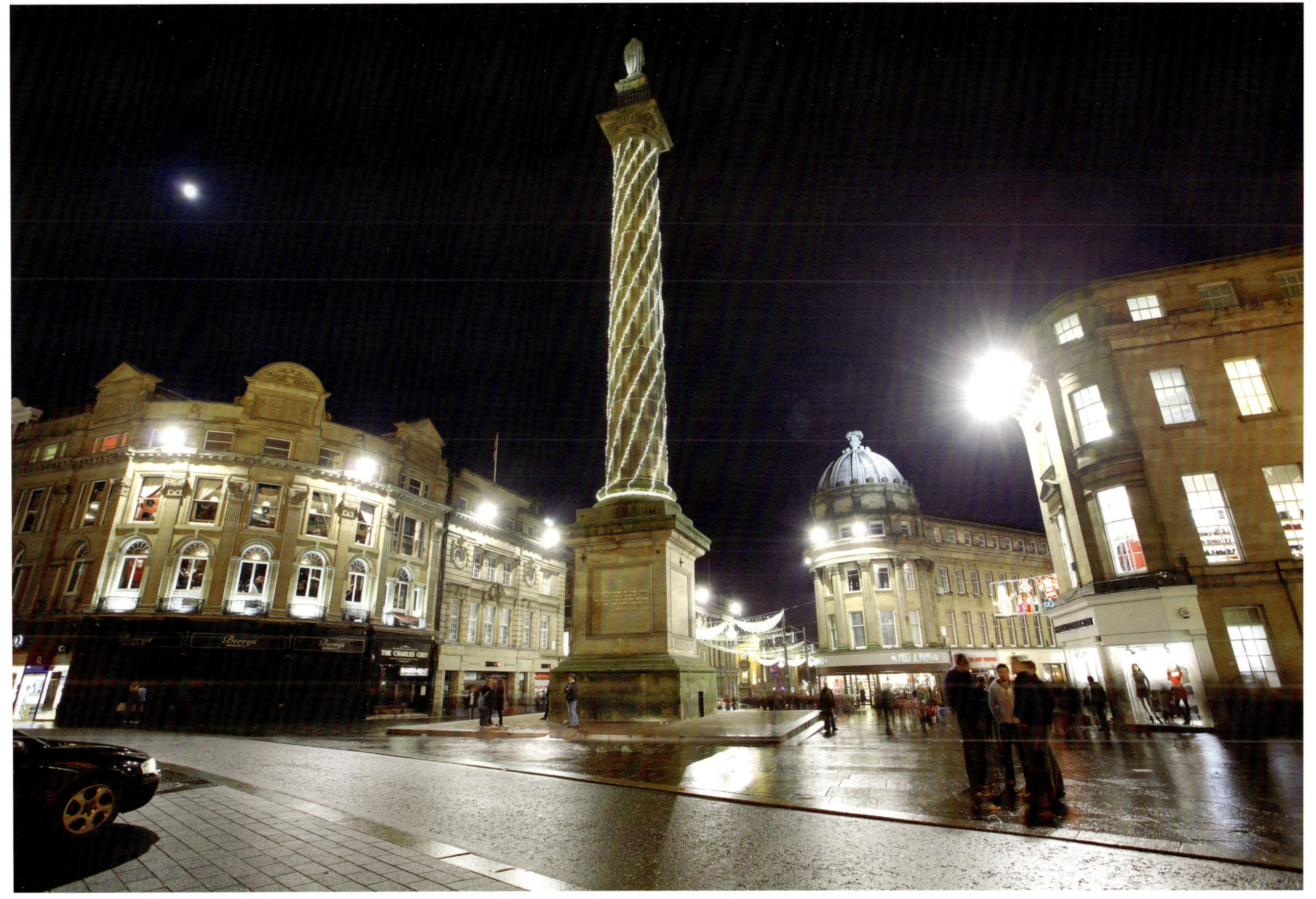

Grey's Monument

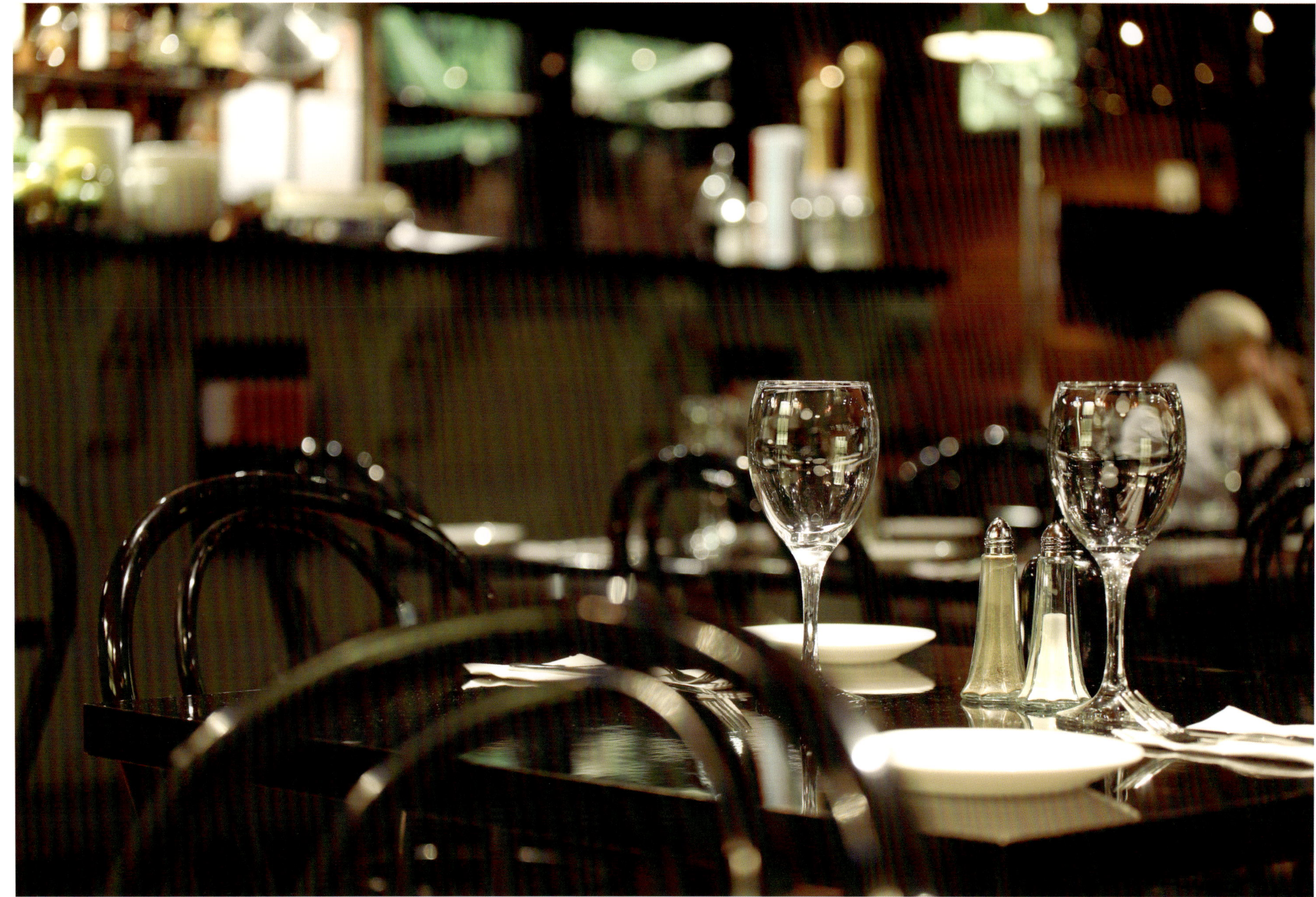

Paradiso Café

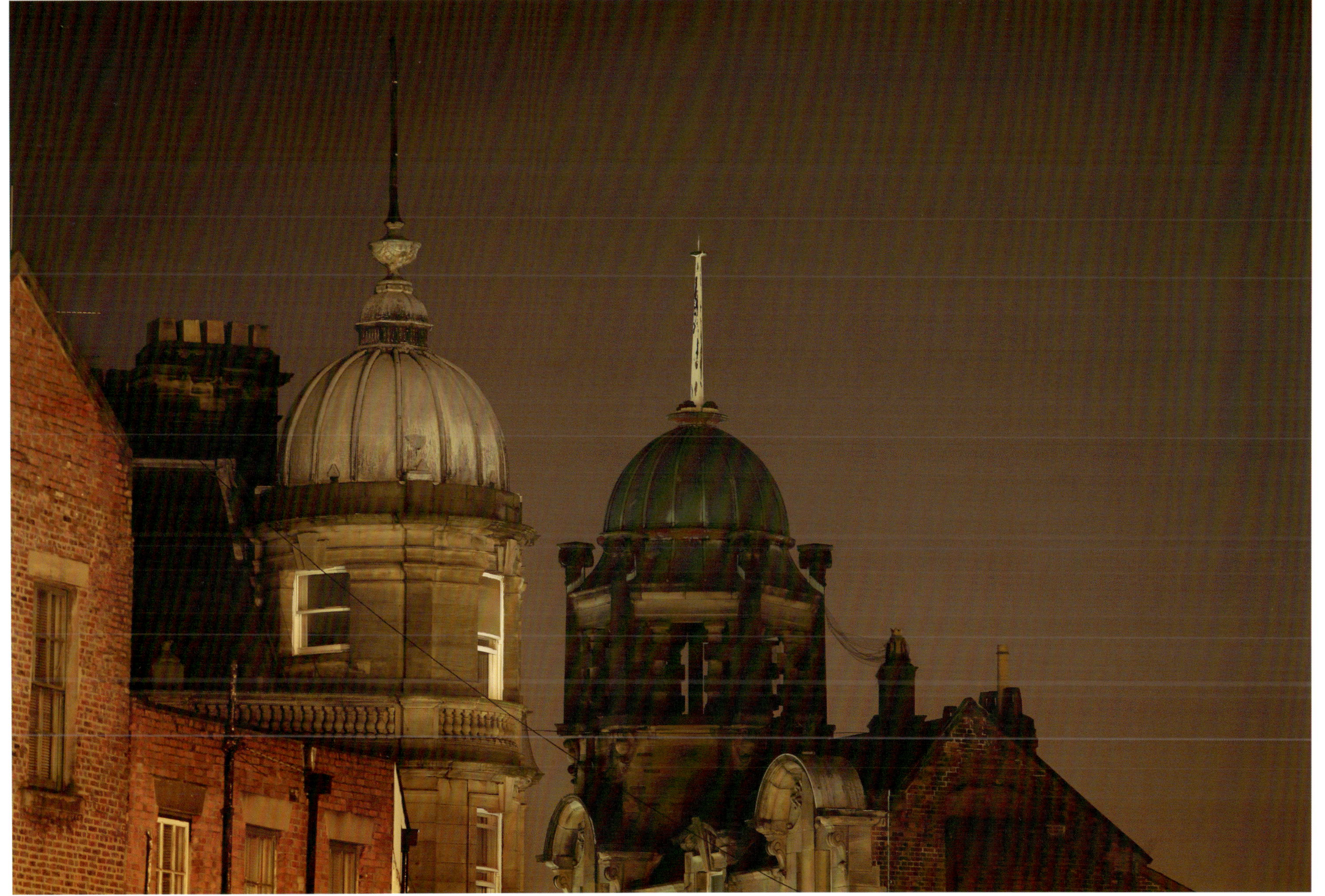

City Rooftops

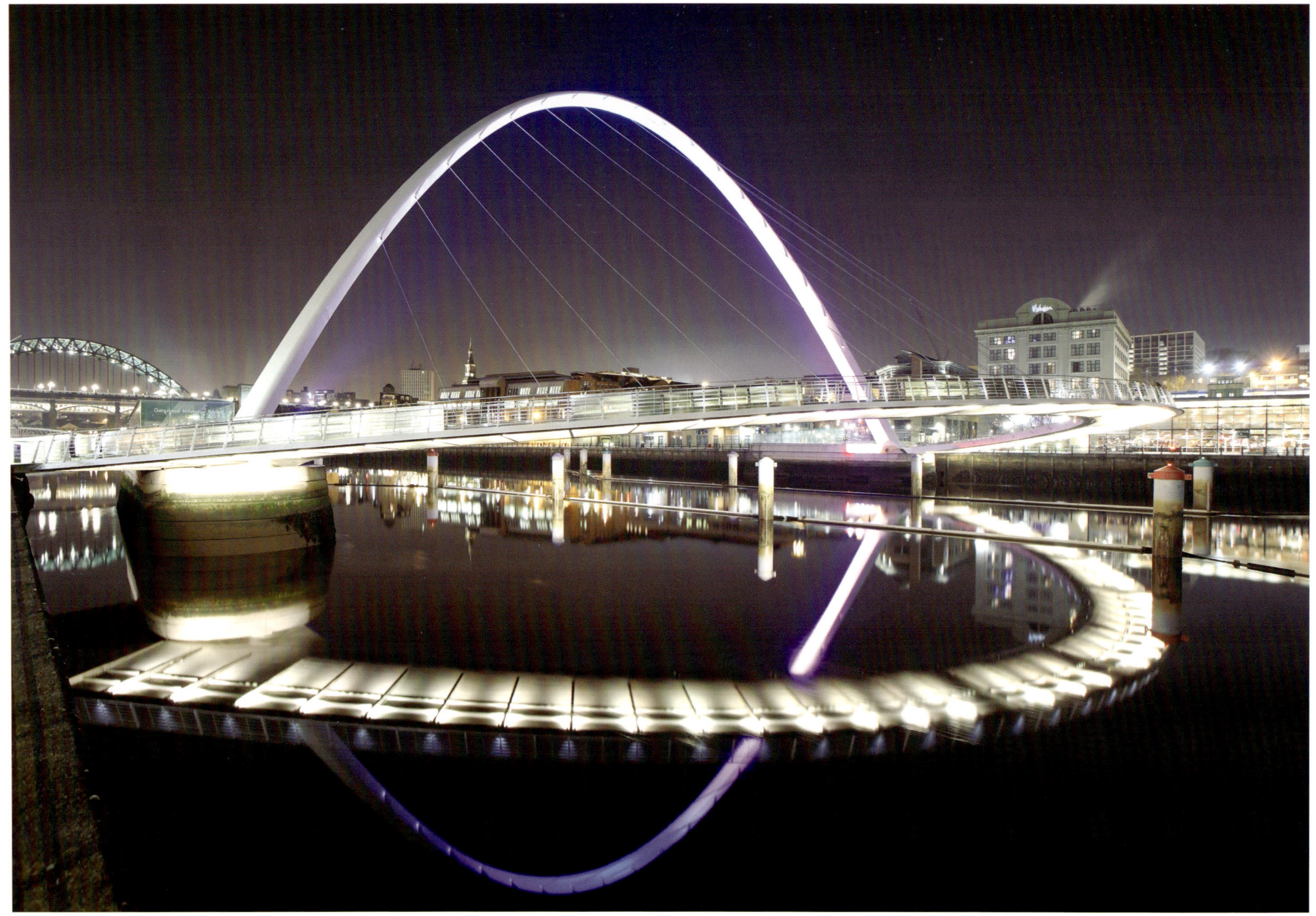

Millenium Bridge

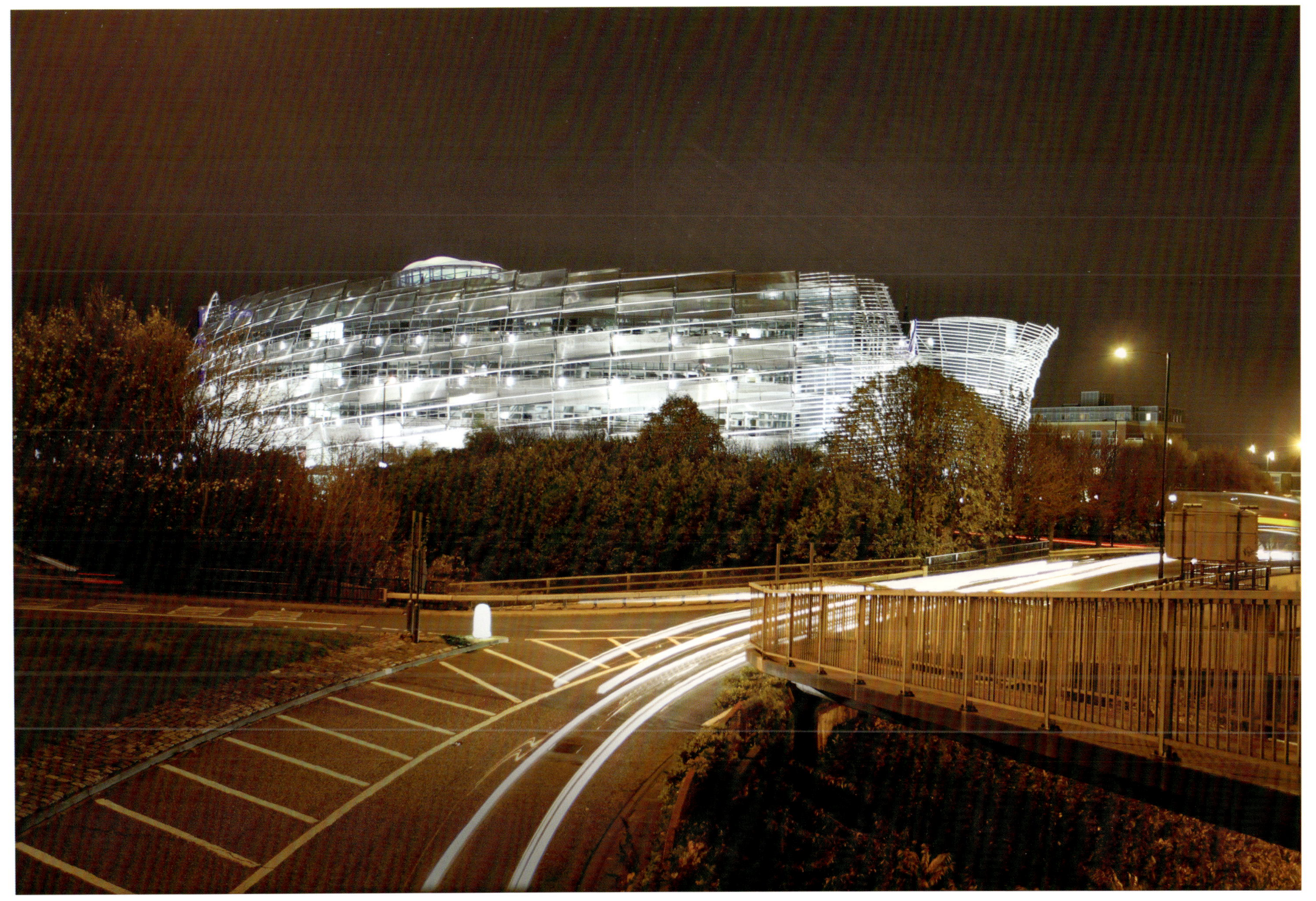

Northumbria University Building

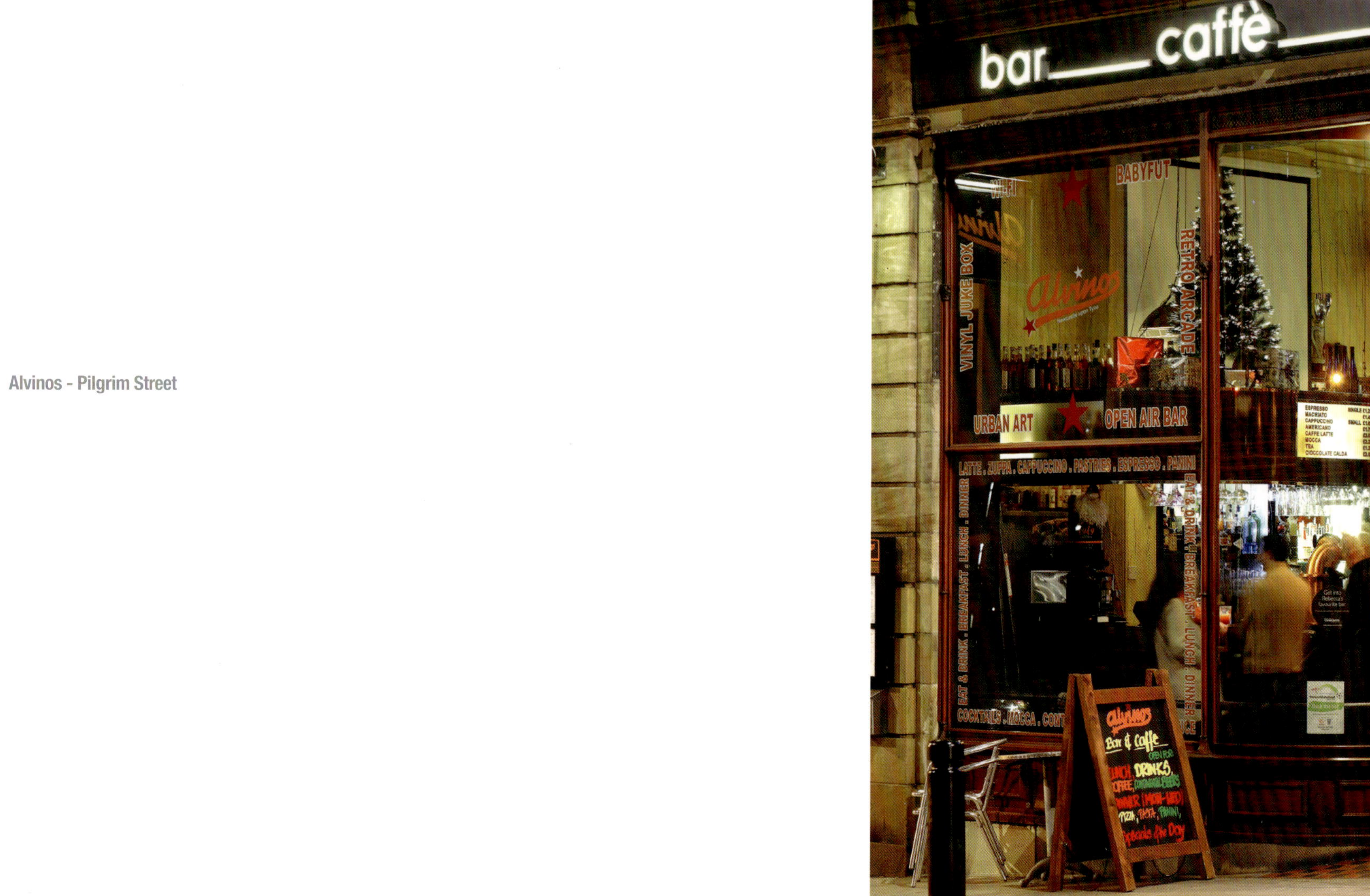

Alvinos - Pilgrim Street

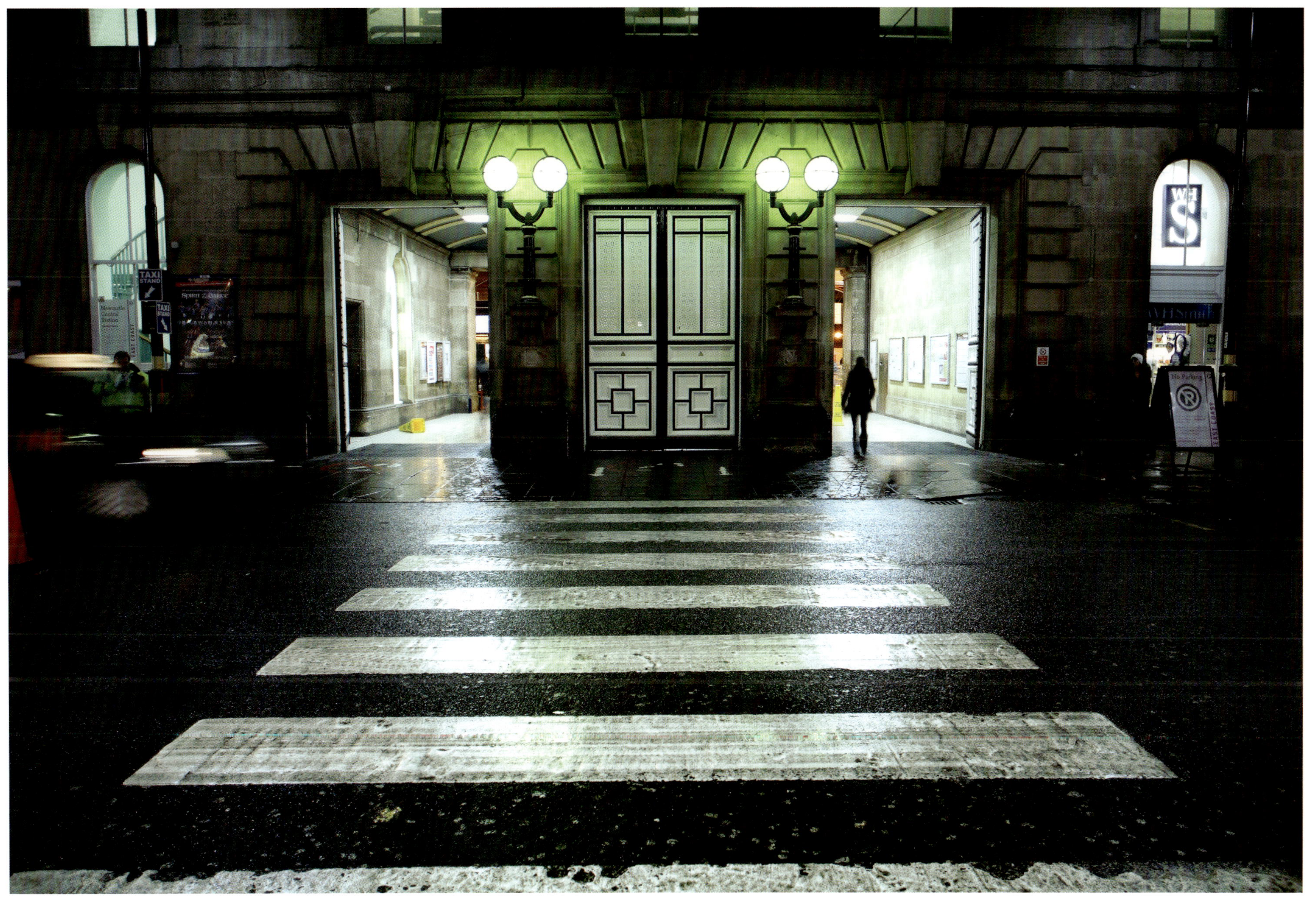

Newcastle Central Station entrance

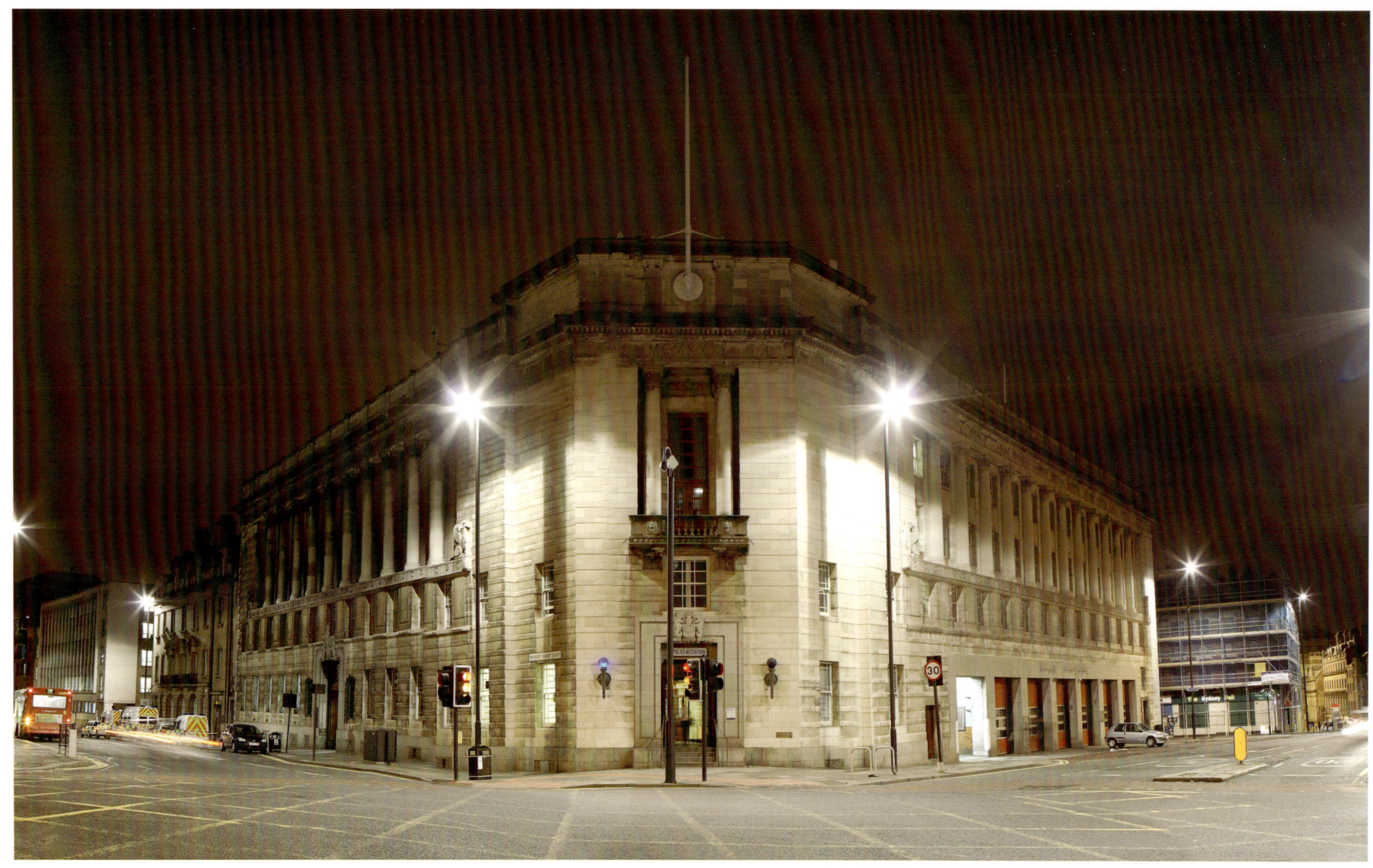

Corner of Market Street East & Pilgrim Street

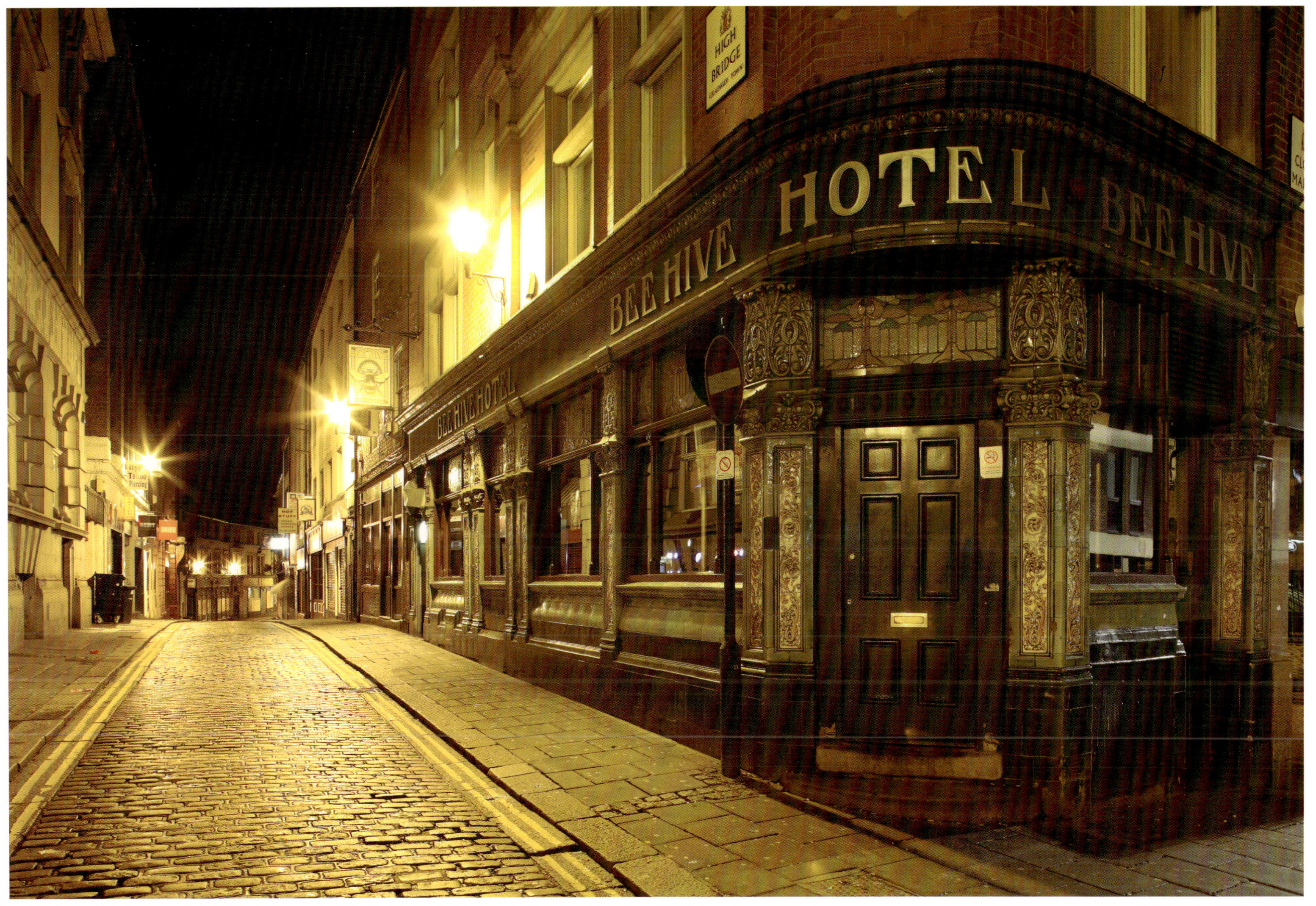

Bee Hive Hotel - High Bridge Street

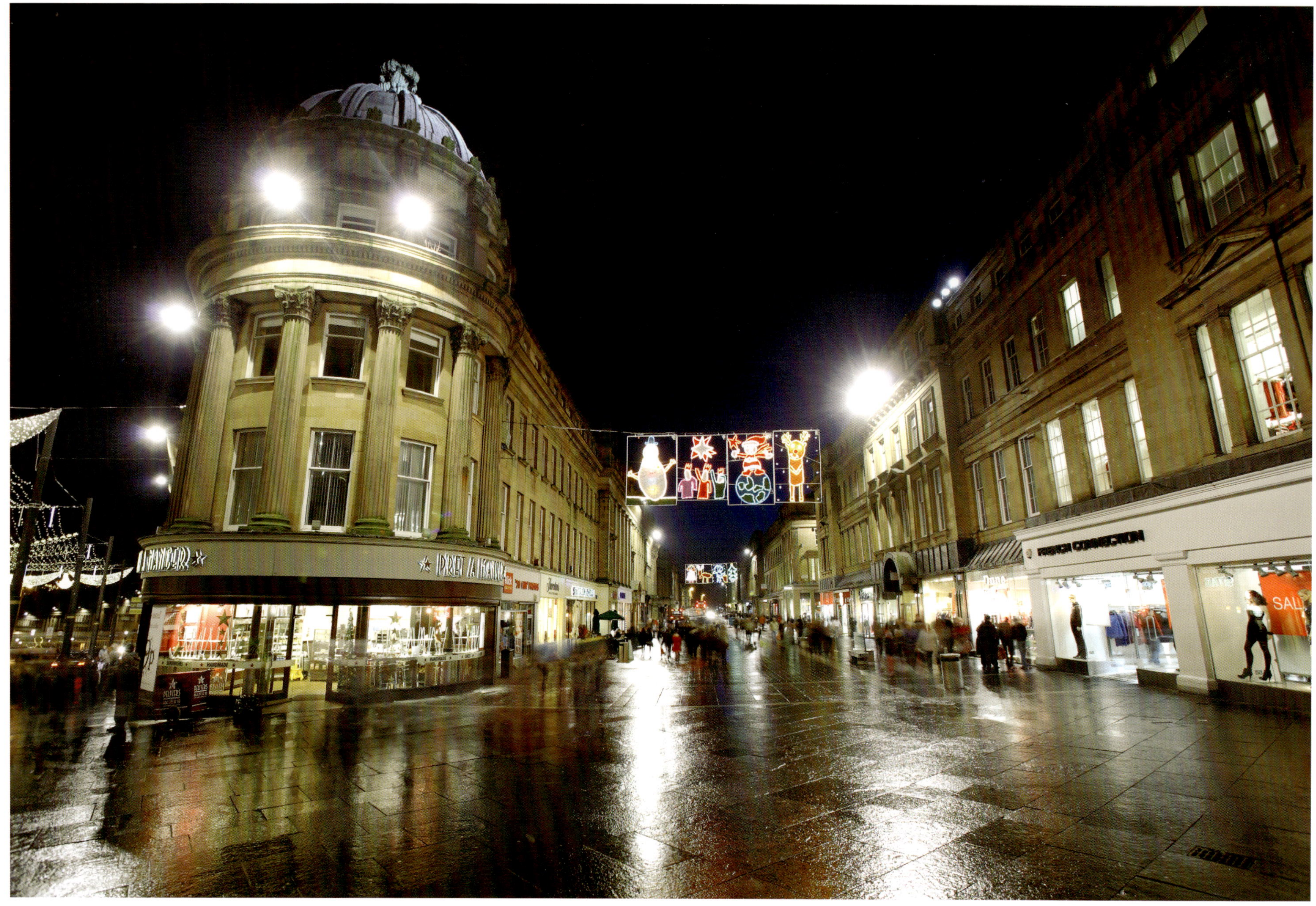

Grainger Street

Barrack Road

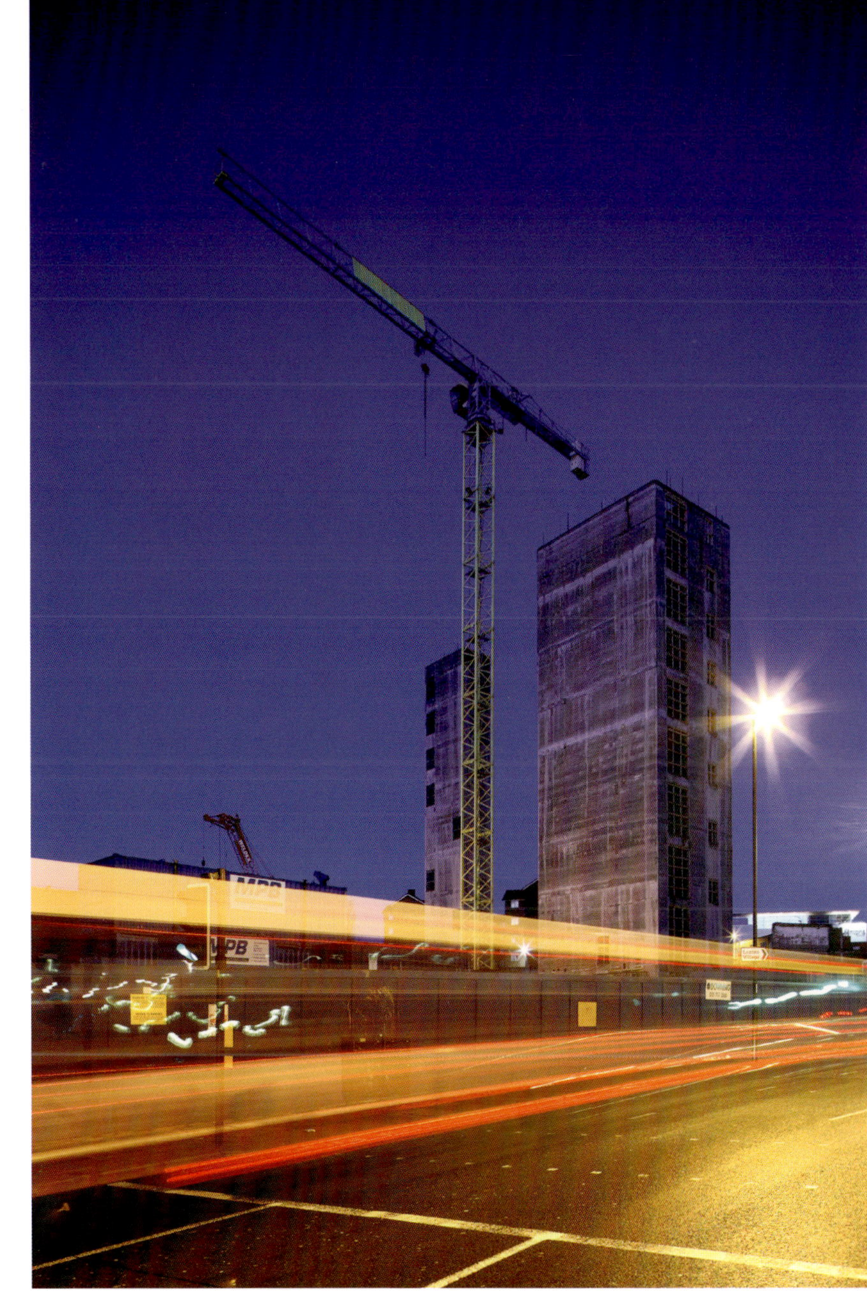

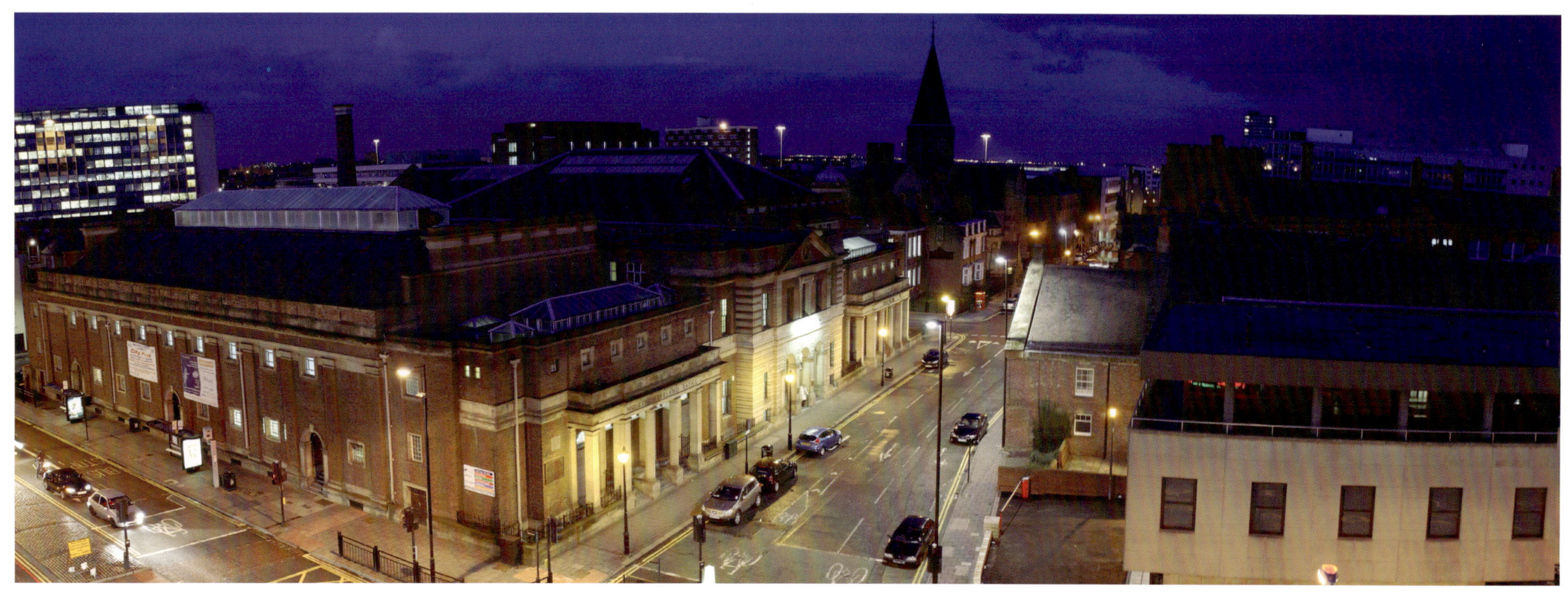

Town Hall Panorama

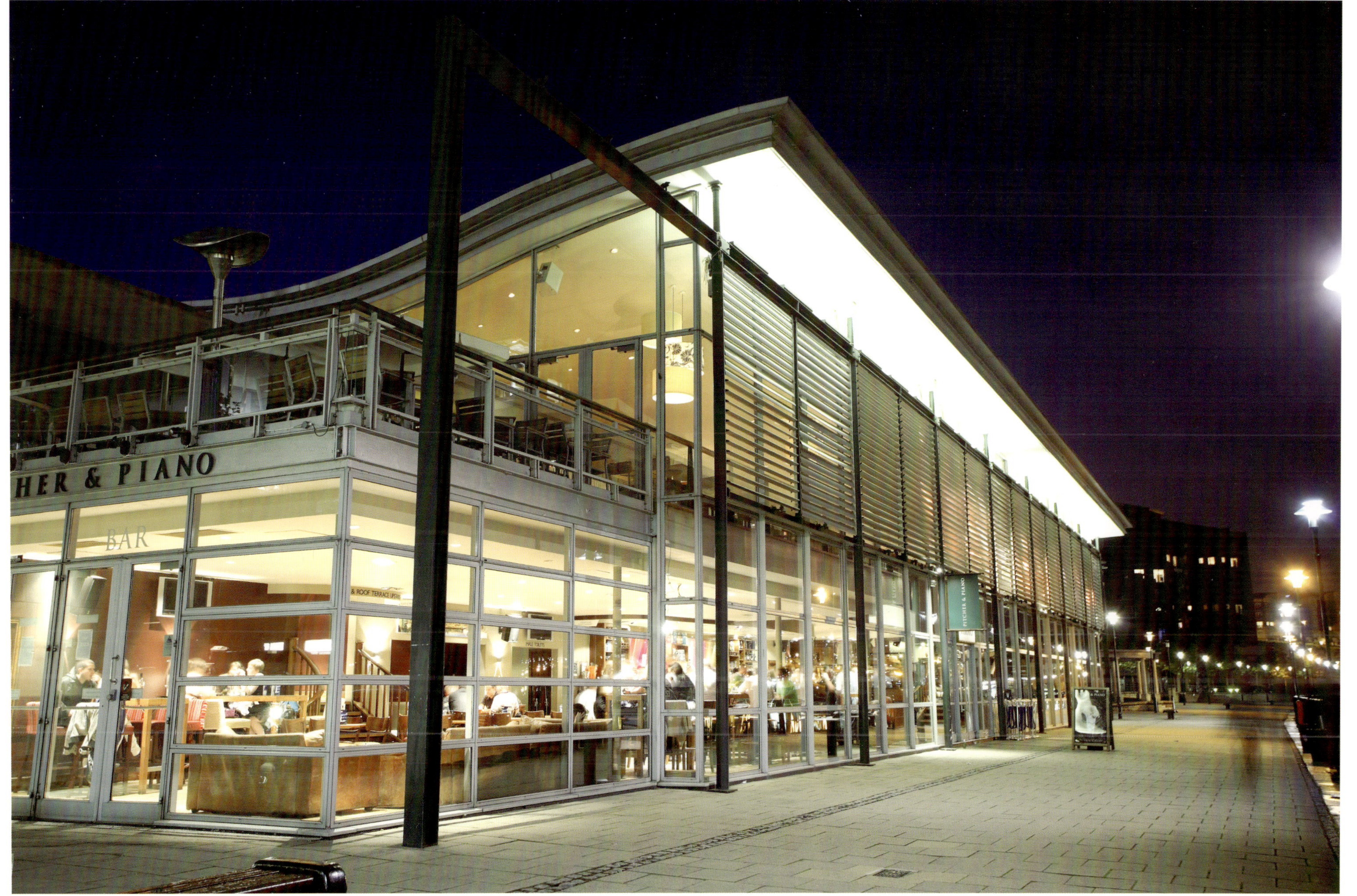

Pitcher and Piano

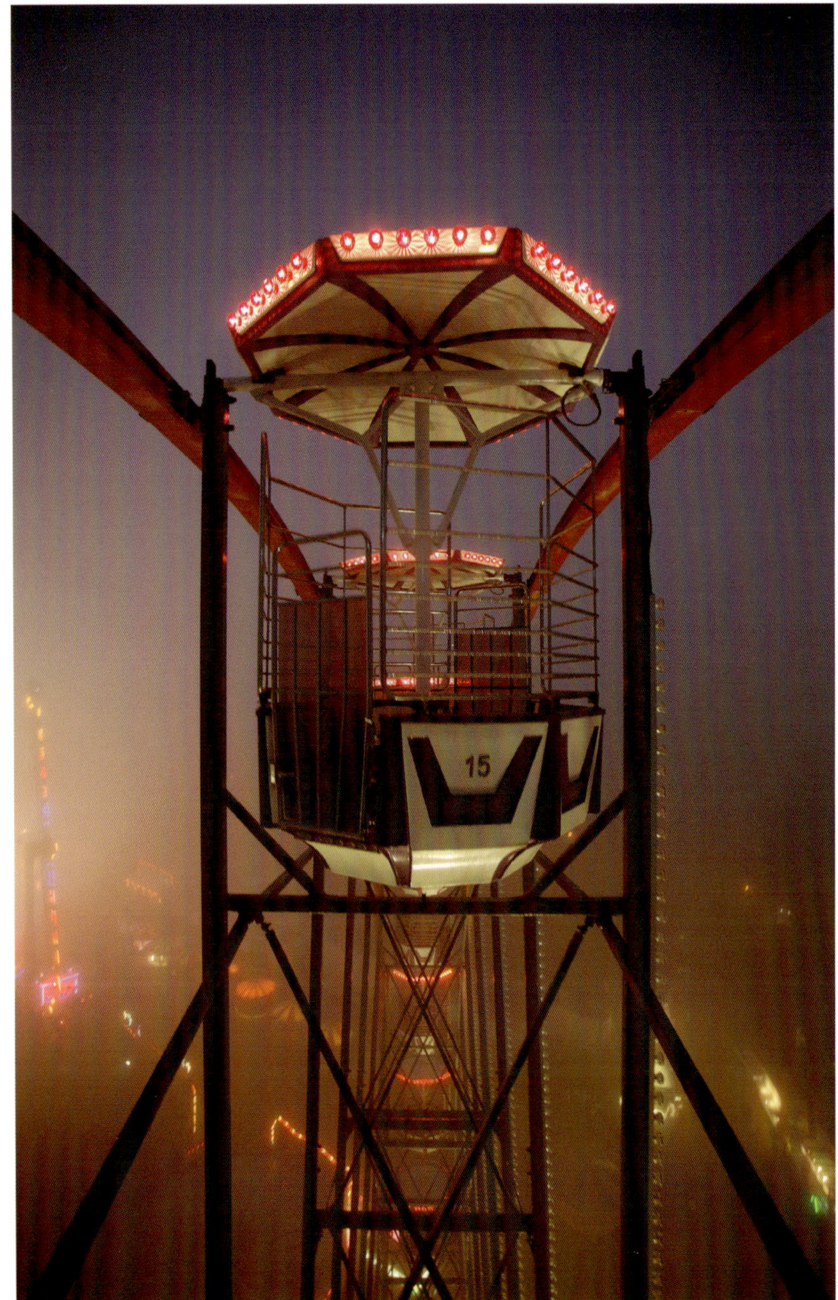

The Hoppings Fair - Town Moor

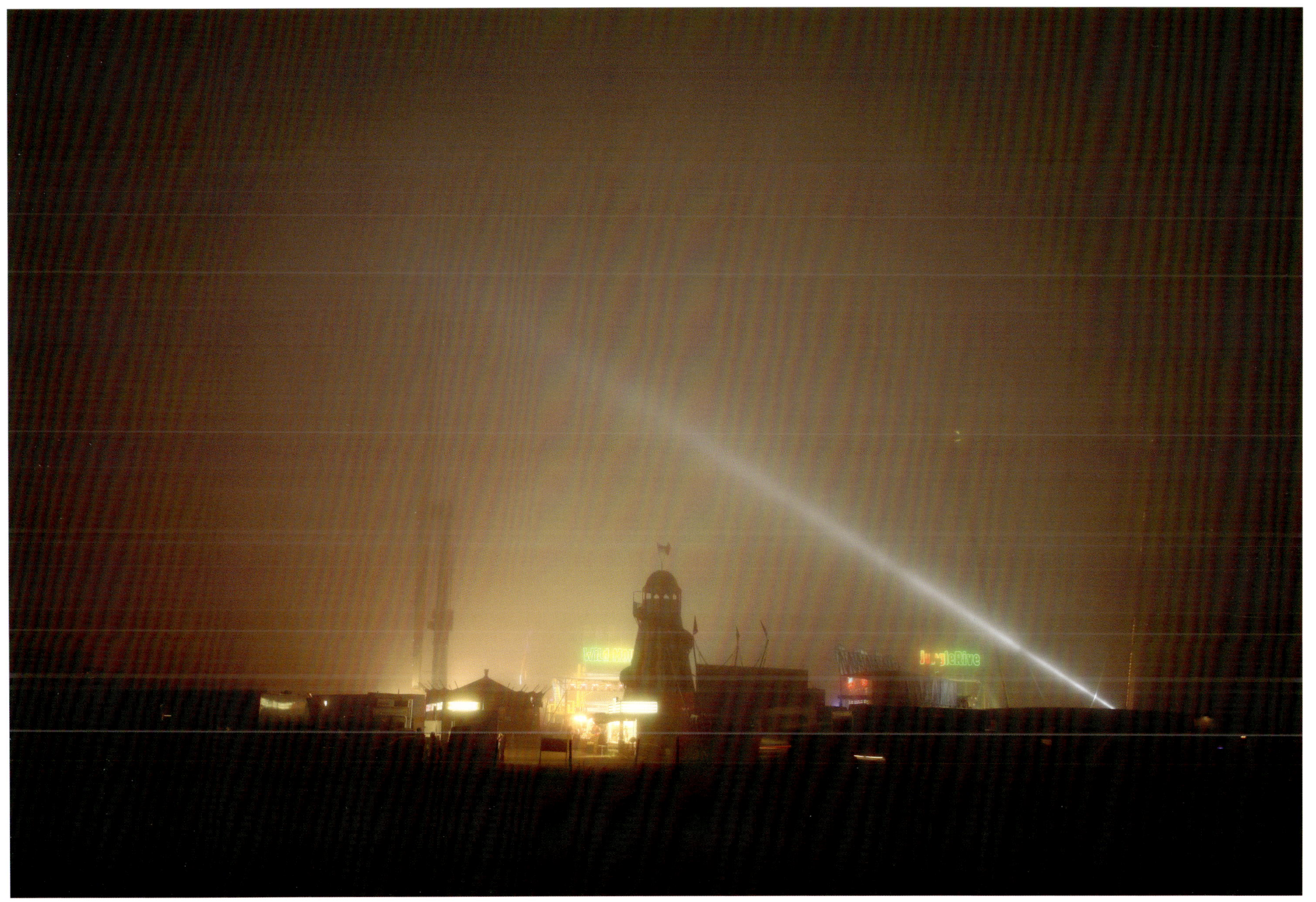

The Hoppings Fair - Town Moor

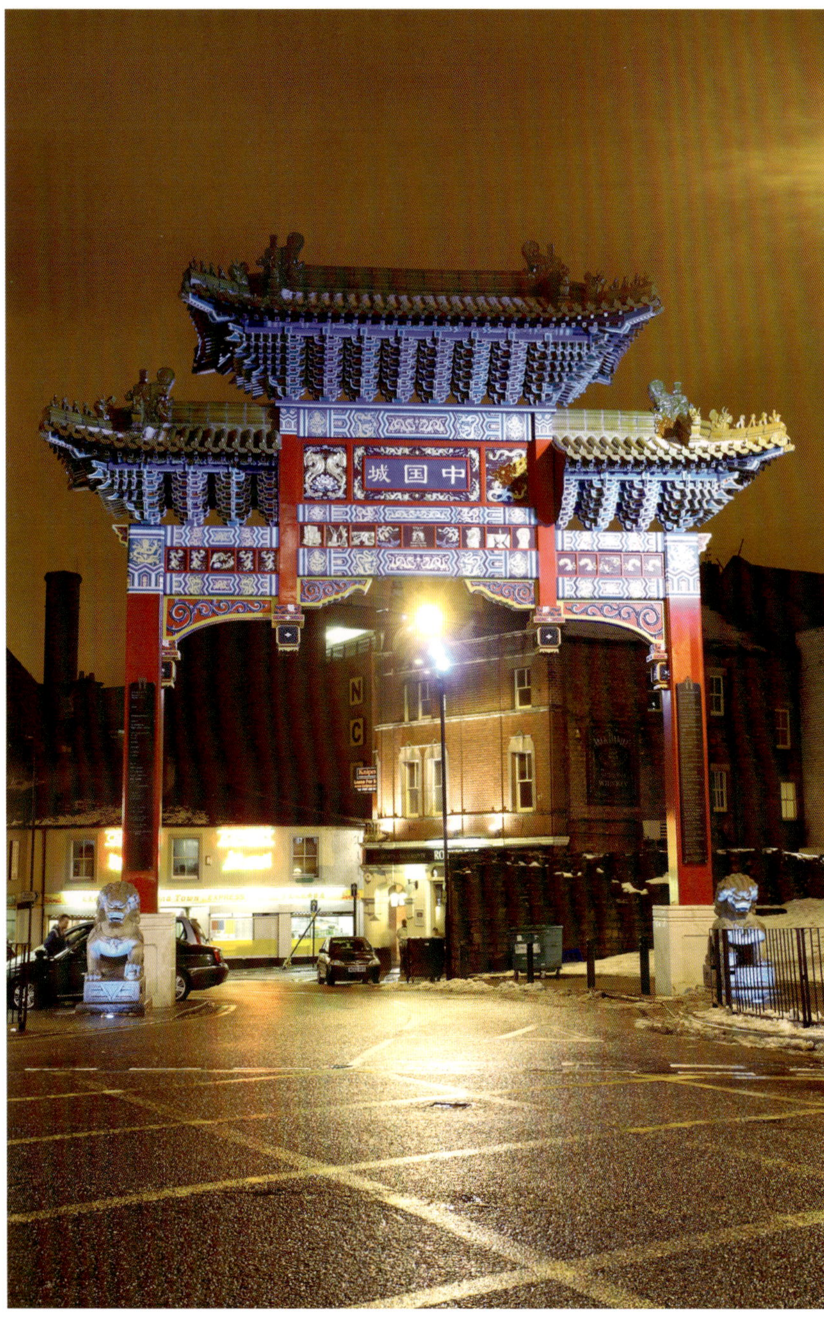

Chinatown Gate

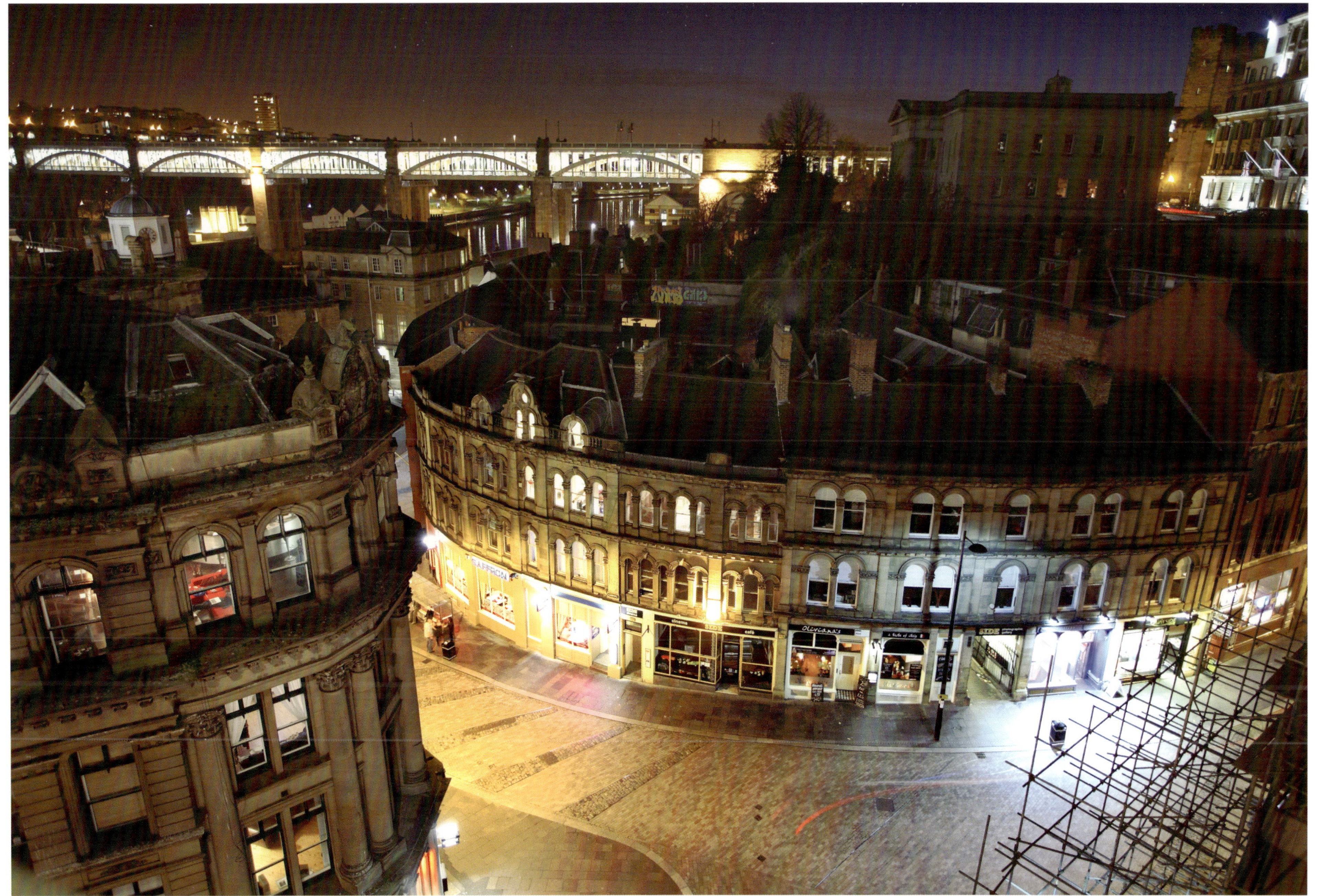

The Side (Quayside)

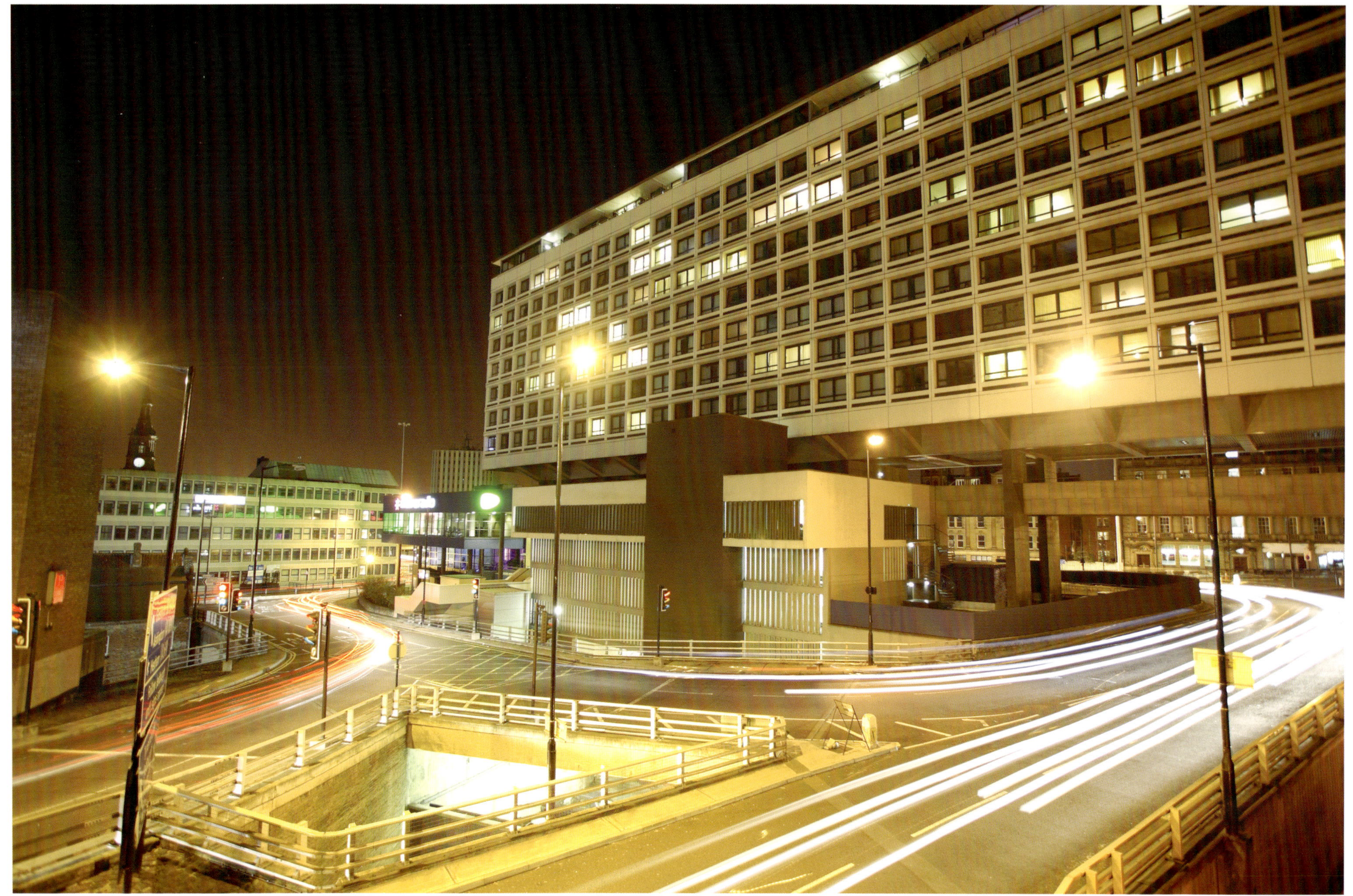

Swan House Roundabout

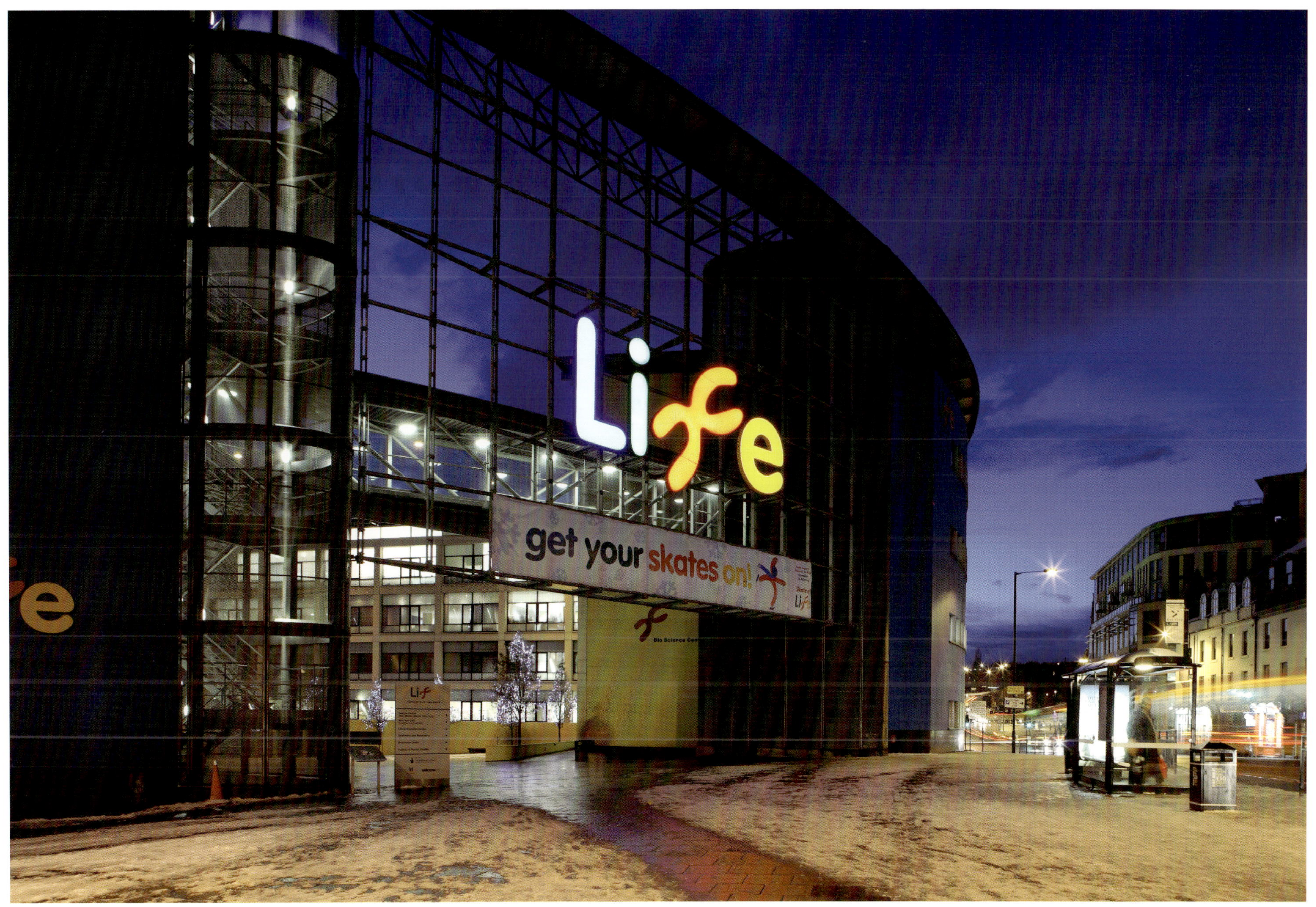

Centre for Life - Times Square

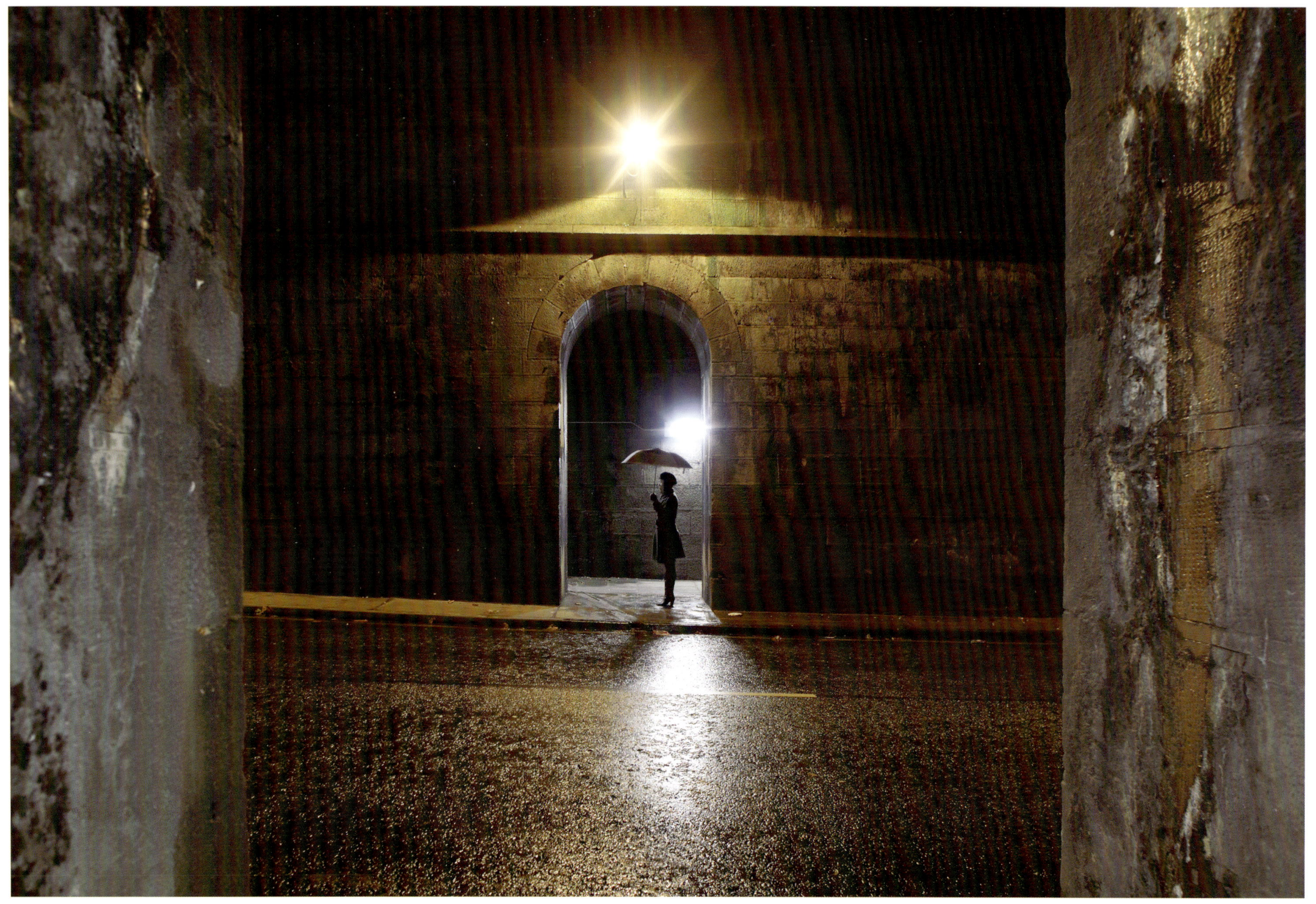

Under arches

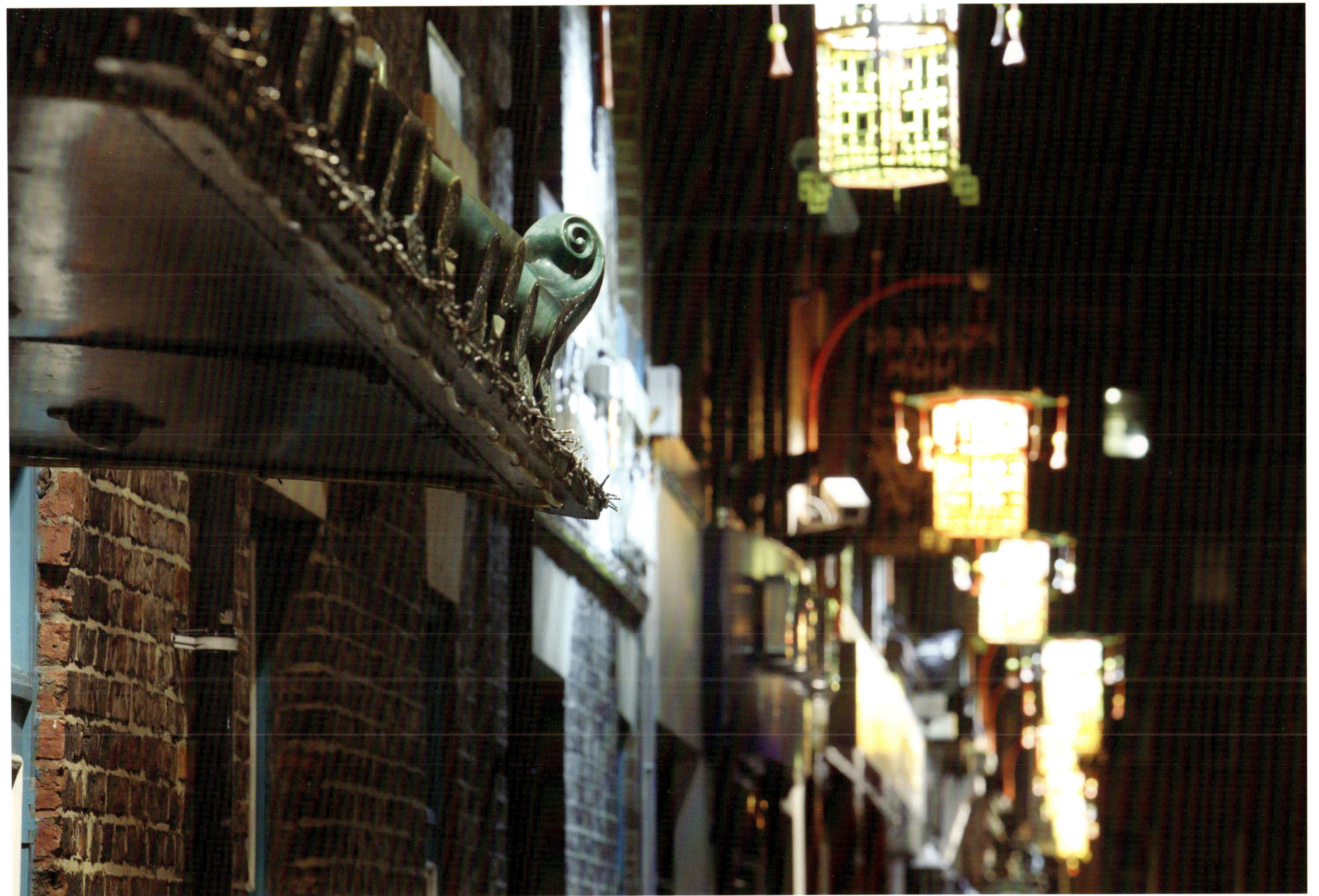

Stowell Street

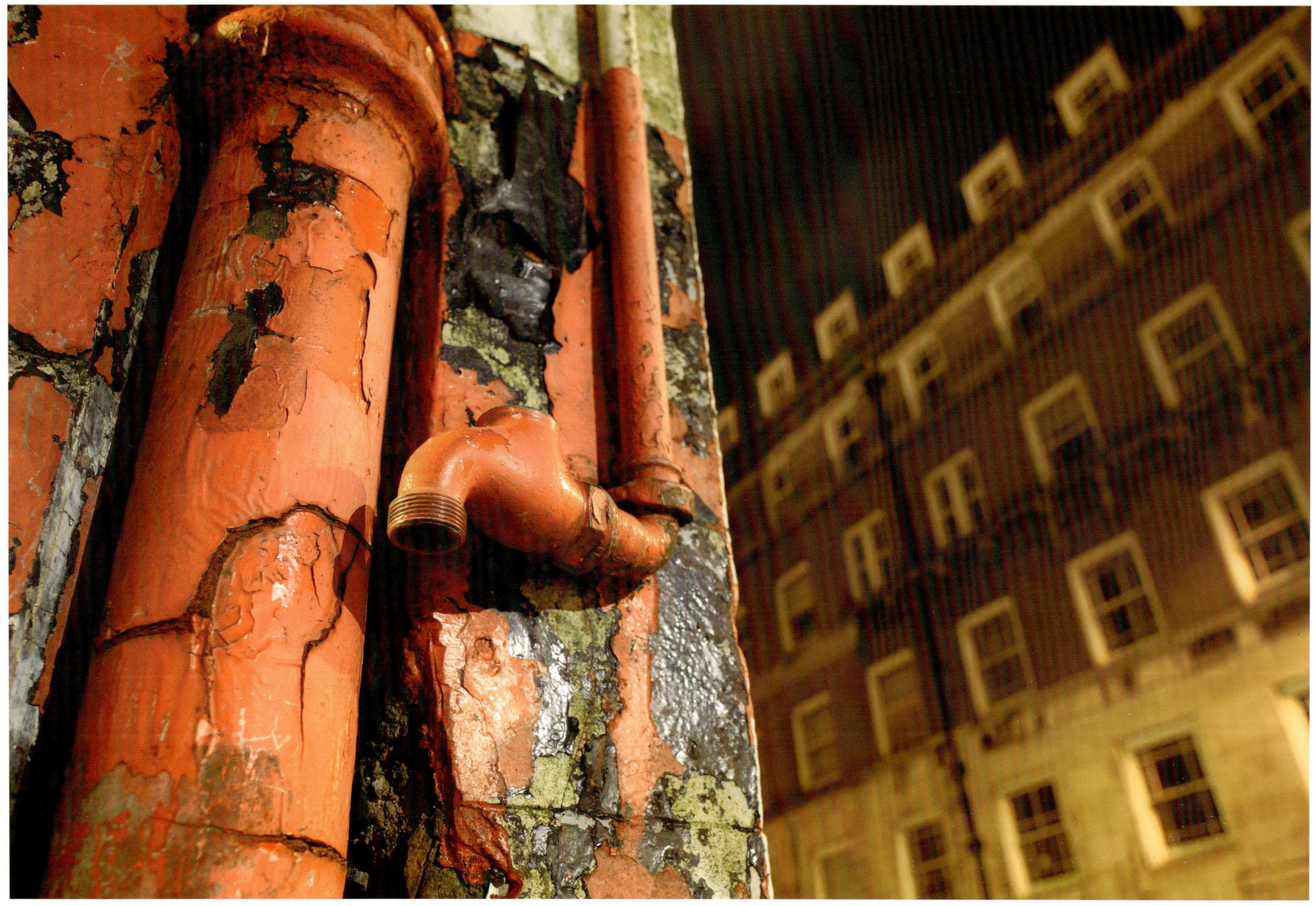

Worswick Street

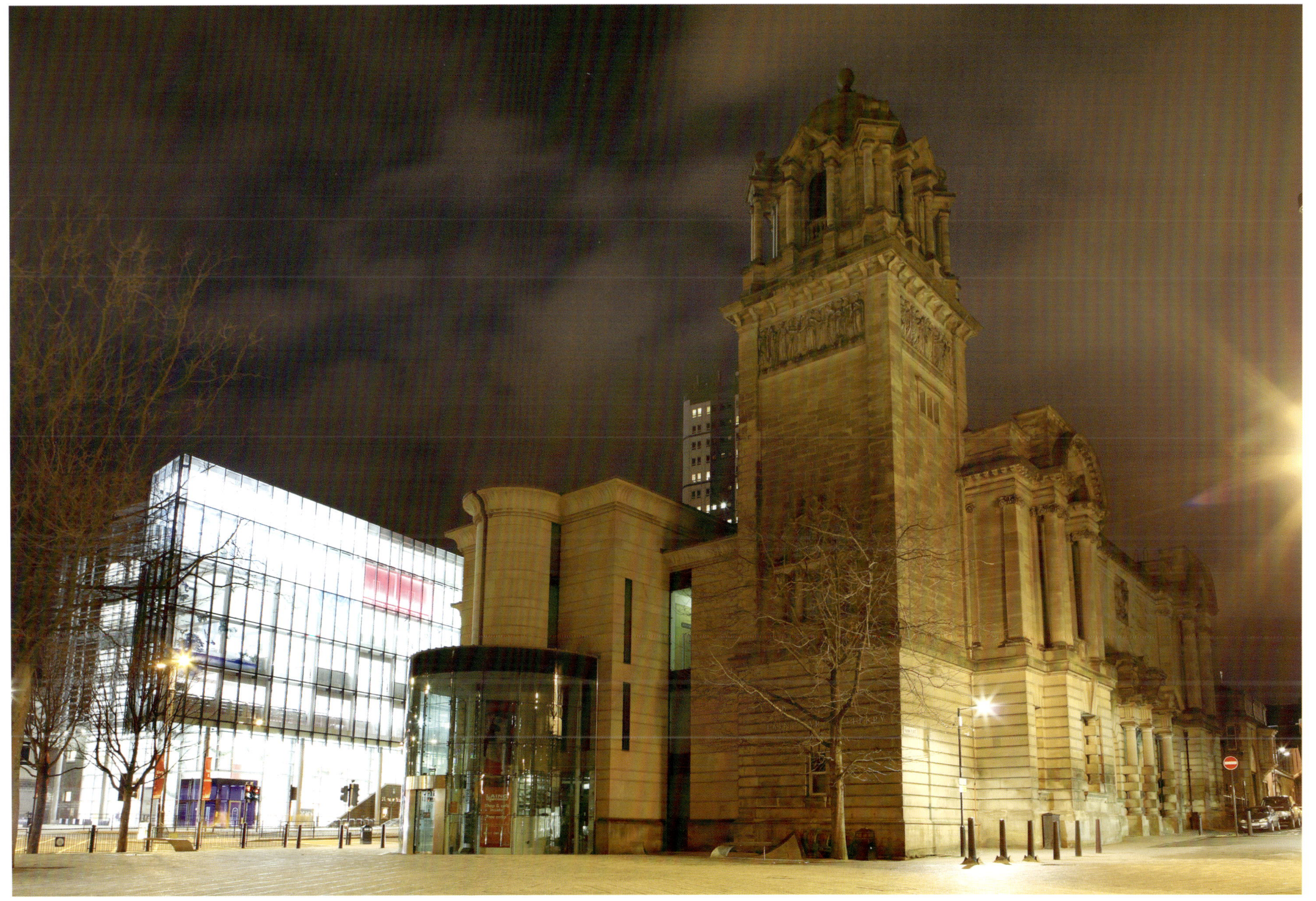

Laing Art Gallery

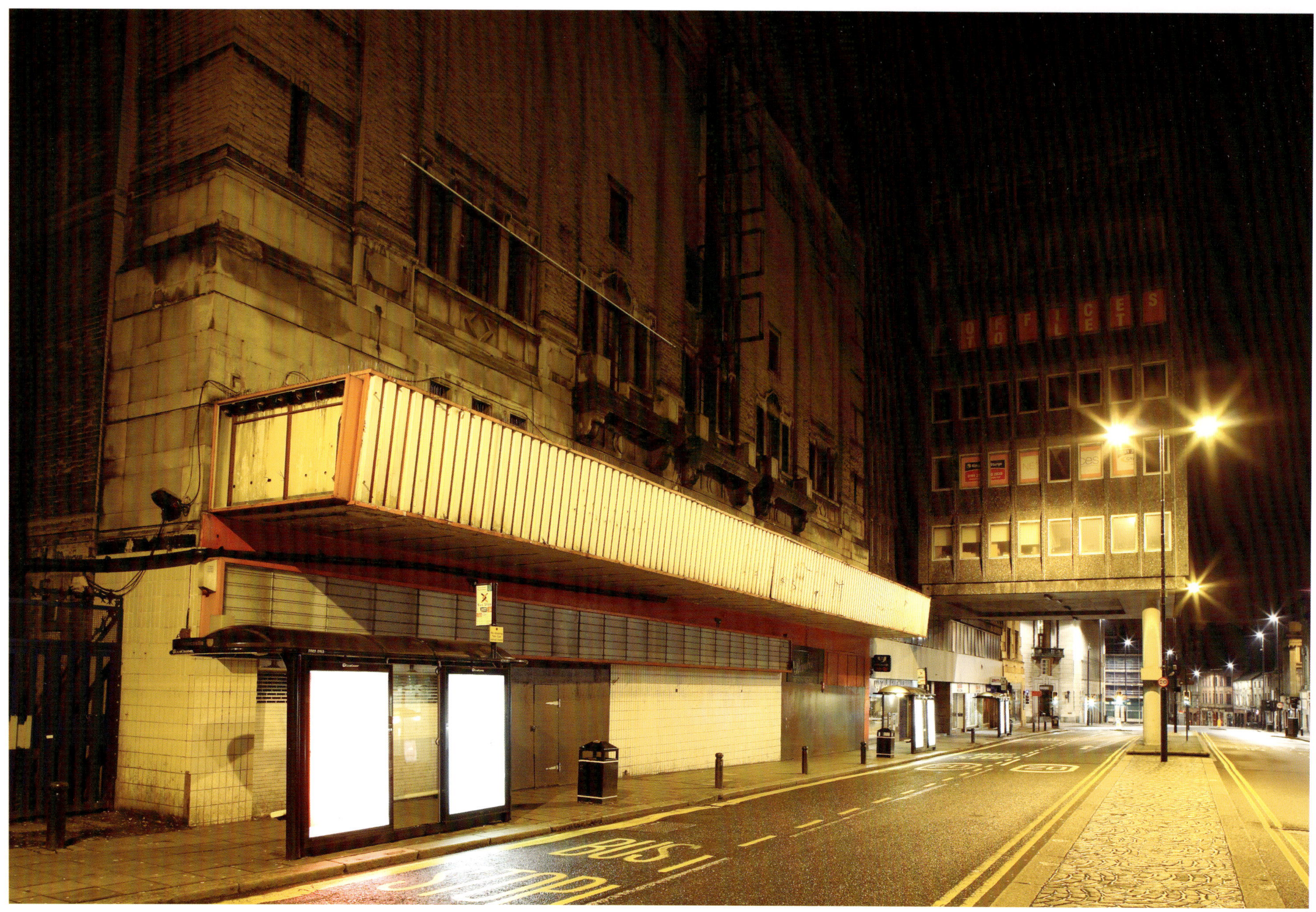

Disused Cinema - Pilgrim Street

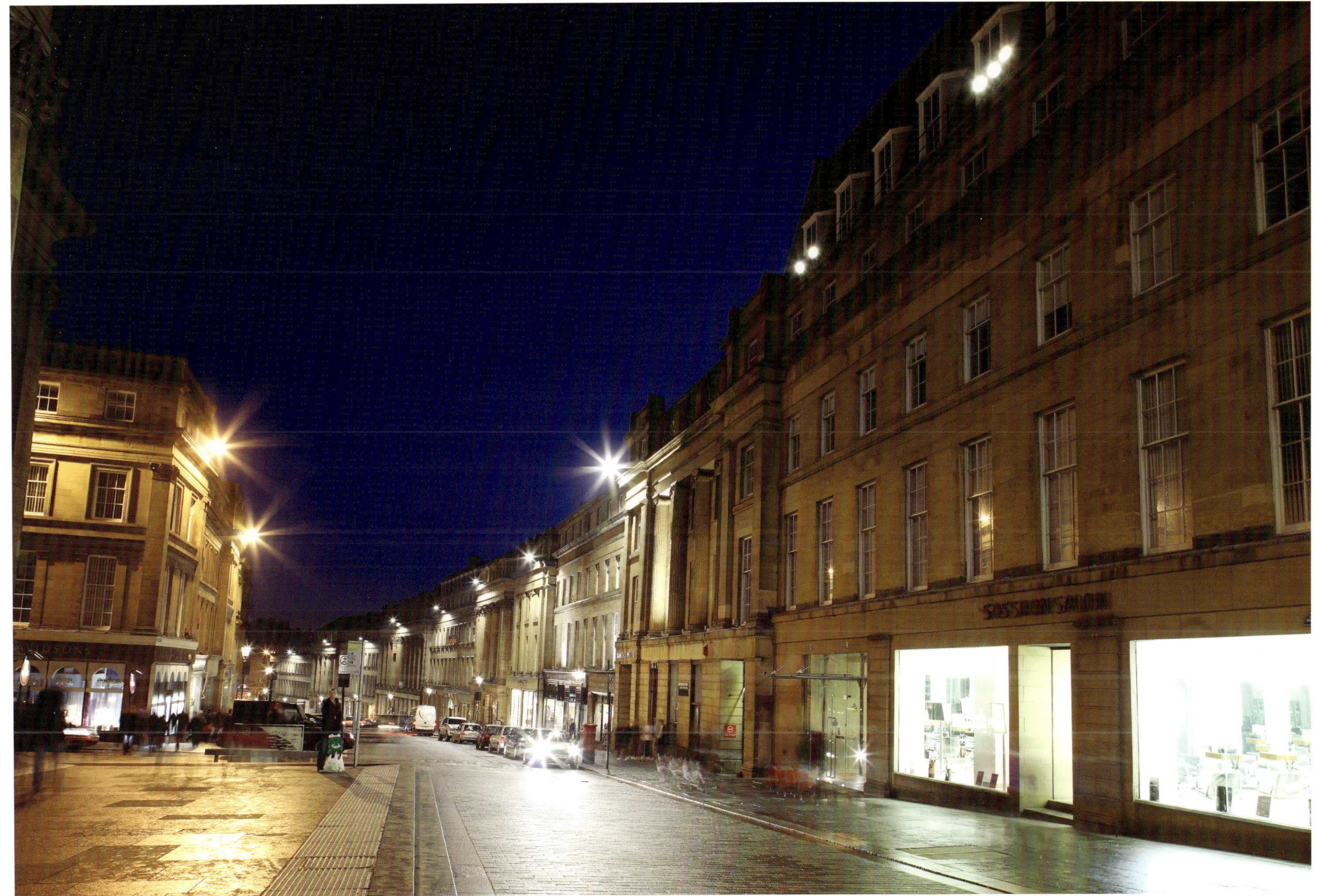

Grey Street

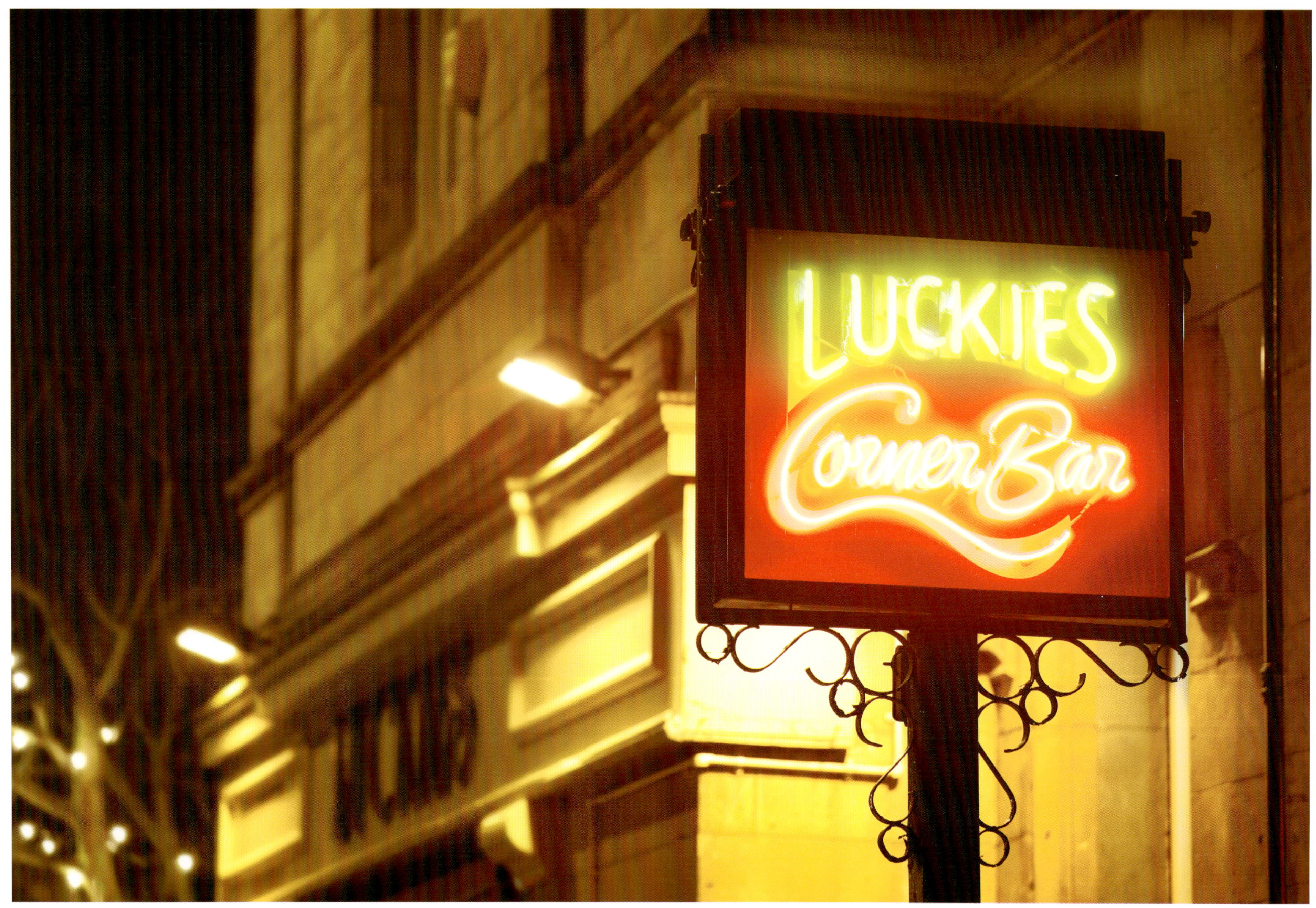

Luckies Corner Bar

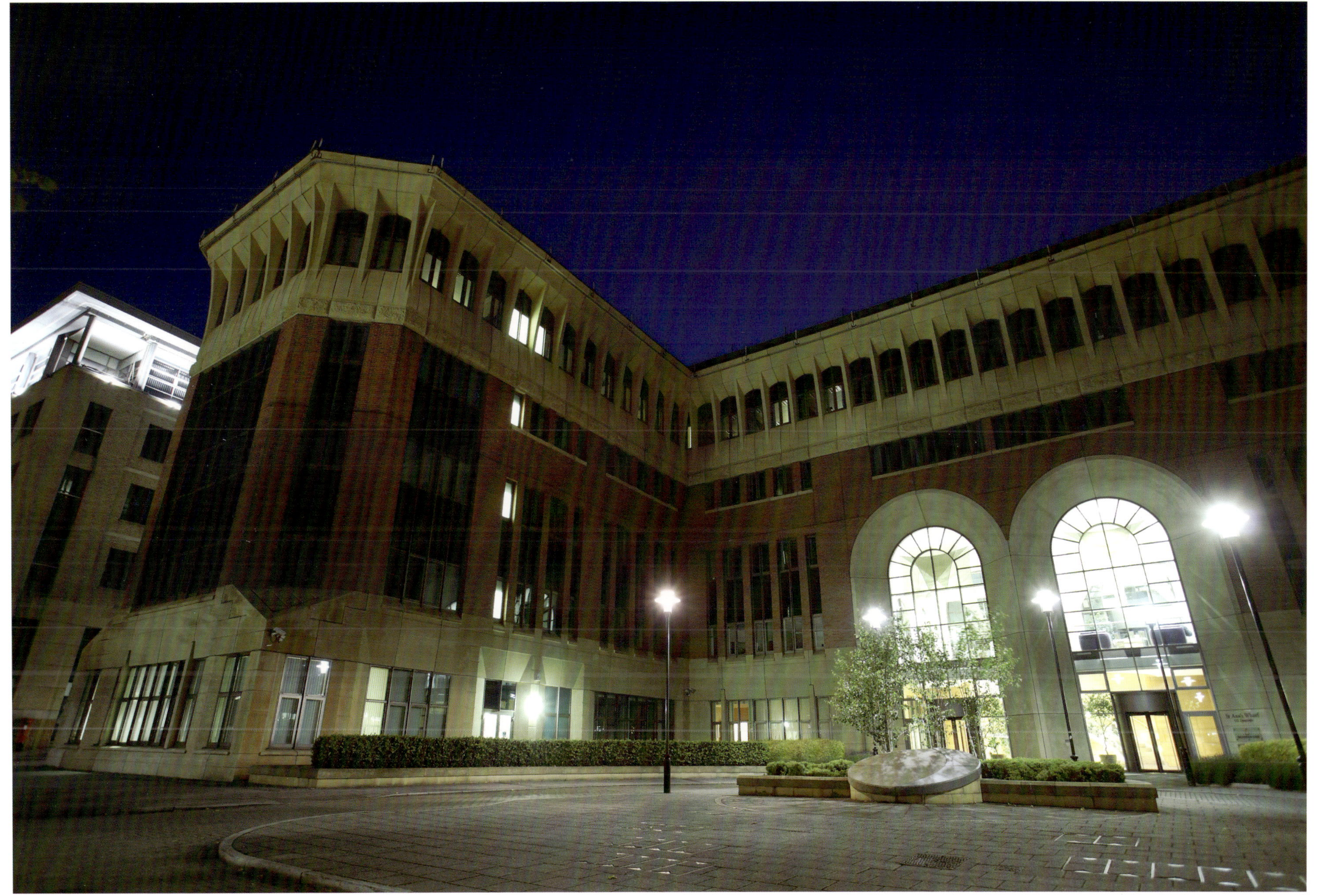

St Ann's Wharf

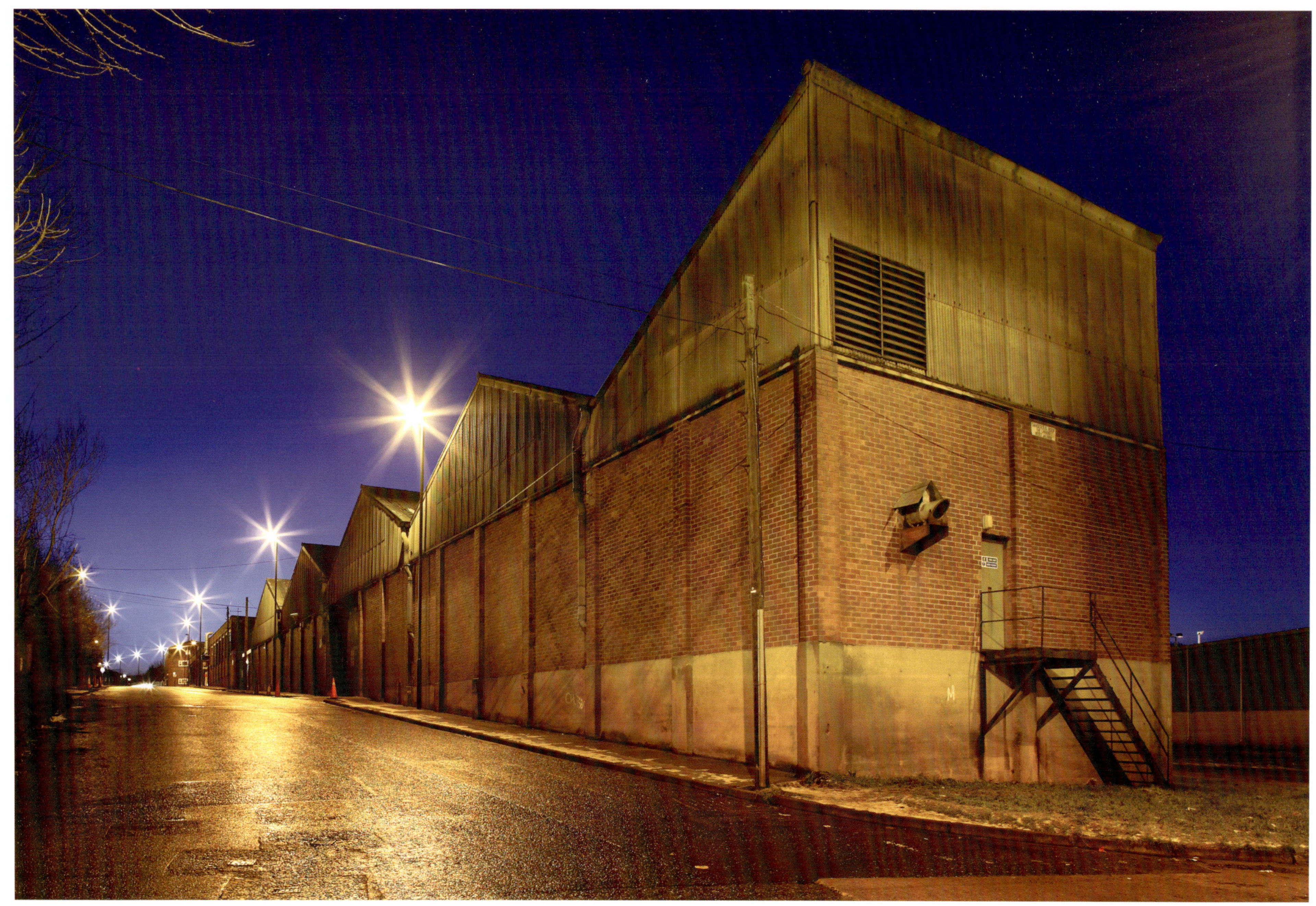

Industrial Building - East Quayside

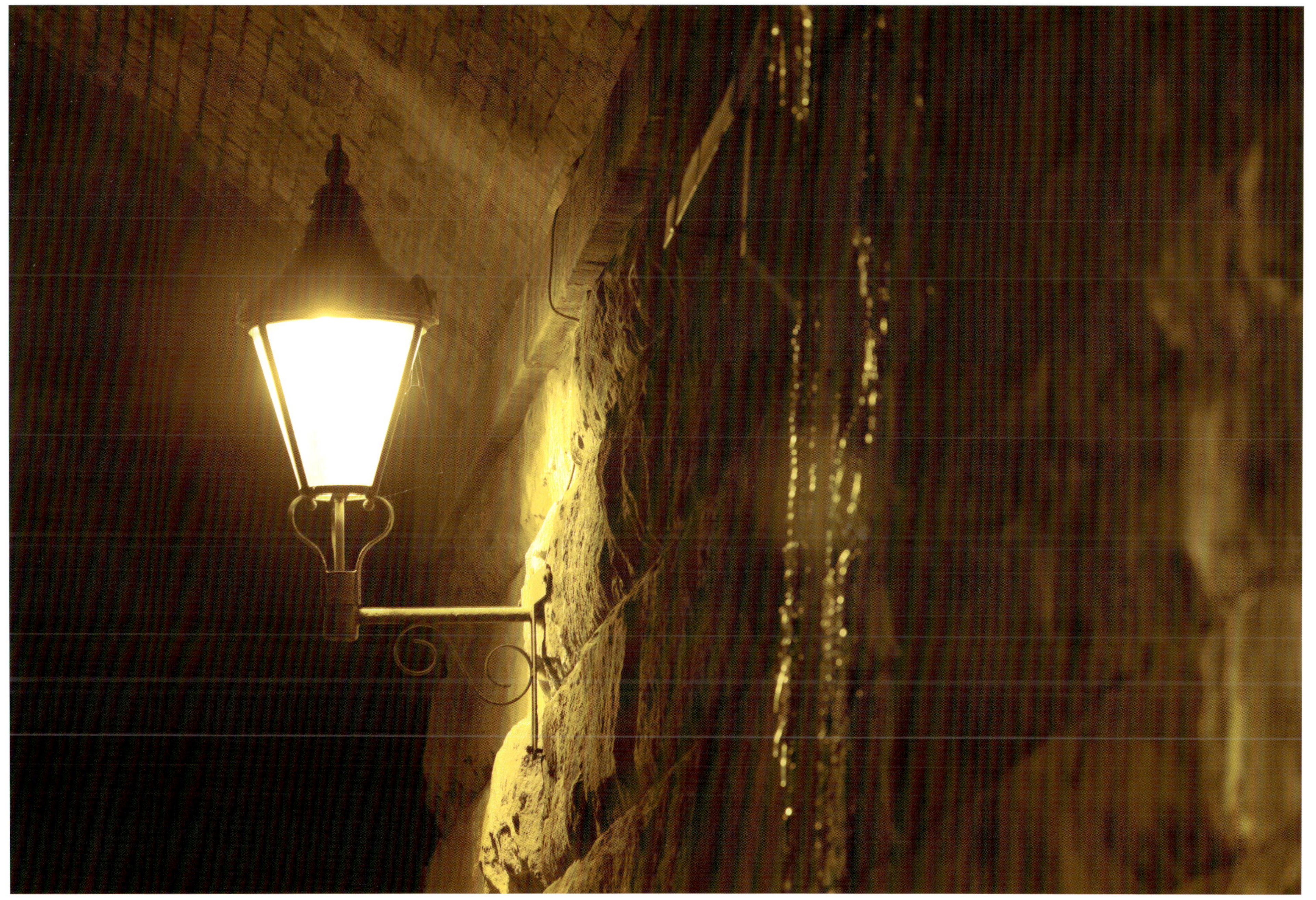

Under Bridge ECM17

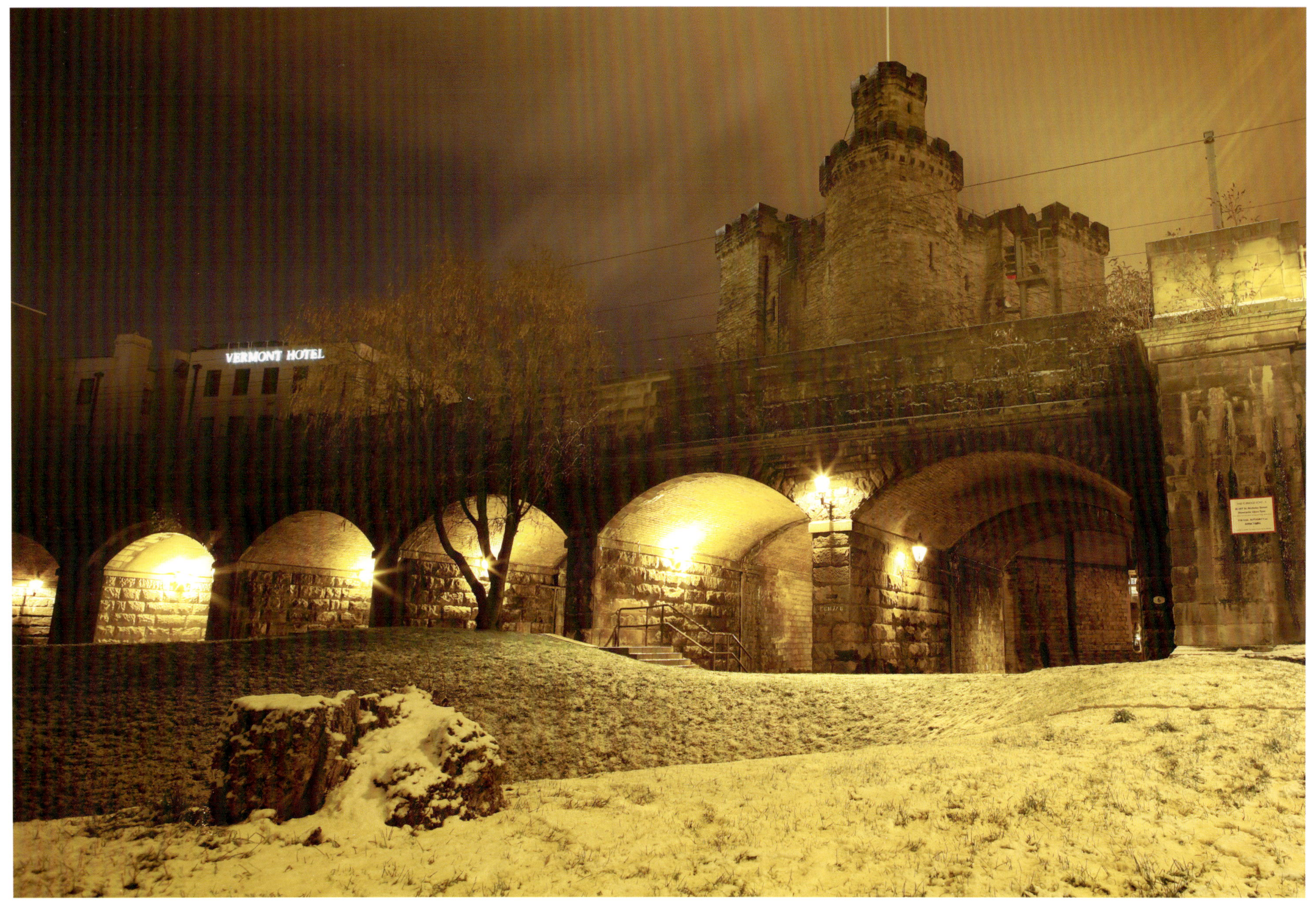

Newcastle Keep

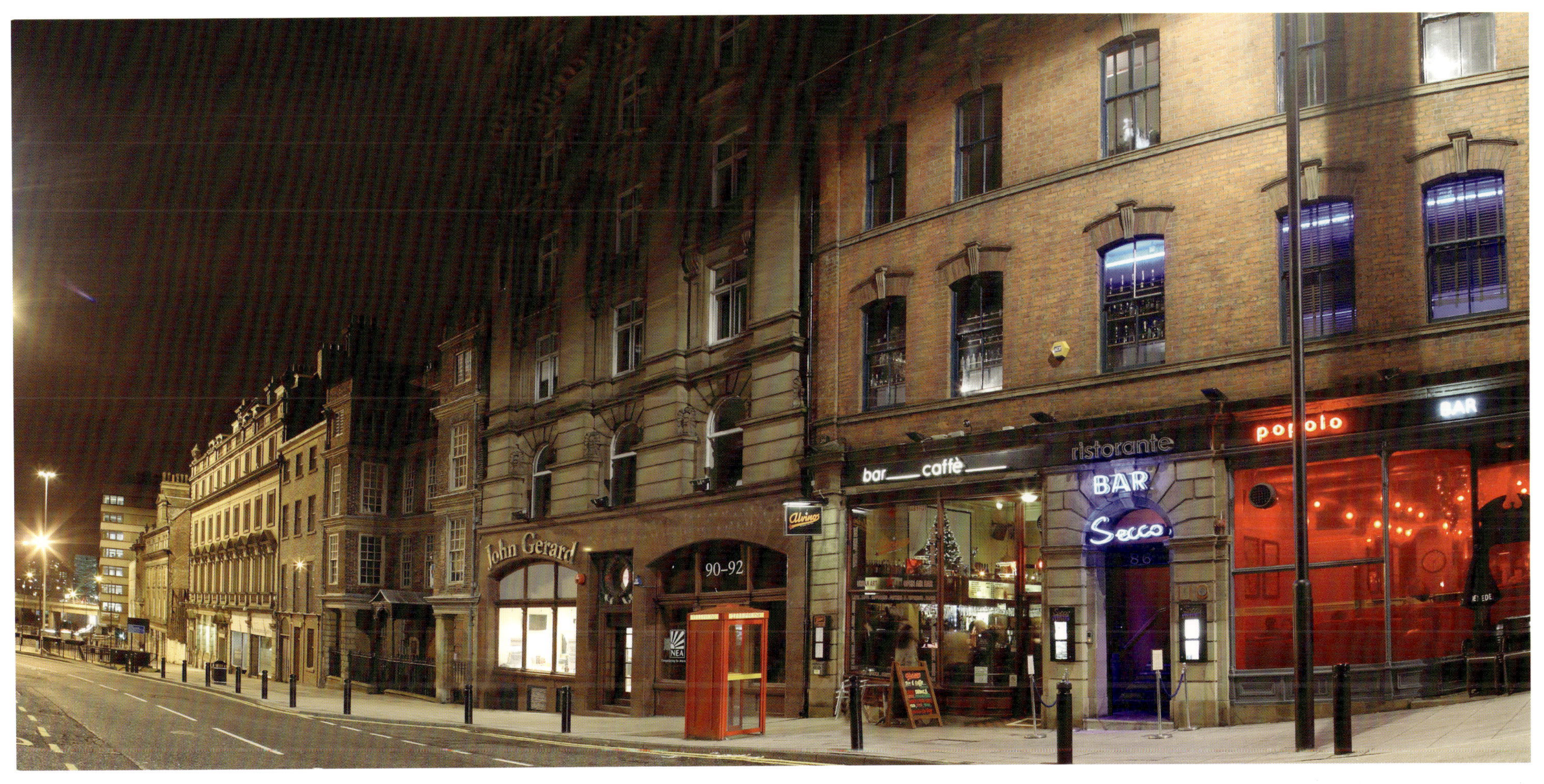

Pilgrim Street

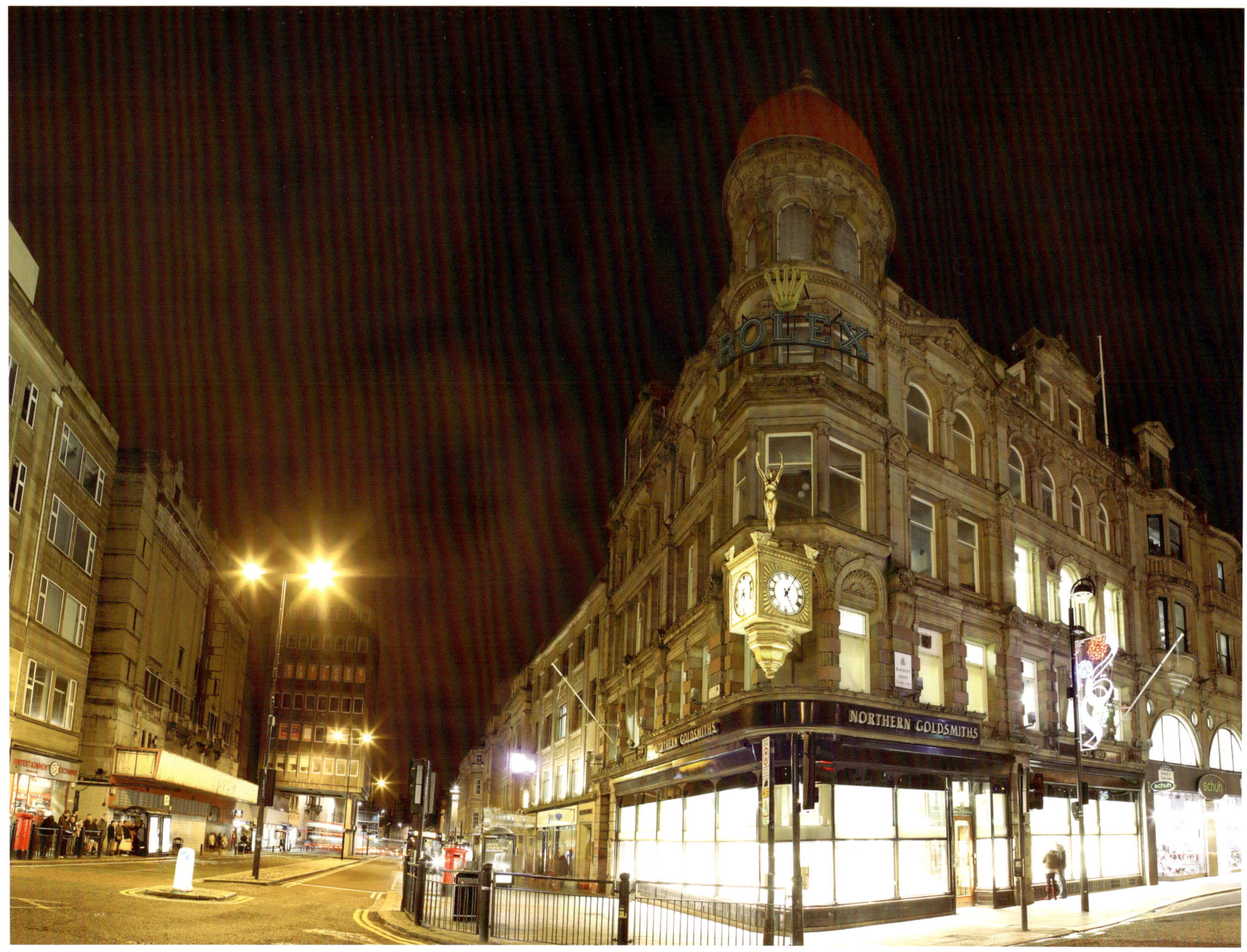

Blackett Street

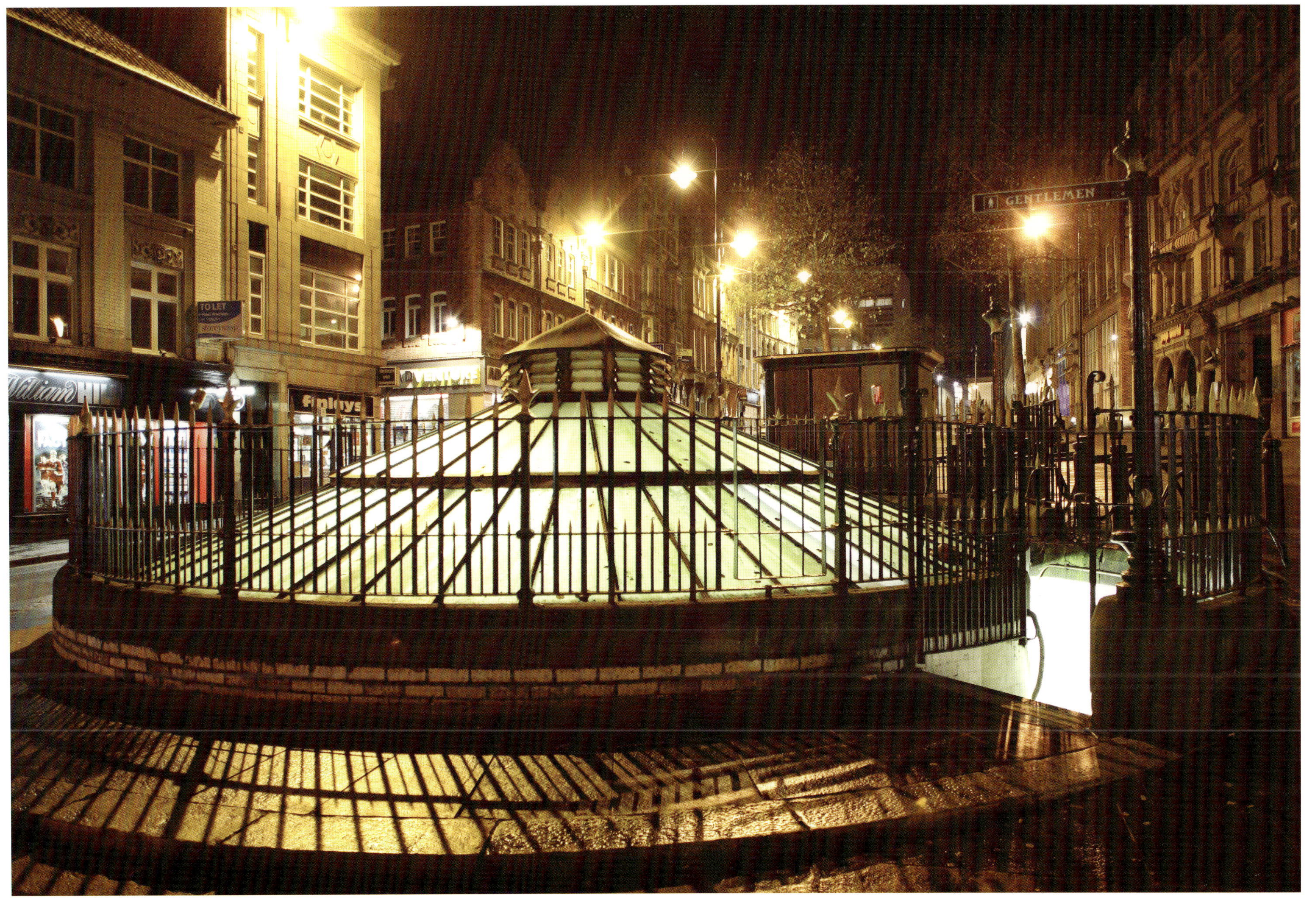

Victorian Toilets - The Bigg Market

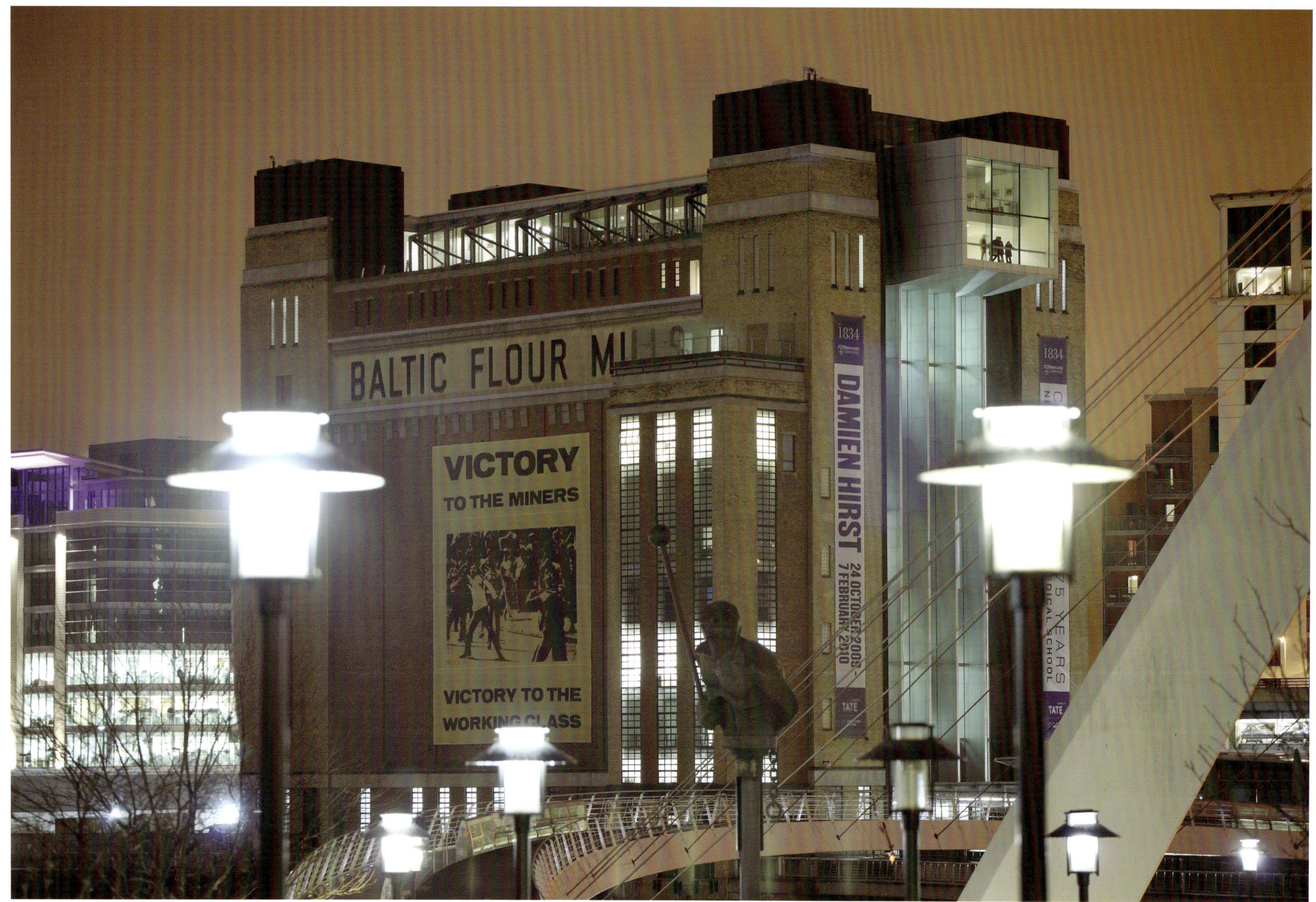

Baltic Flour Mills

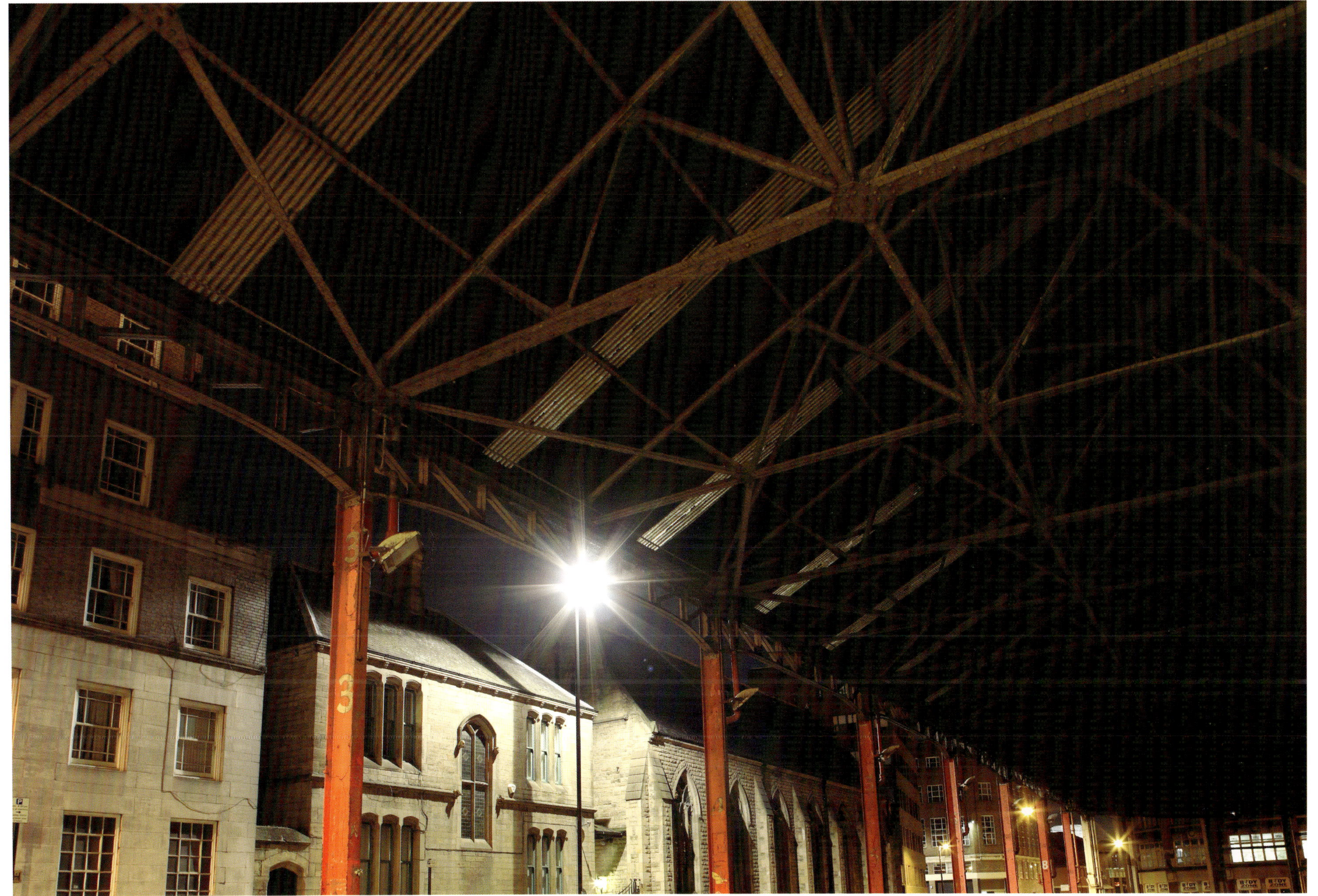

Worsick Street

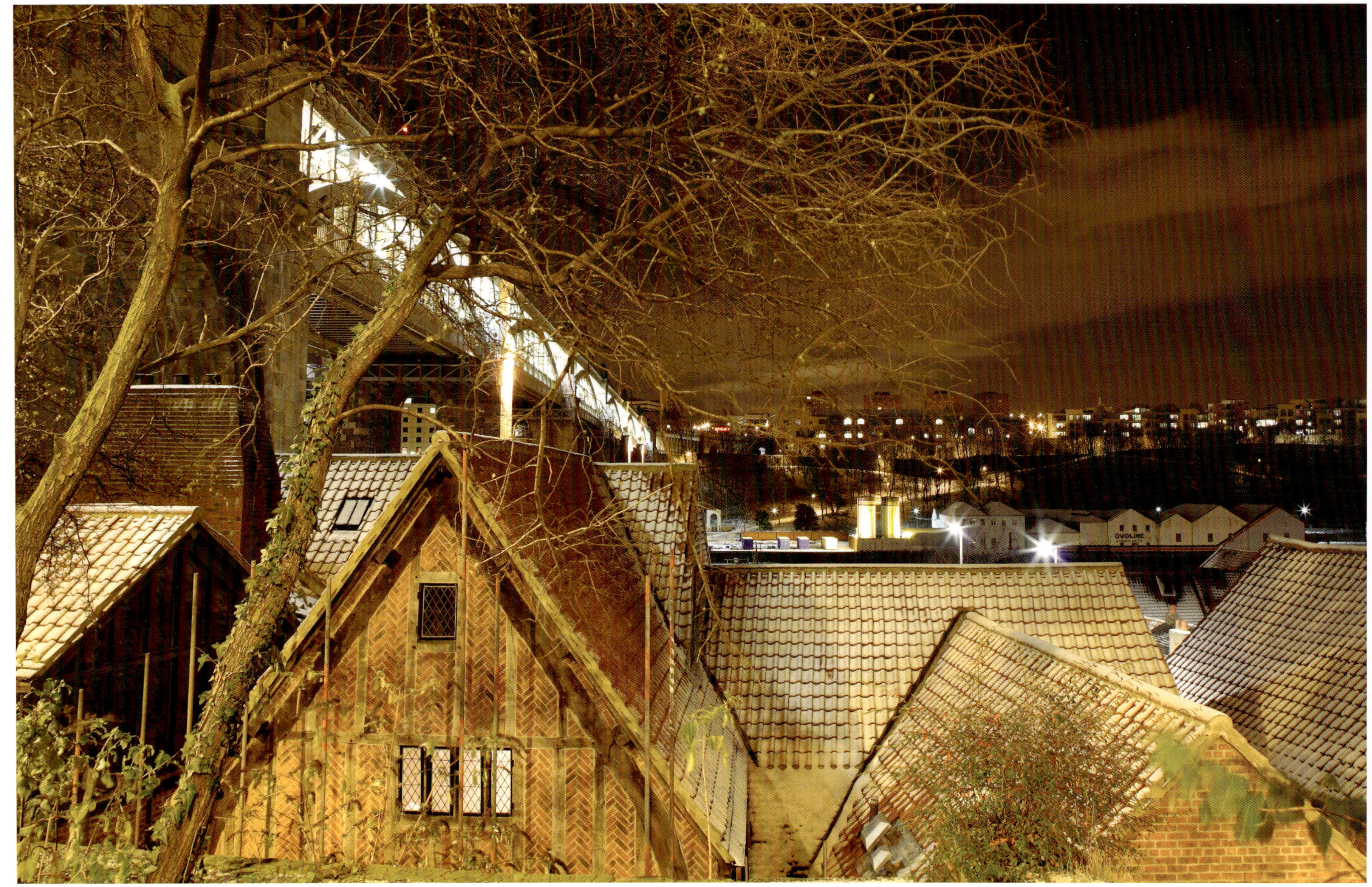

Behind Buttress House

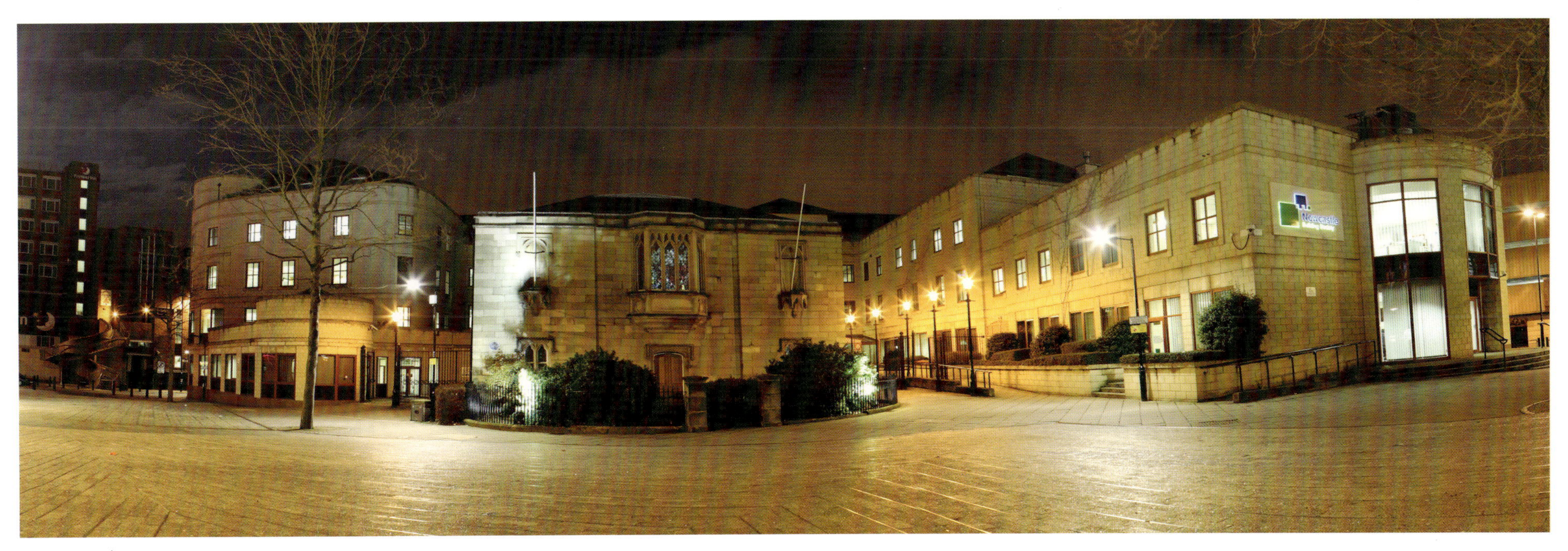

Higham Place

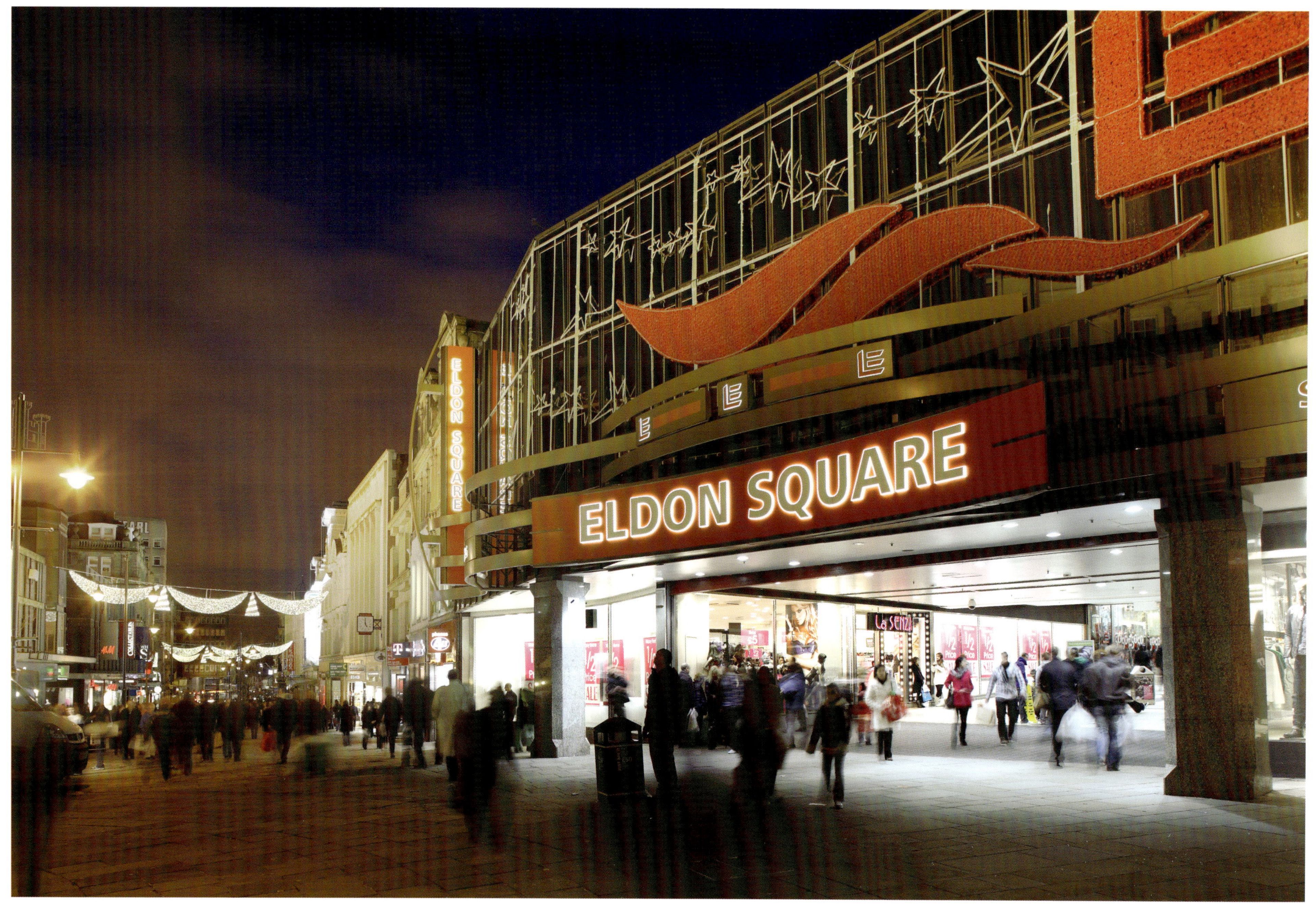

Eldon Square - Northumberland Street

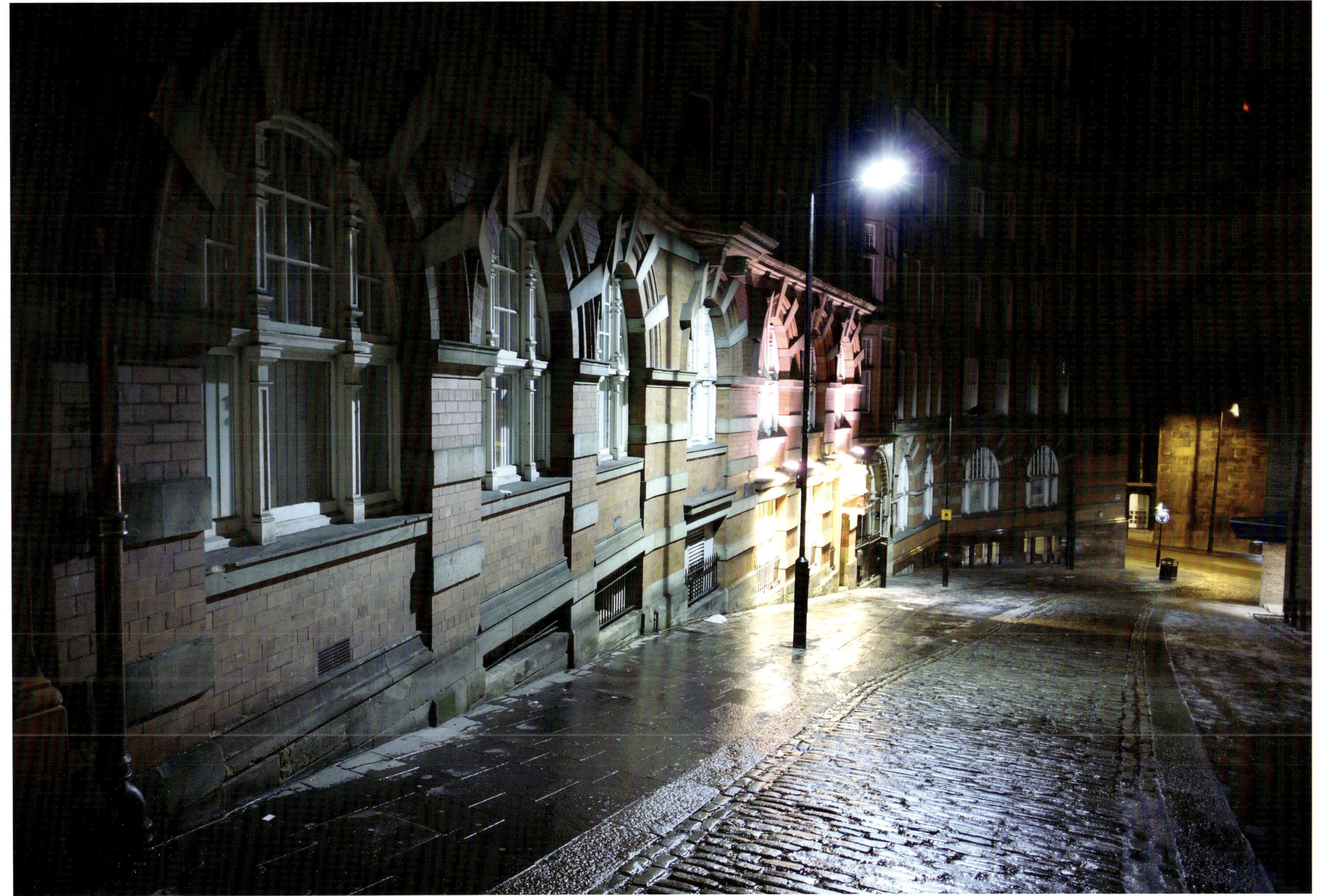

The Side

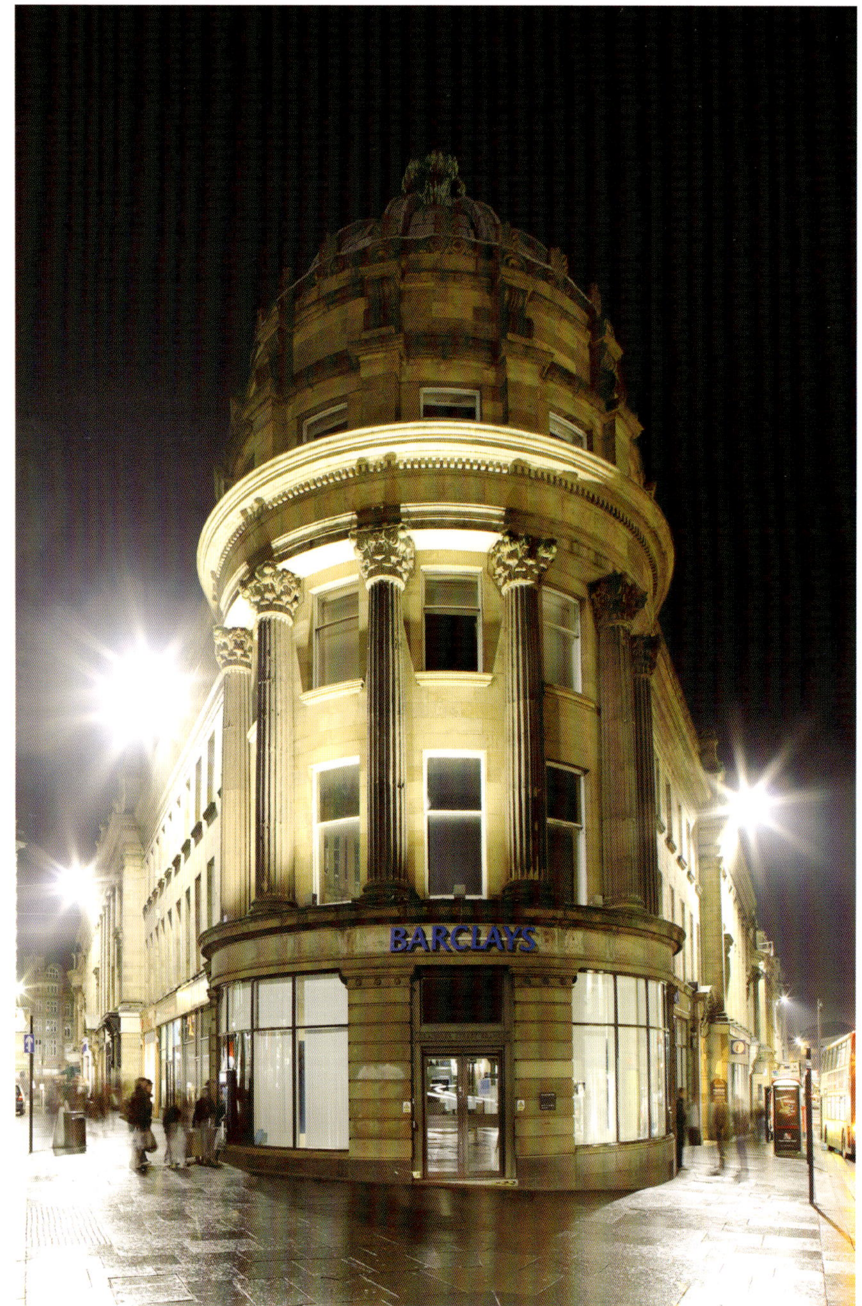

Grainger Street Corner

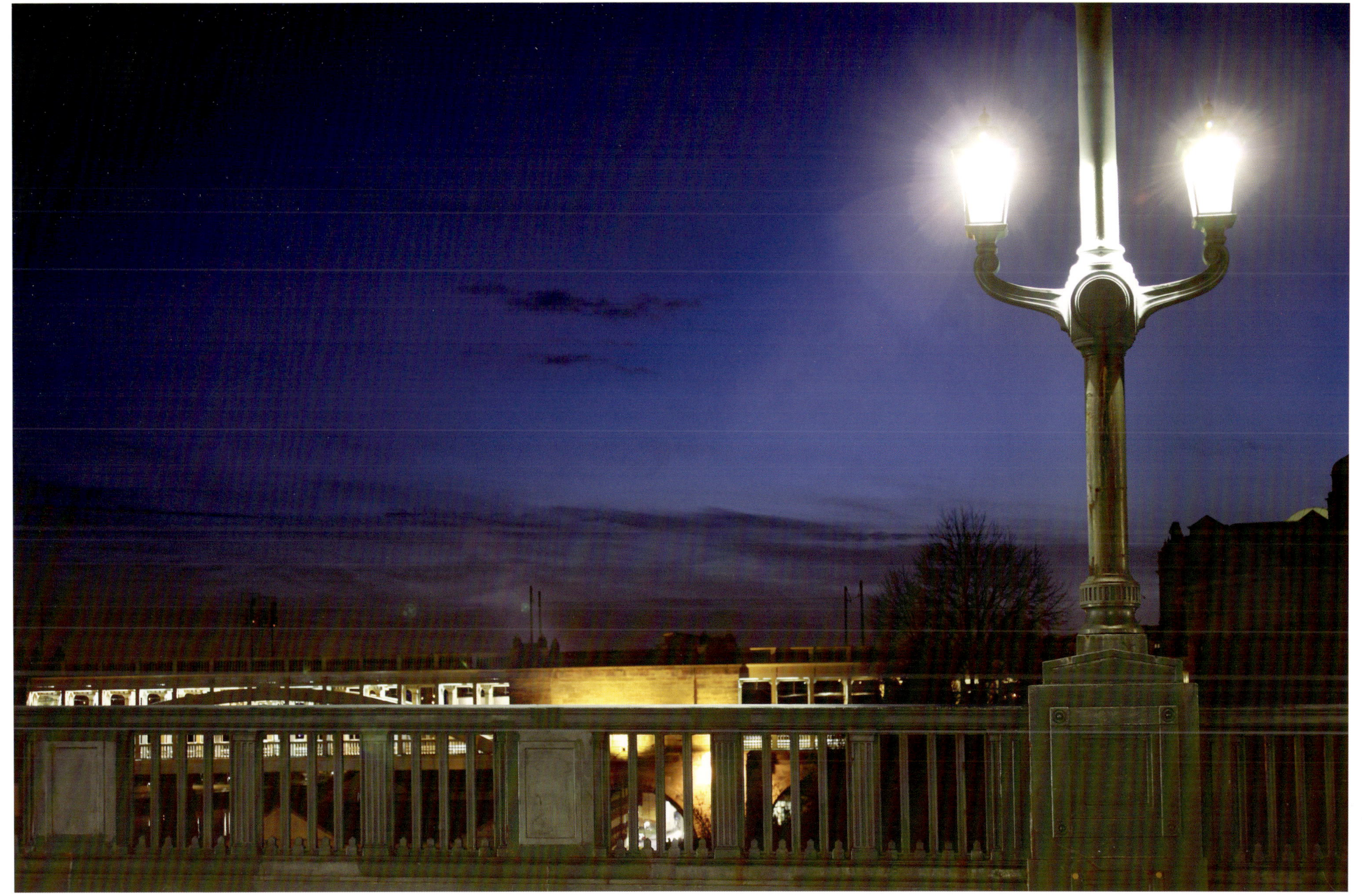

Tyne Bridge

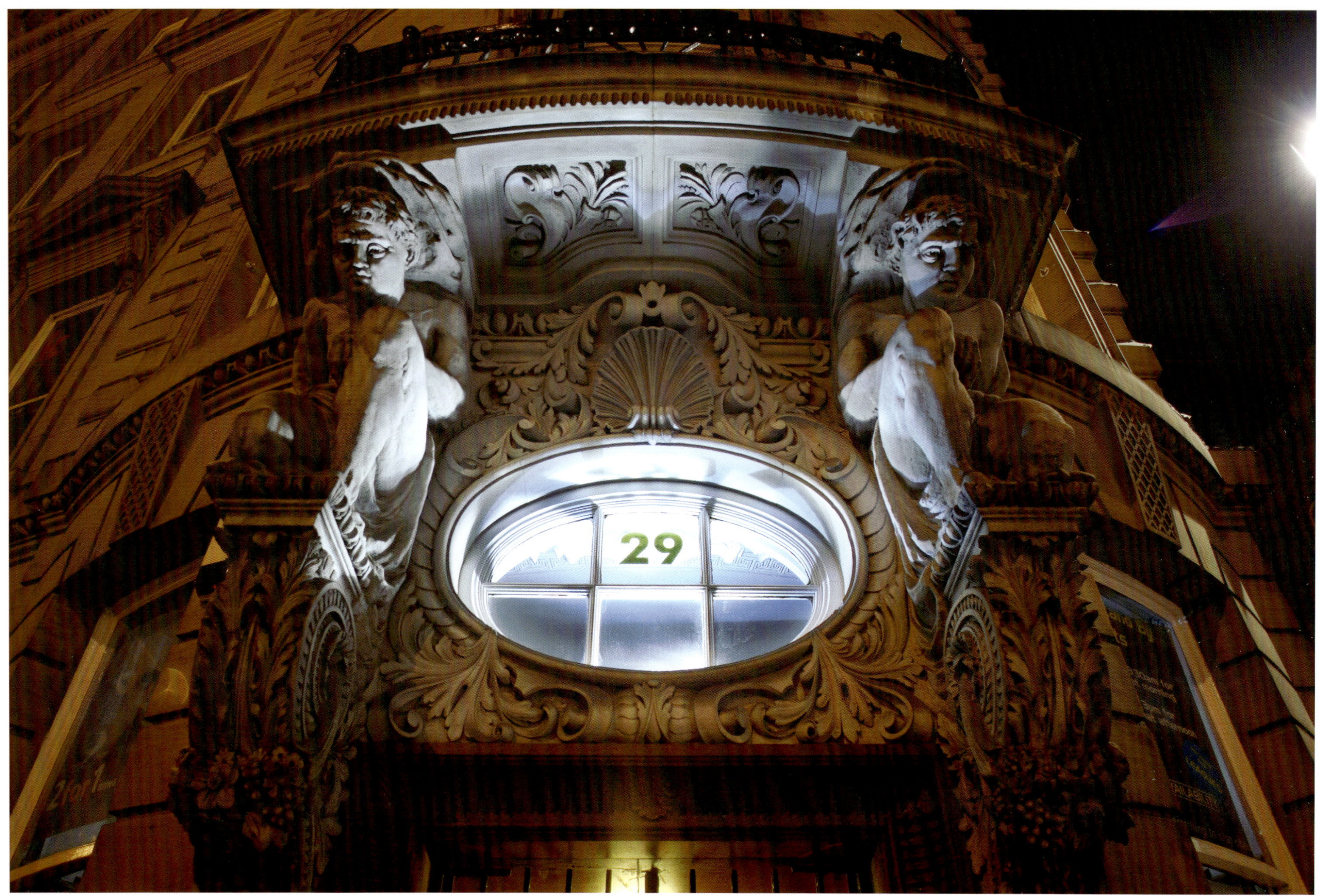

Collingwood Street Doorway

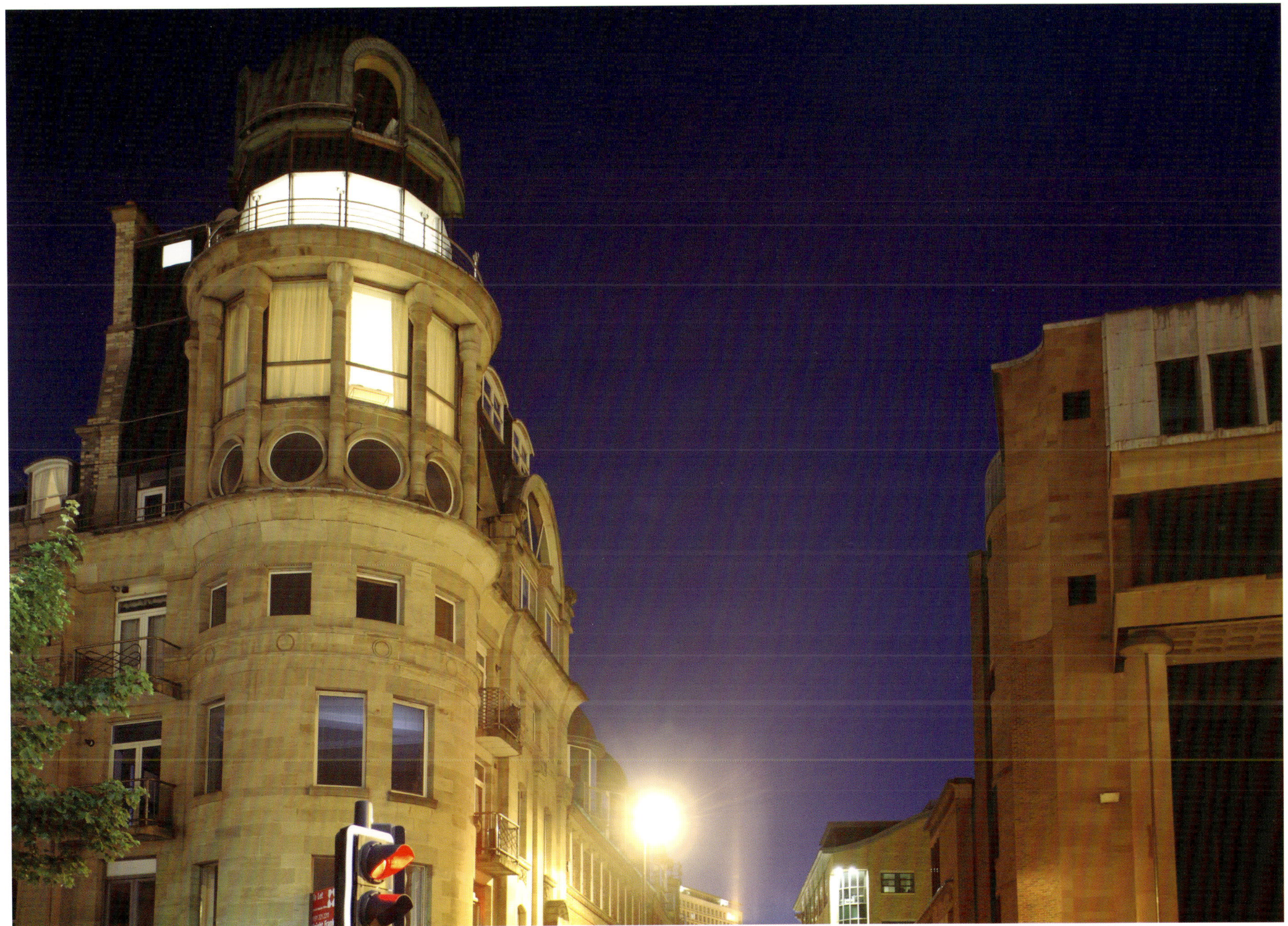

The Quayside

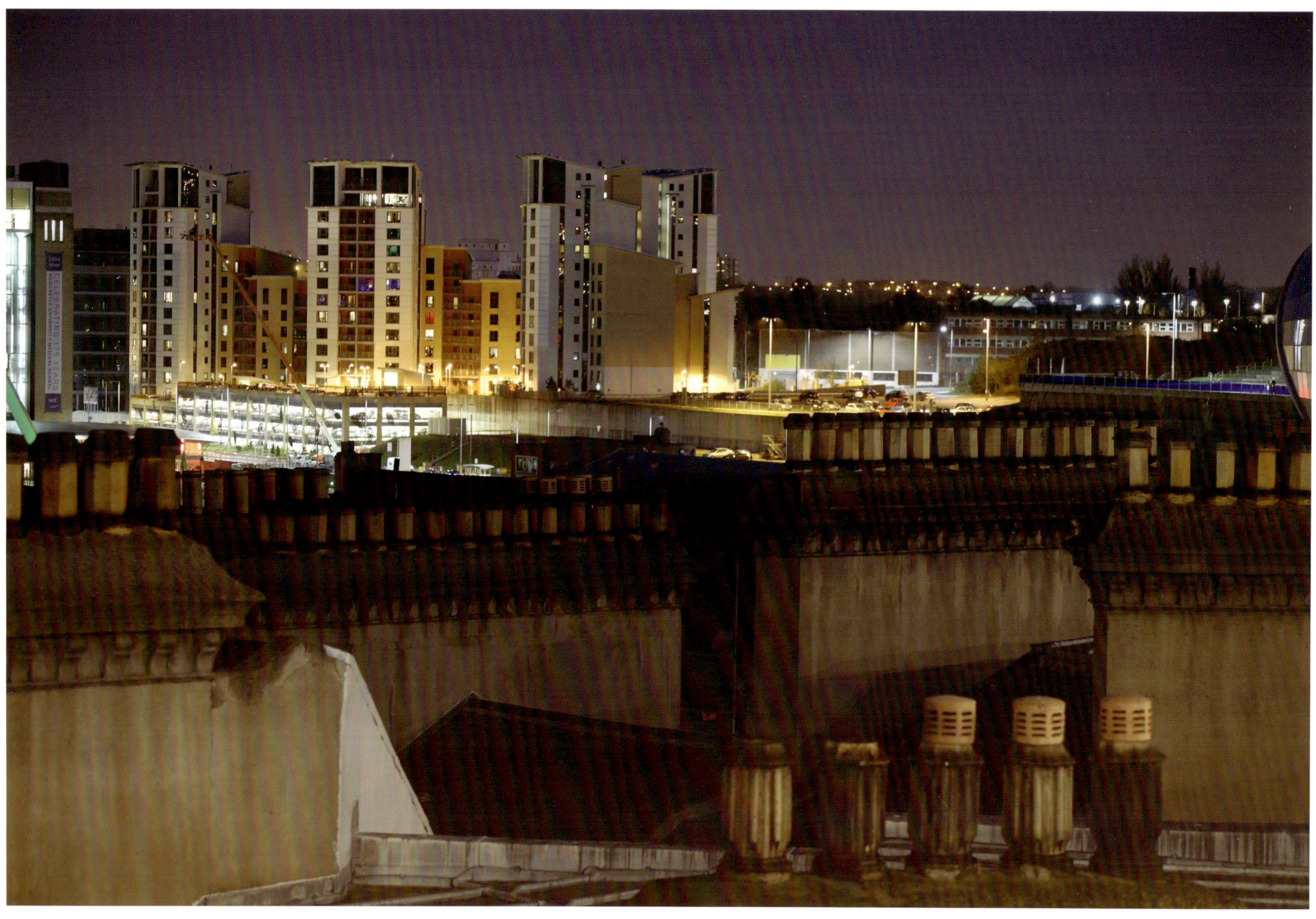

Chimney Pots with Gateshead in the Background

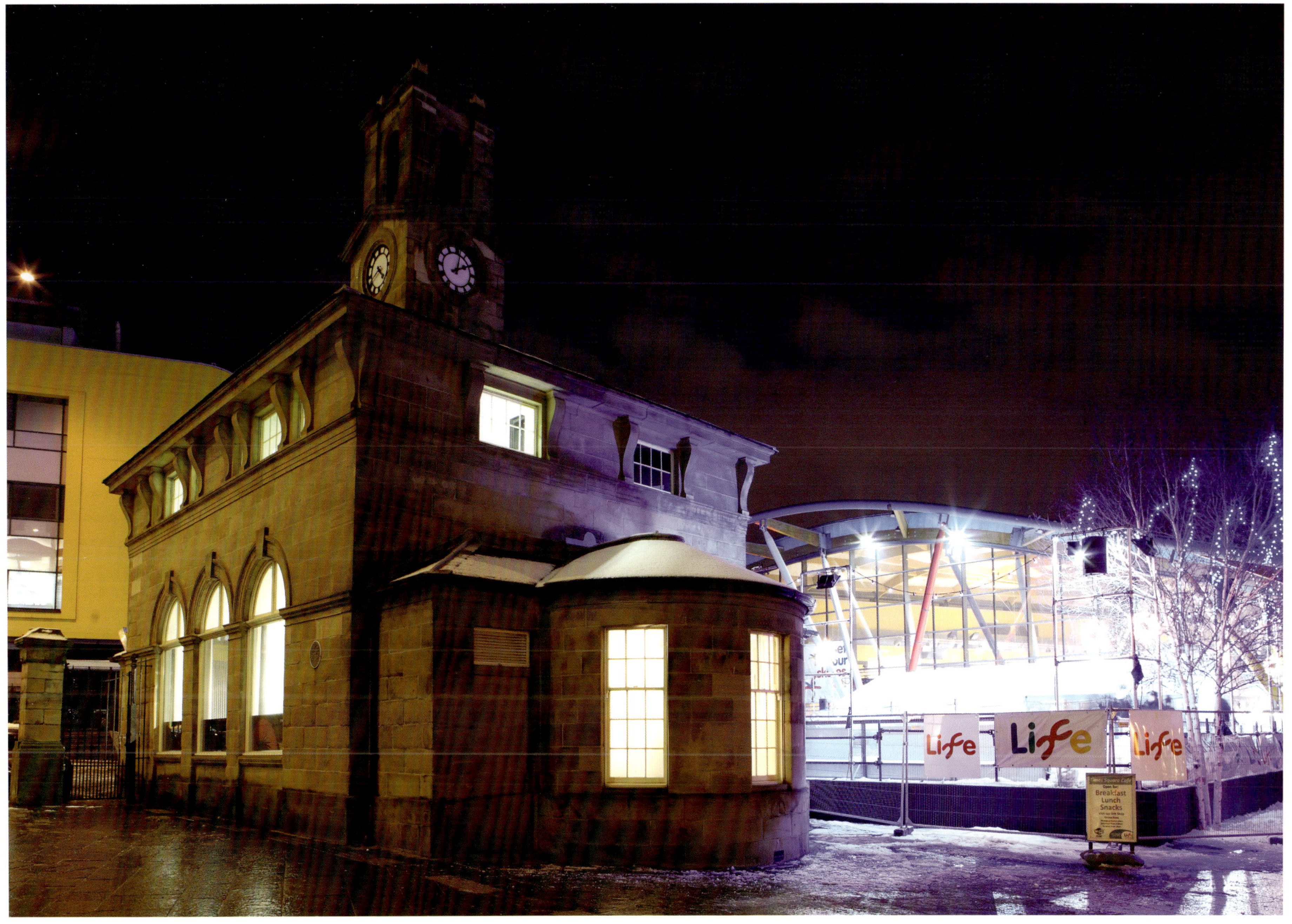

Cattle Market Office

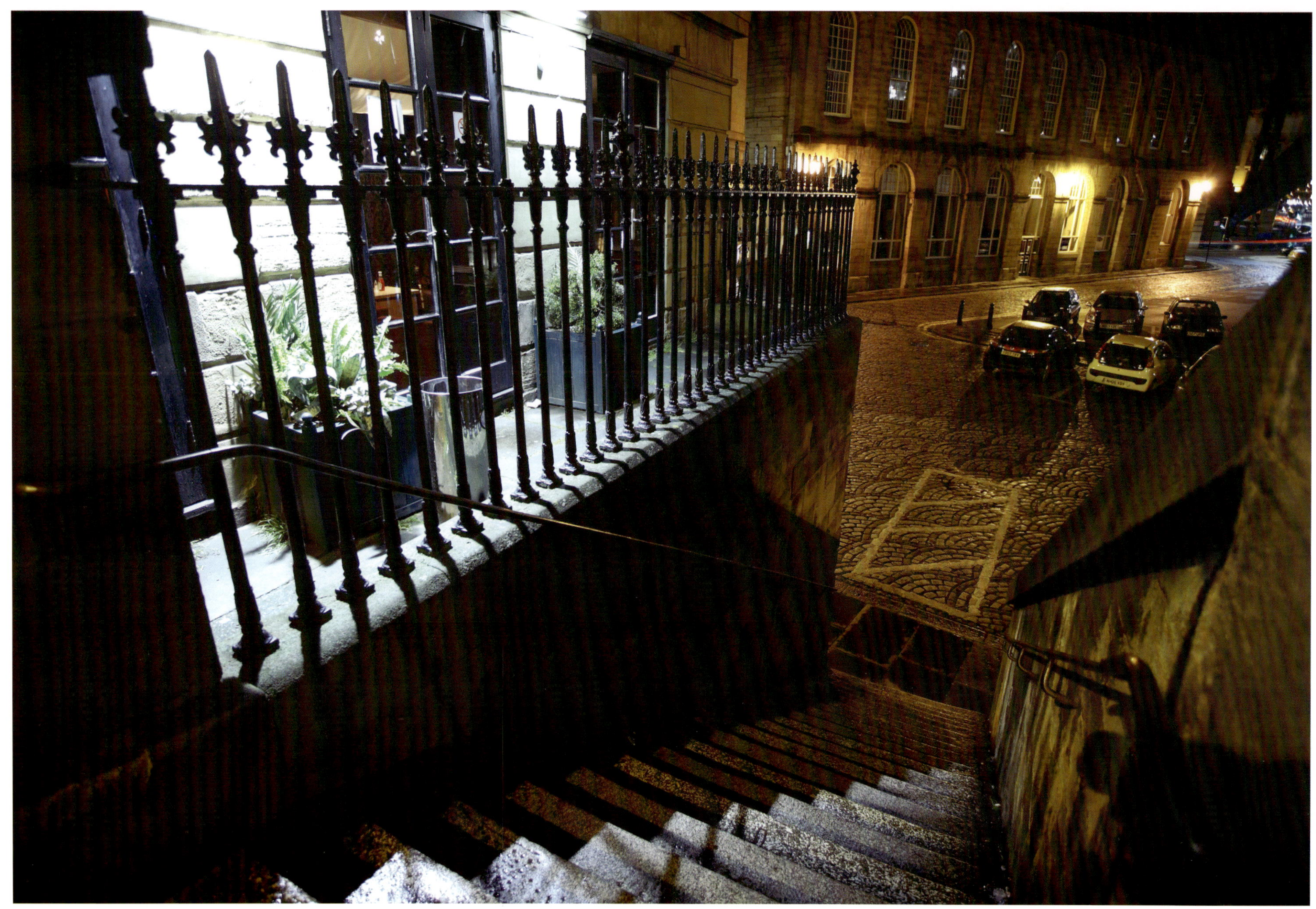

Staircase near Swing Bridge

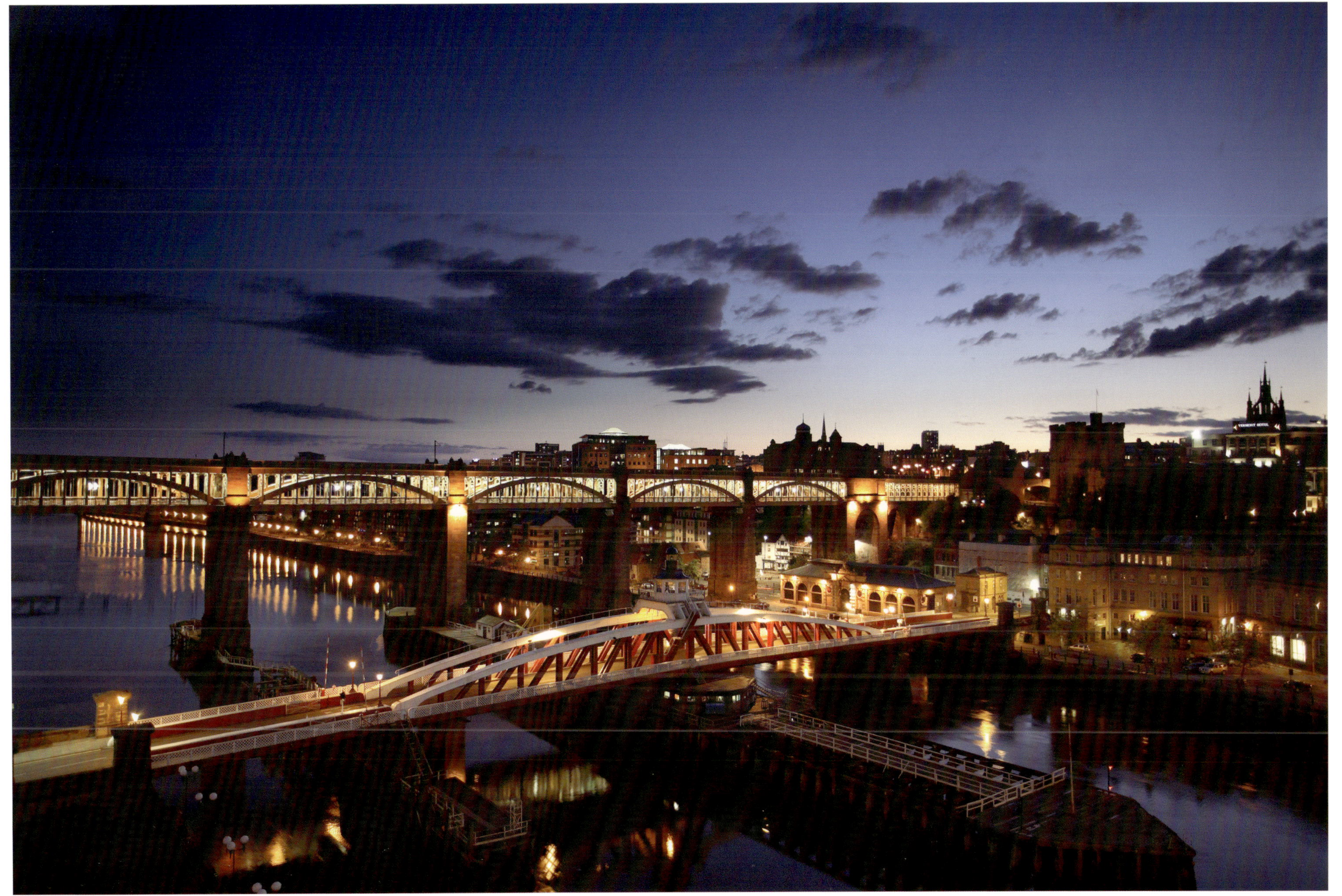

Tyne View

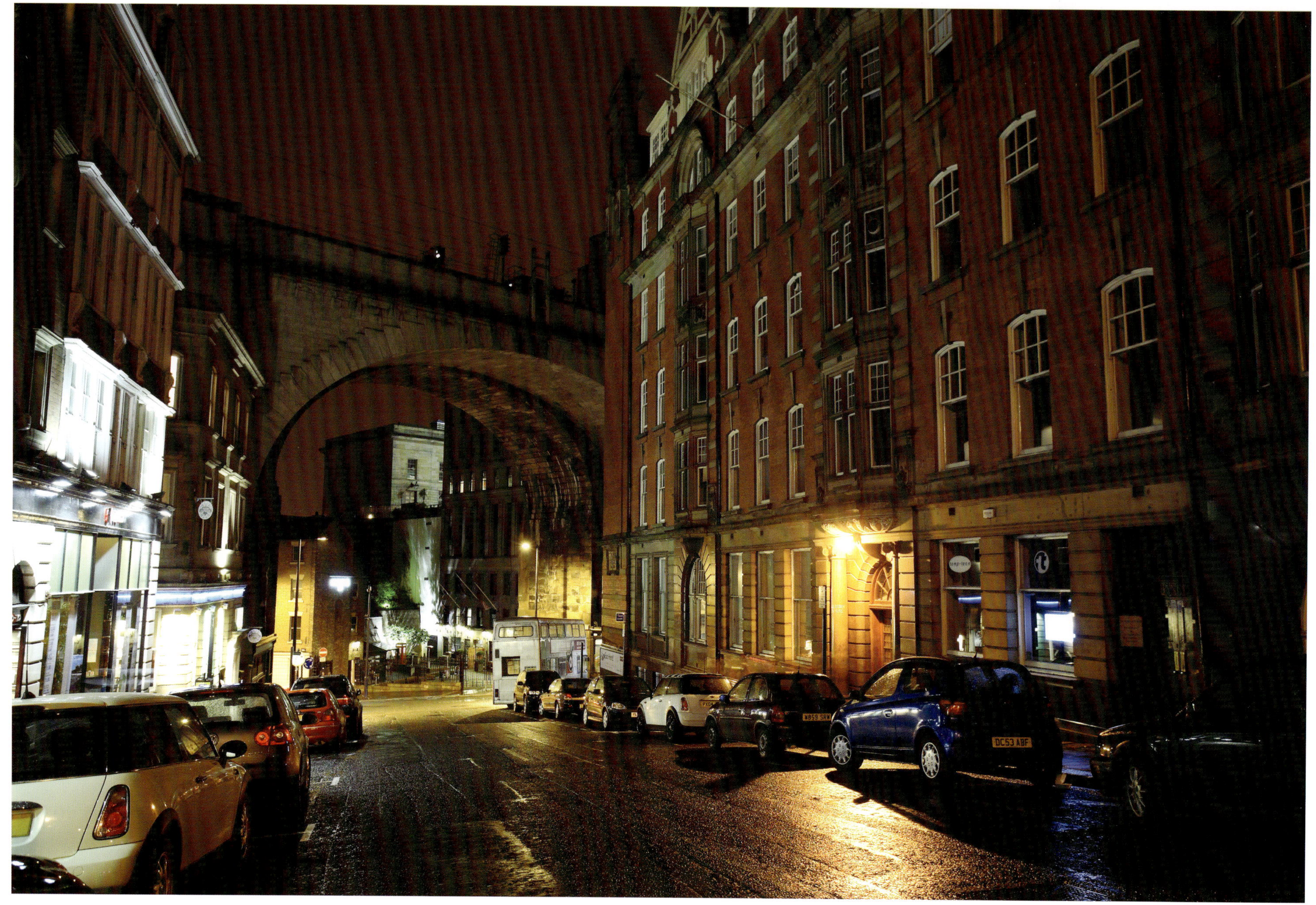

Dean Street

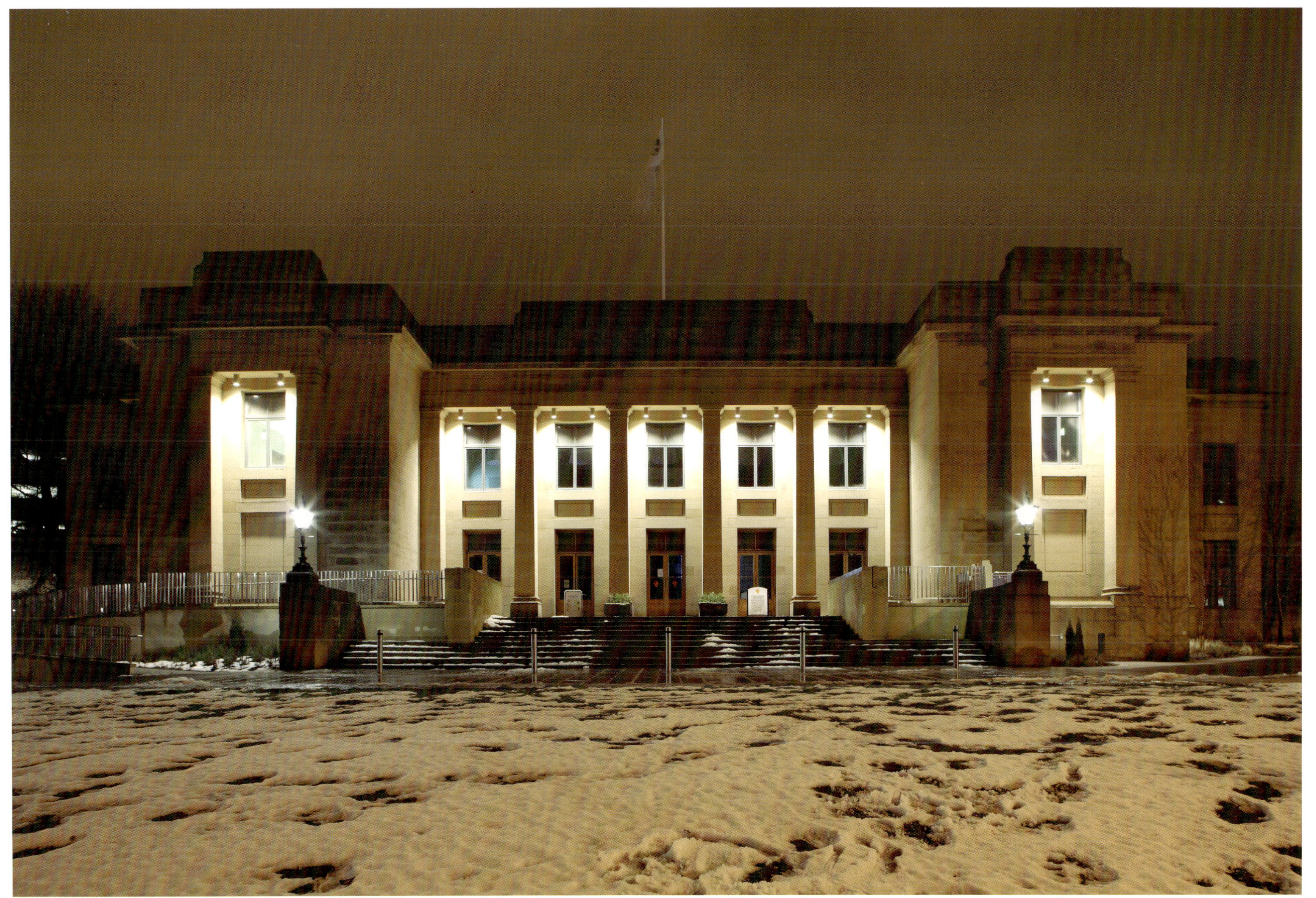

Hancock Museum

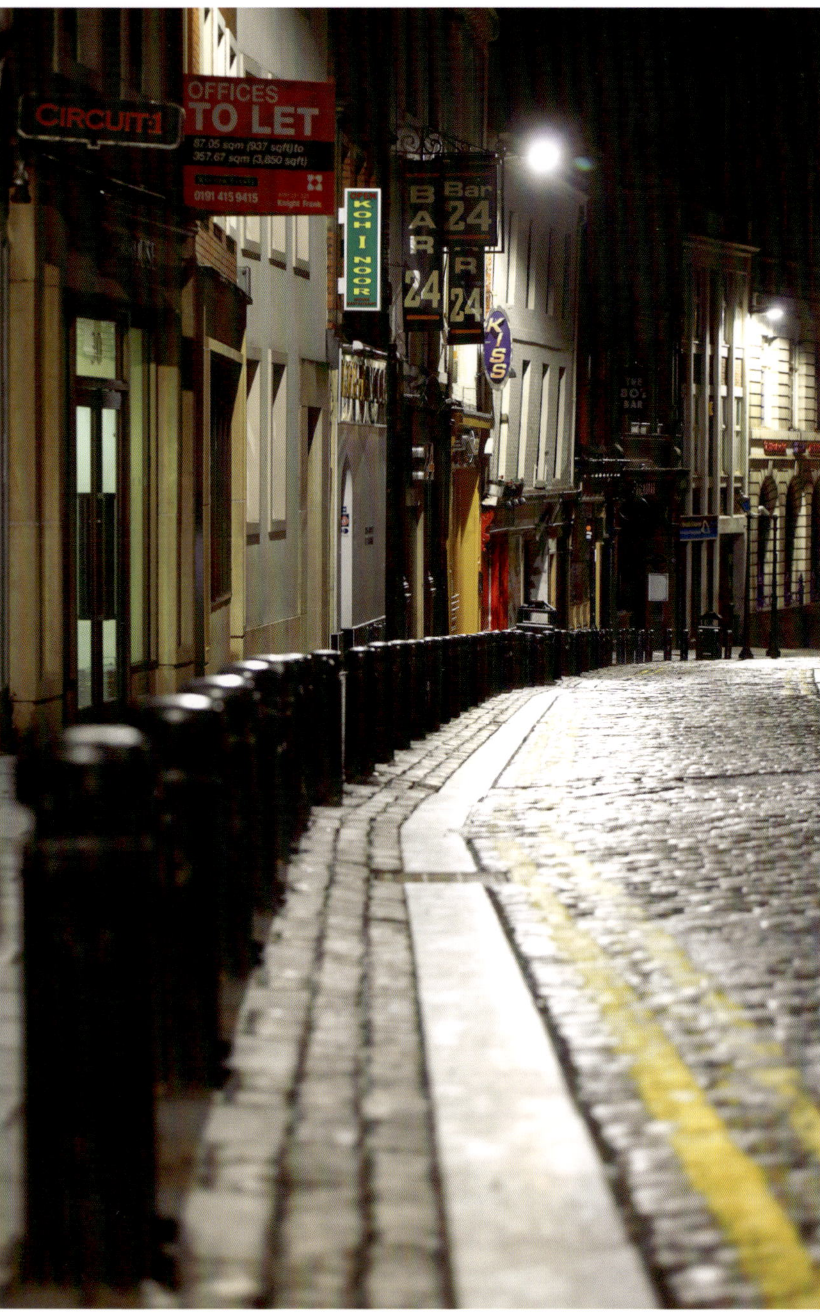

Cloth Market

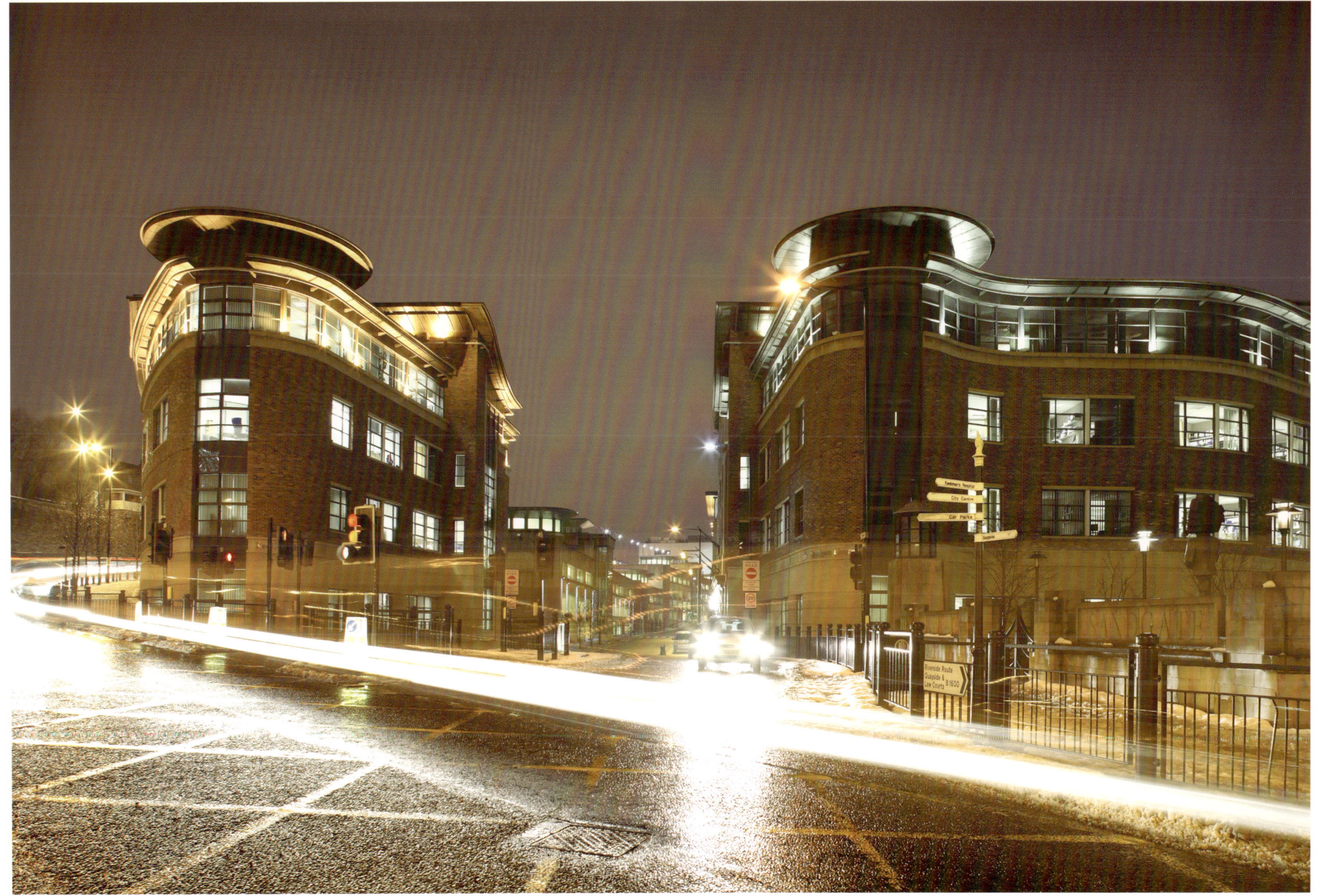

Sandgate House

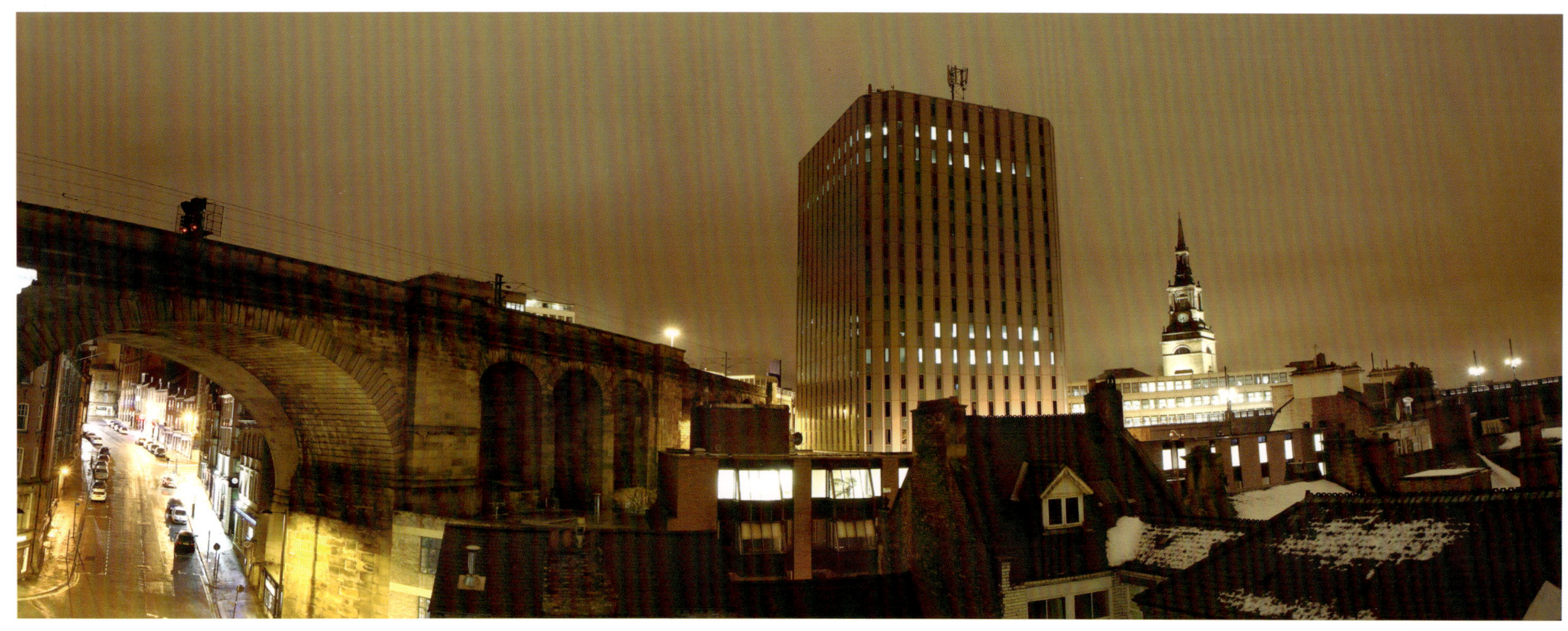

Rutherford Street

The High Level Bridge

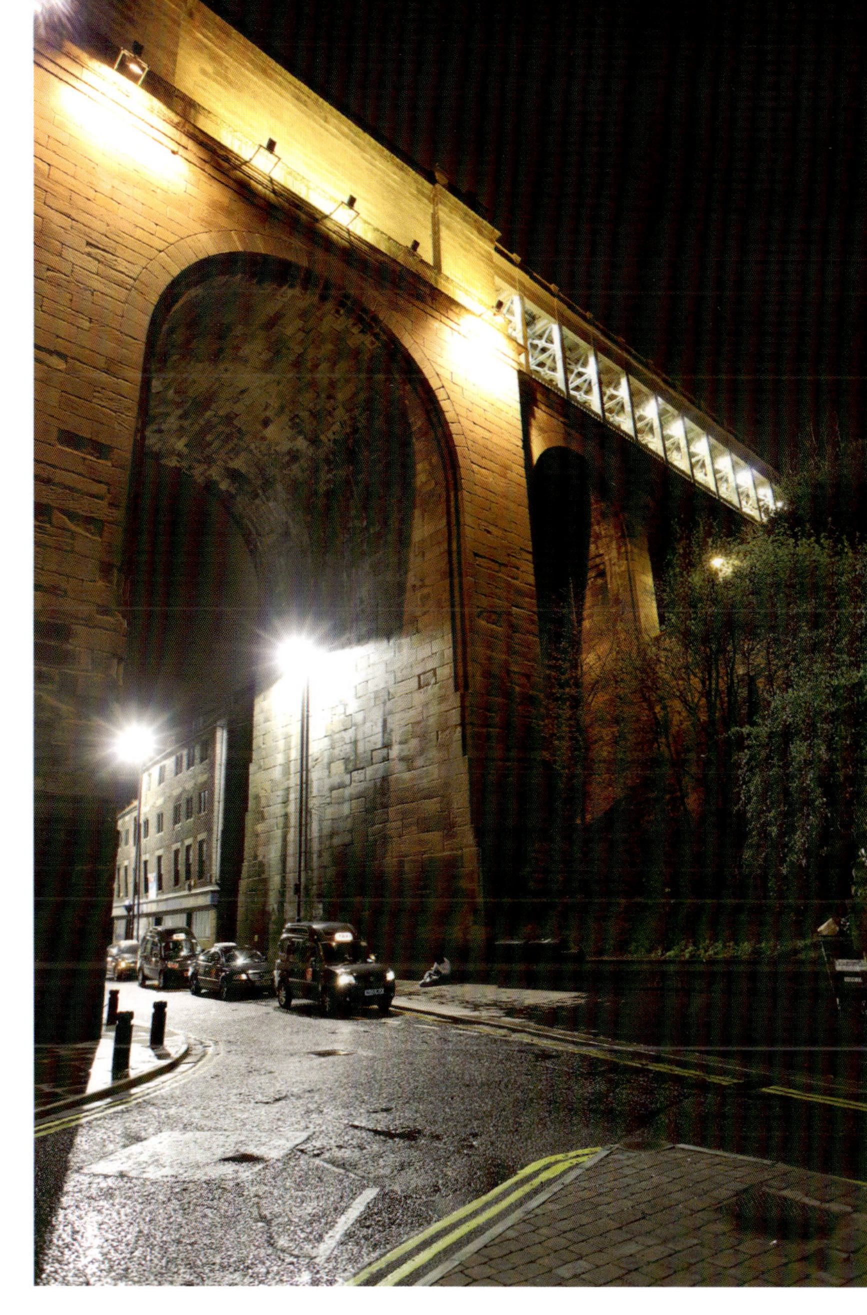

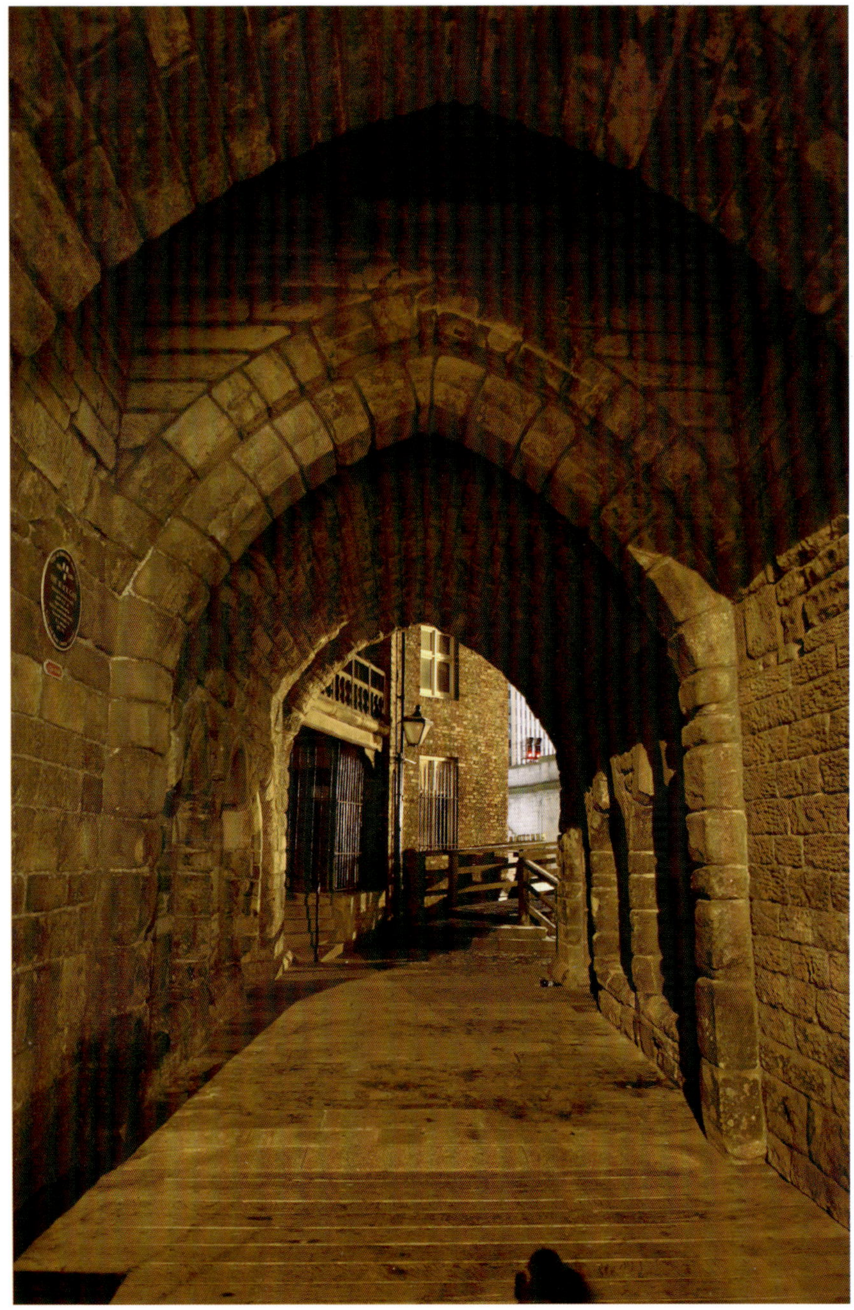

Black Gate Archway

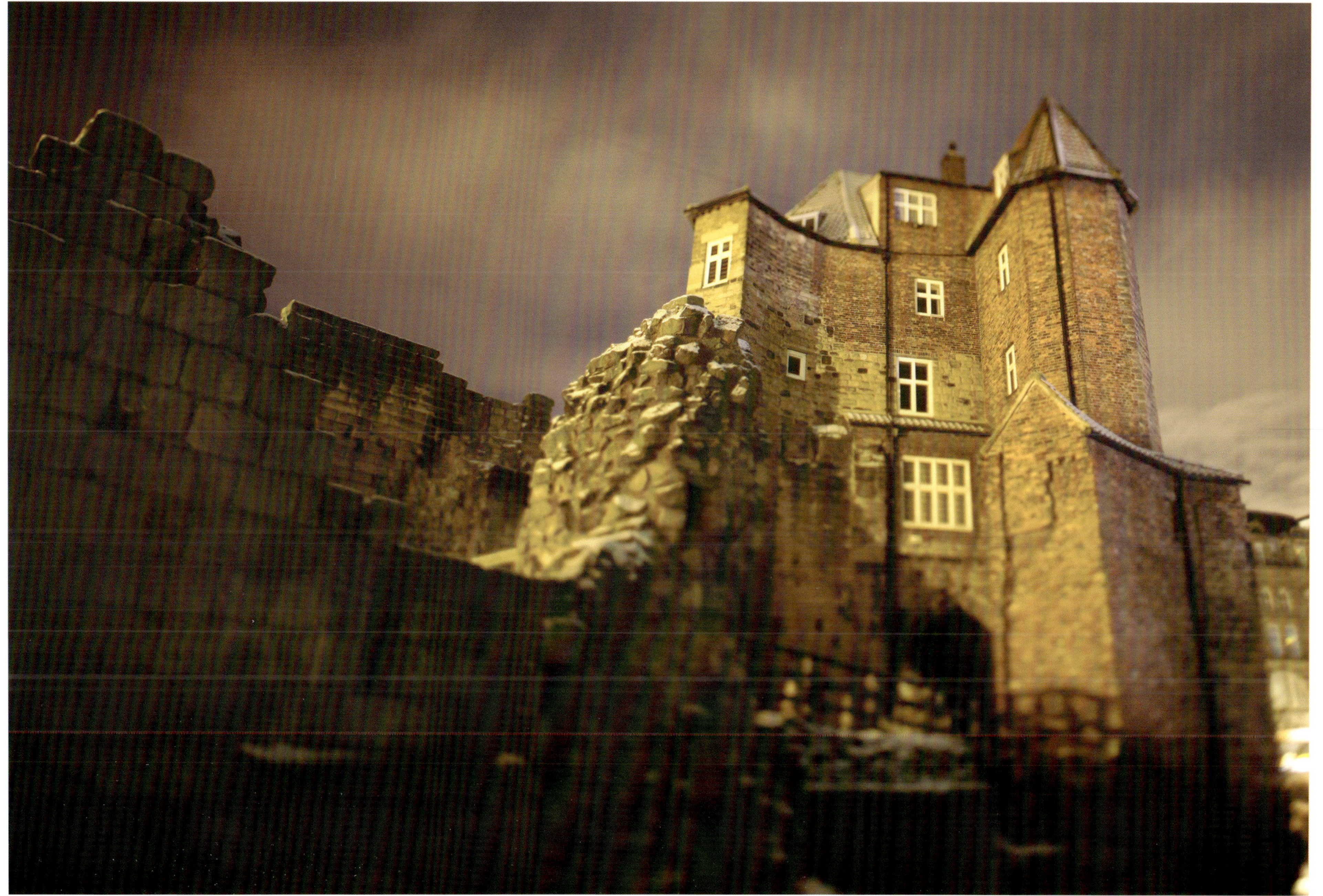

The Black Gate

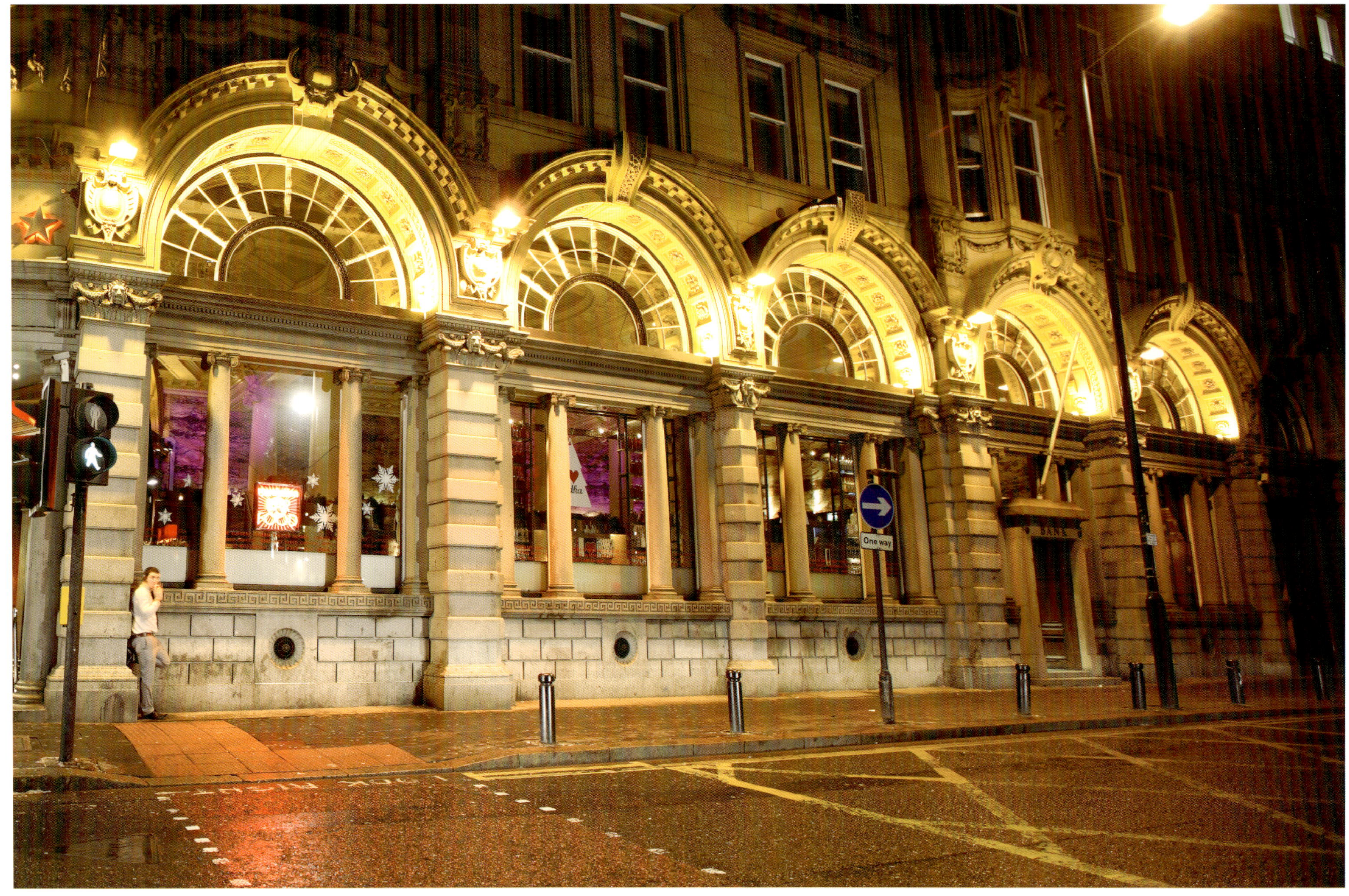

Barclays Bank Chambers

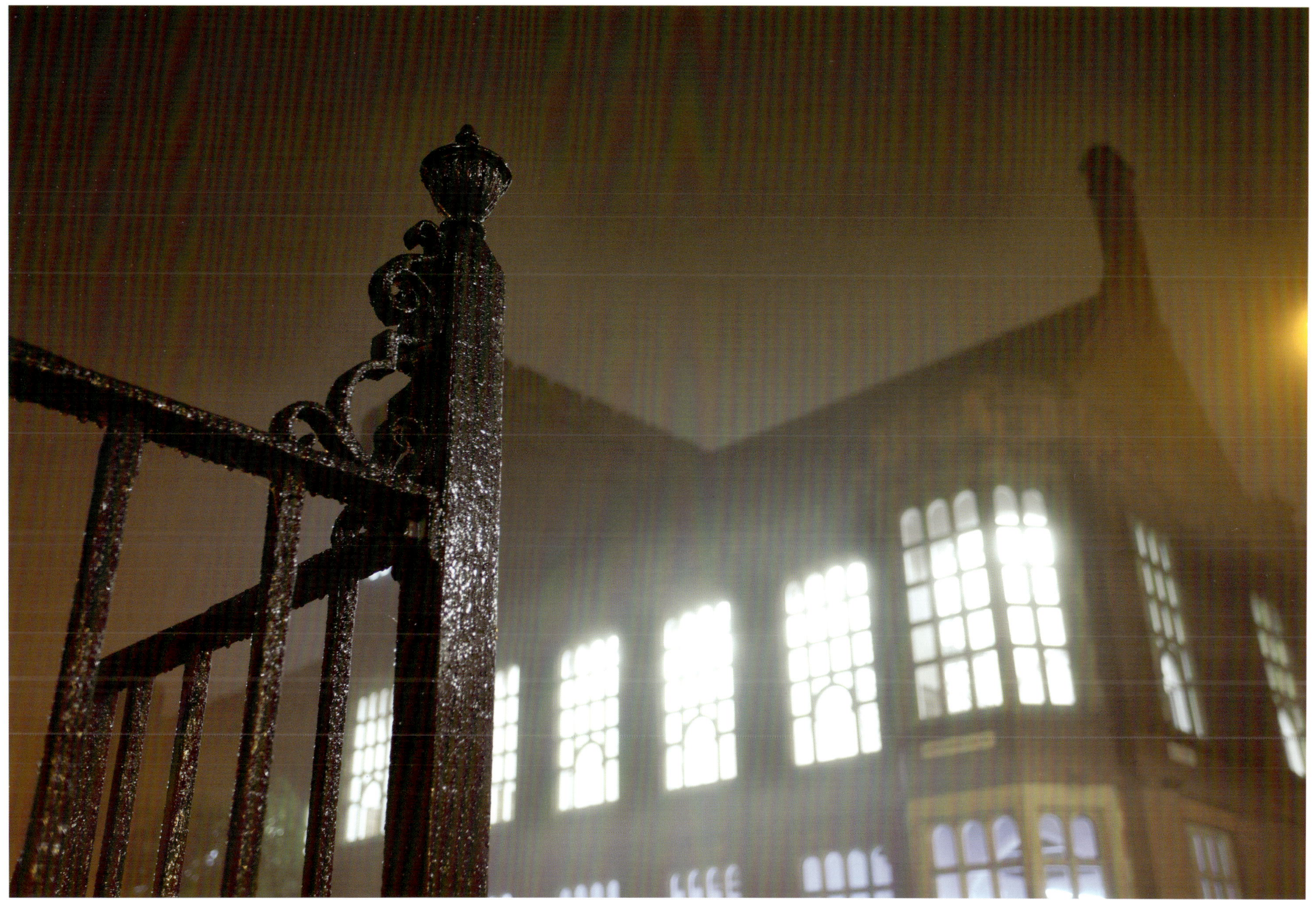

College Street

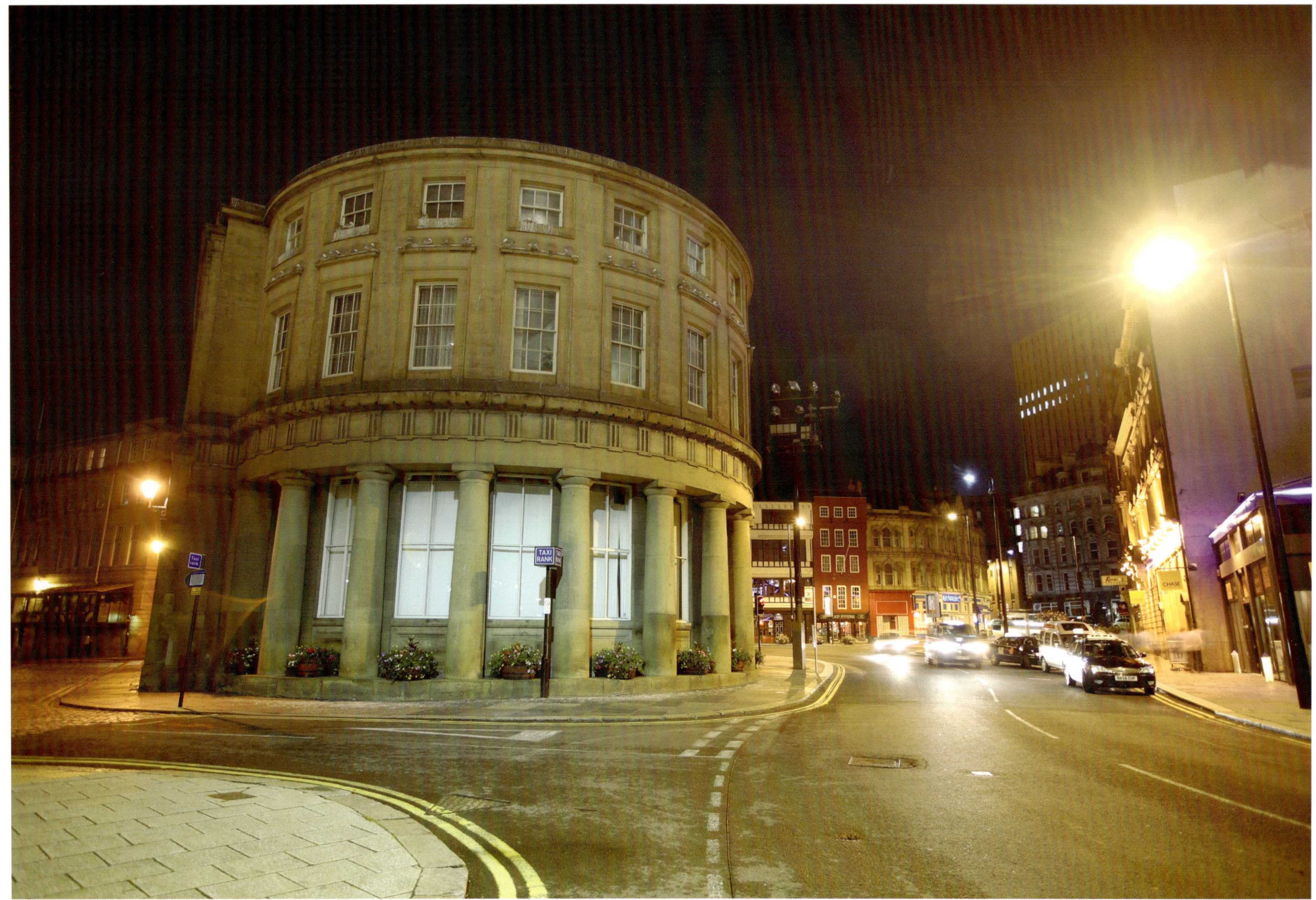

The Guild Hall

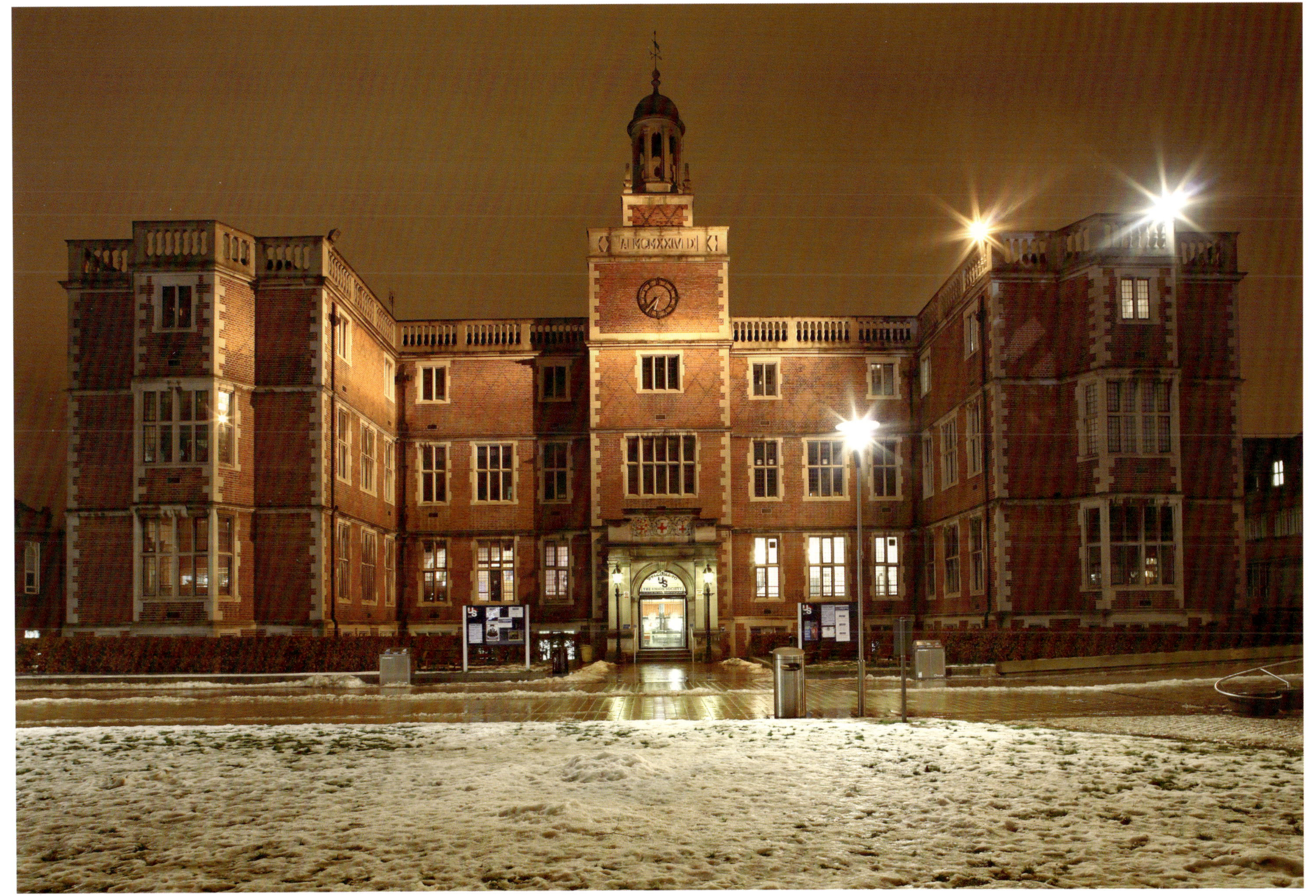

Union Society

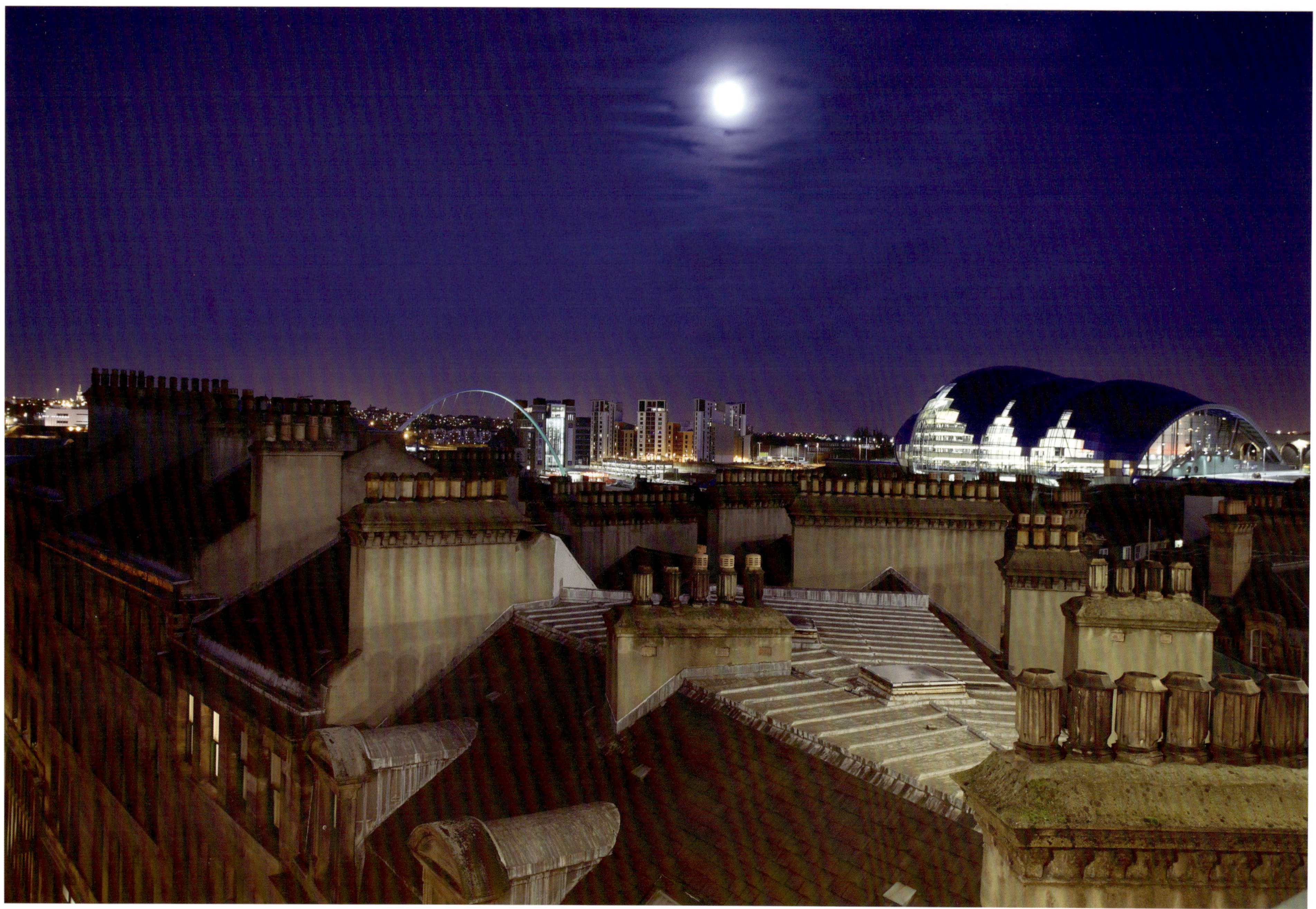

Rooftops and the Sage

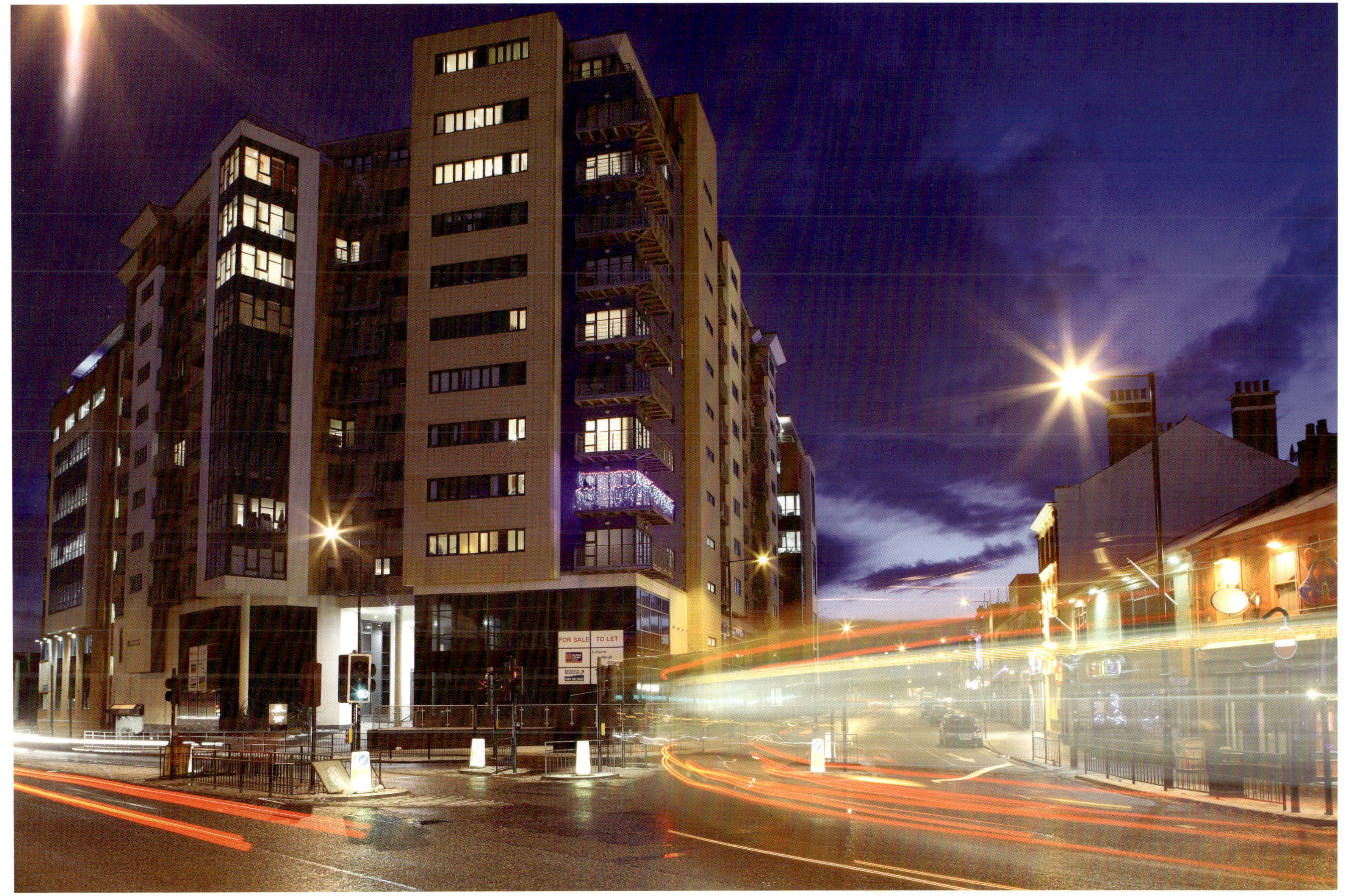

Scotswood Road

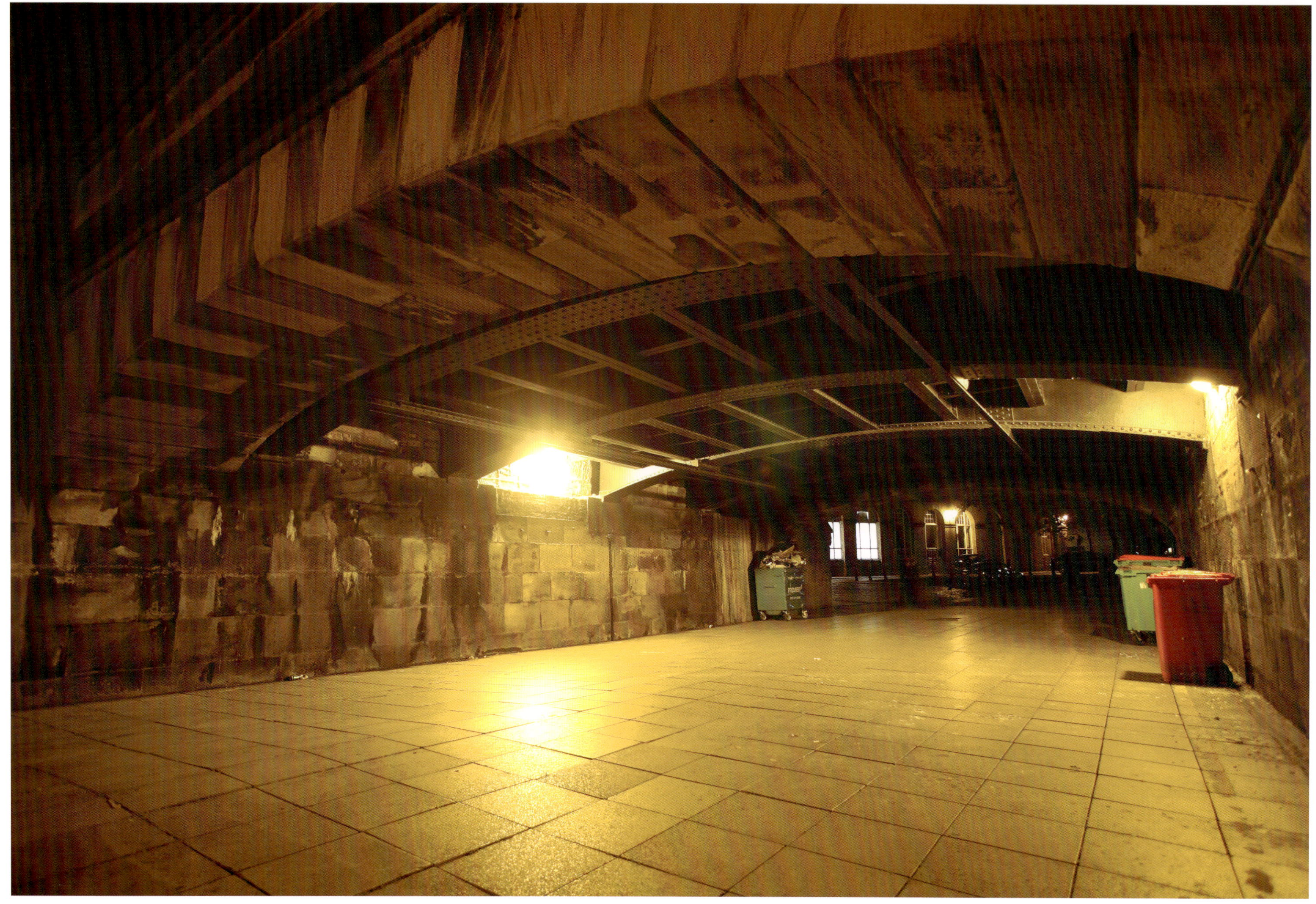

Under Swing Bridge

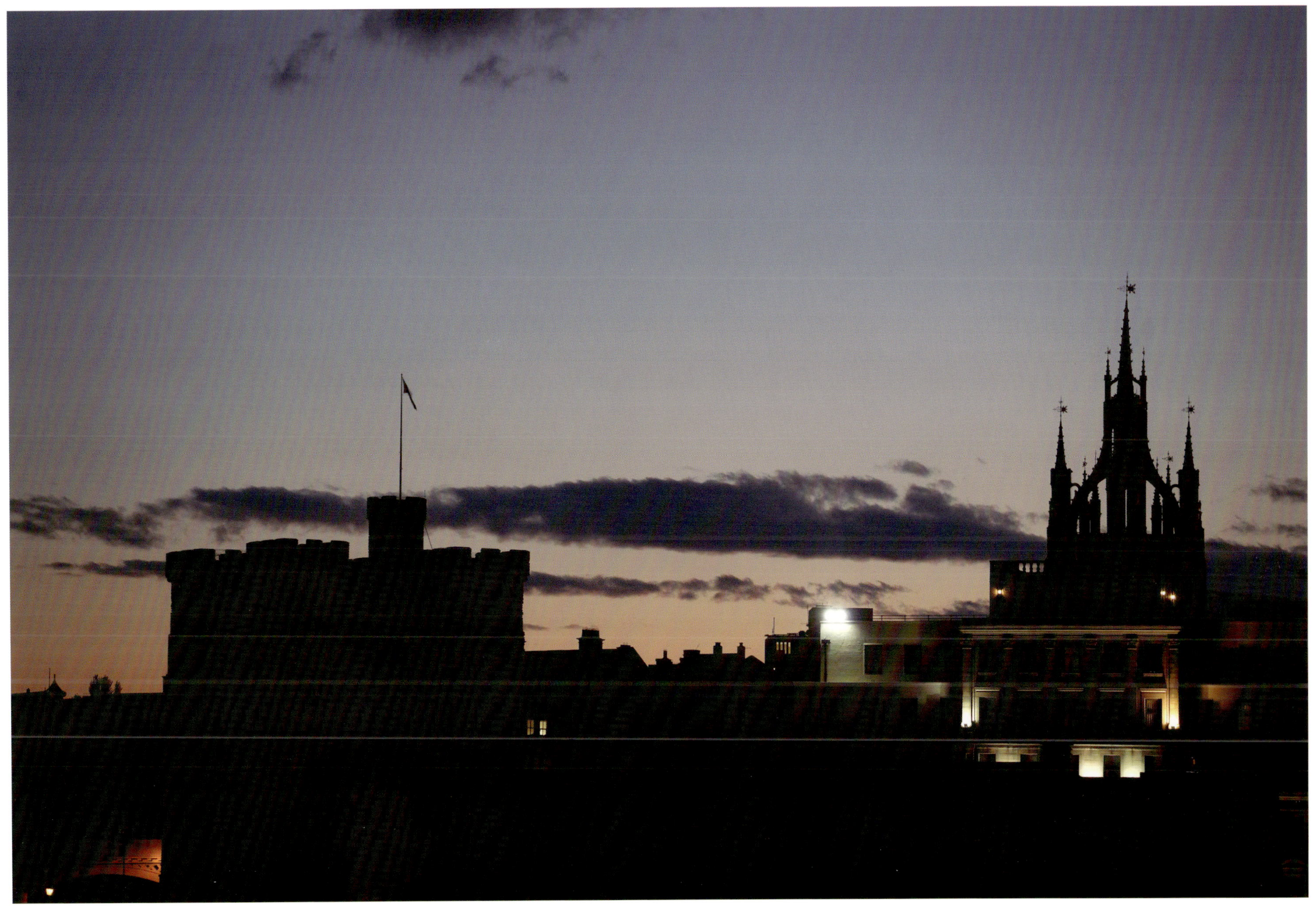

Newcastle Skyline

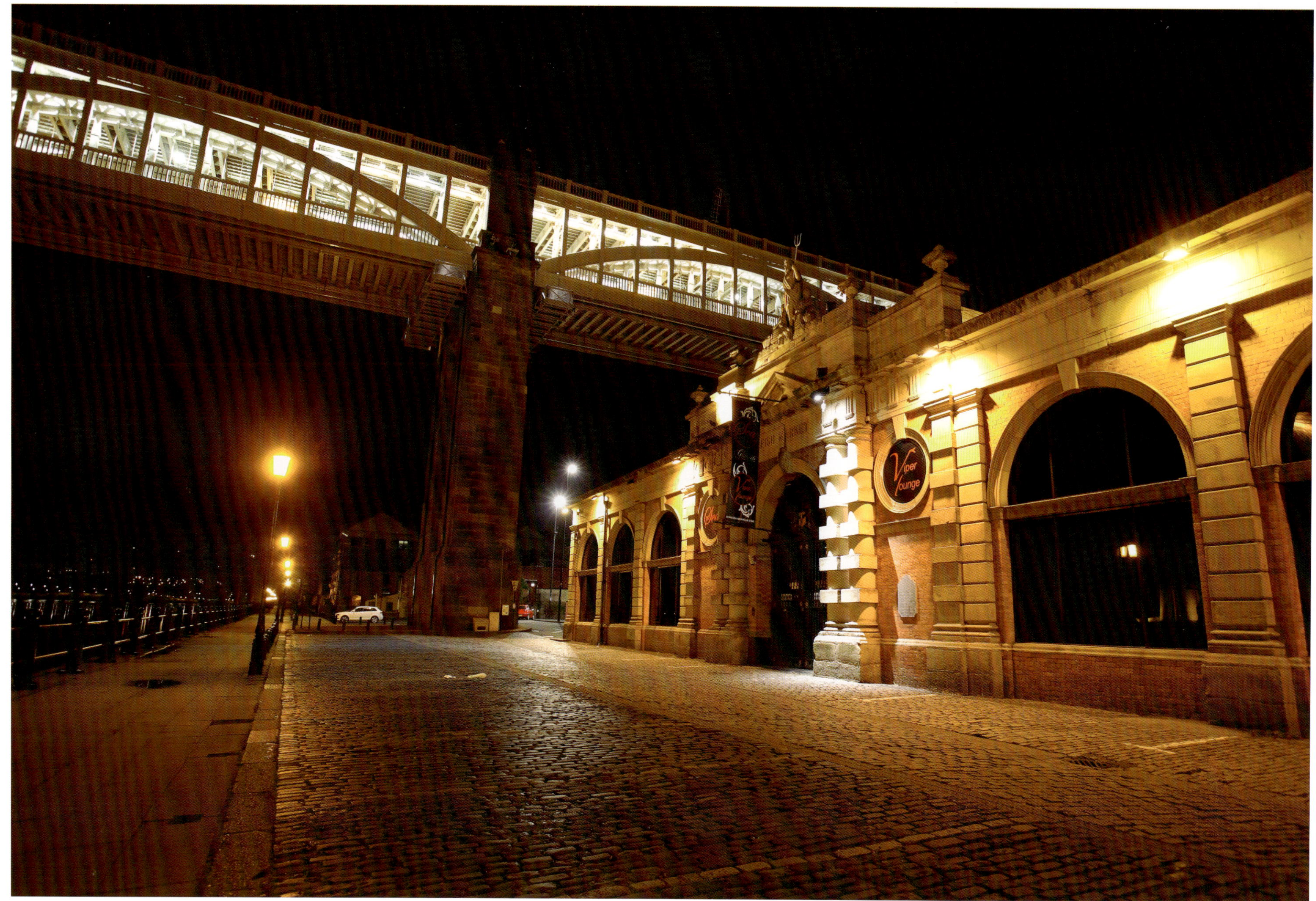

The Old Fish Market

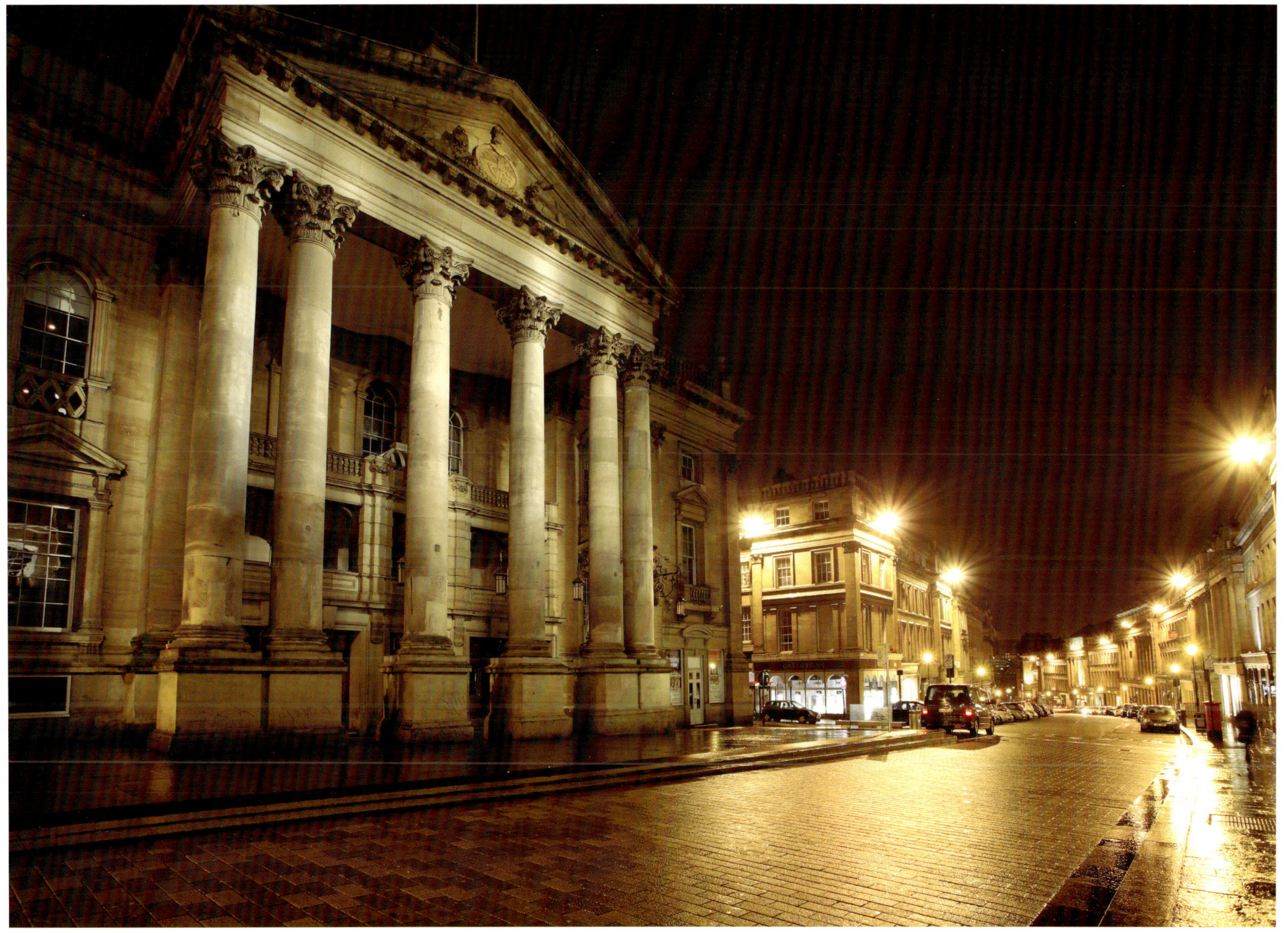

The Theatre Royal

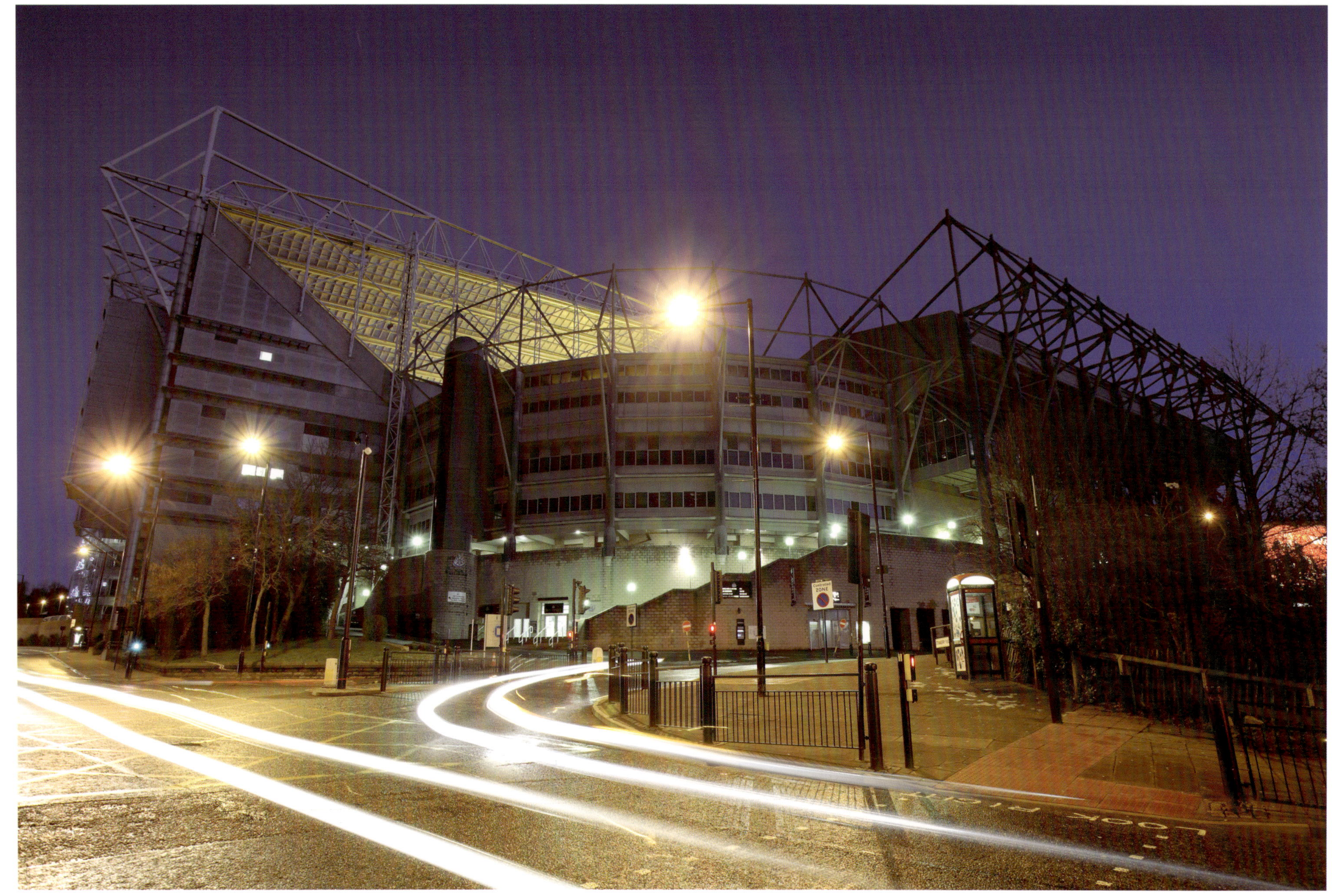

St James' Park

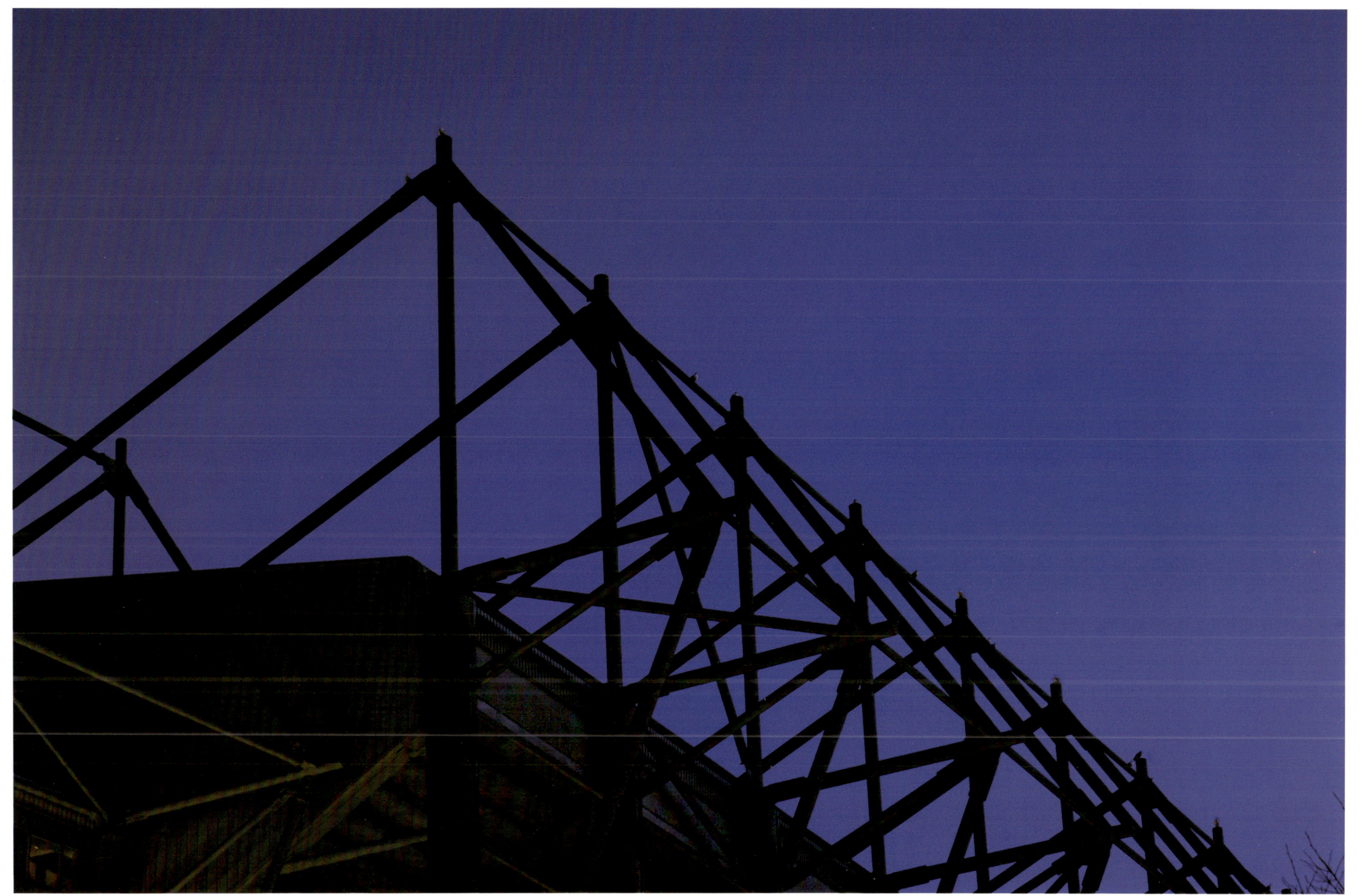

St James' Park

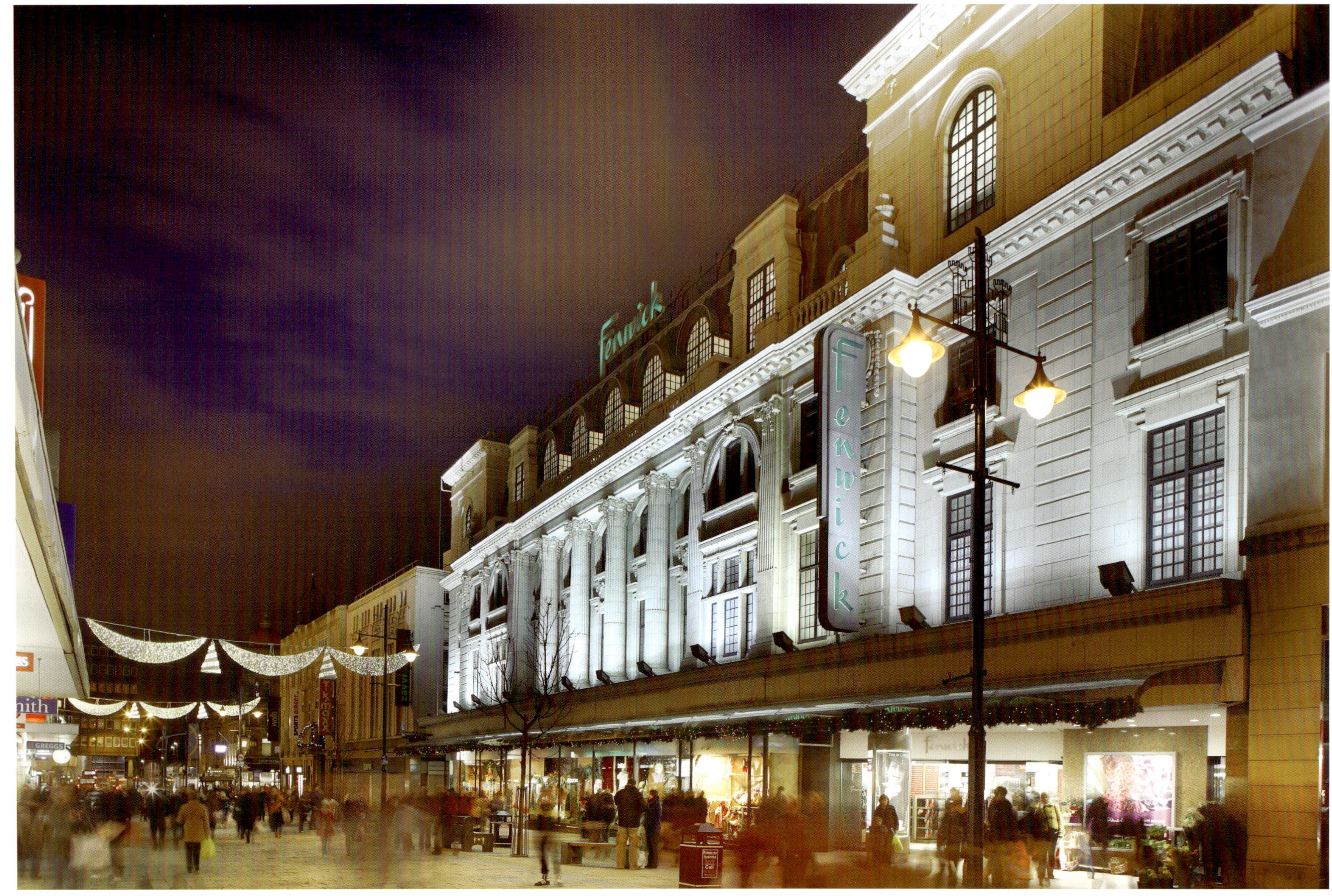

Fenwick - Northmberland Street

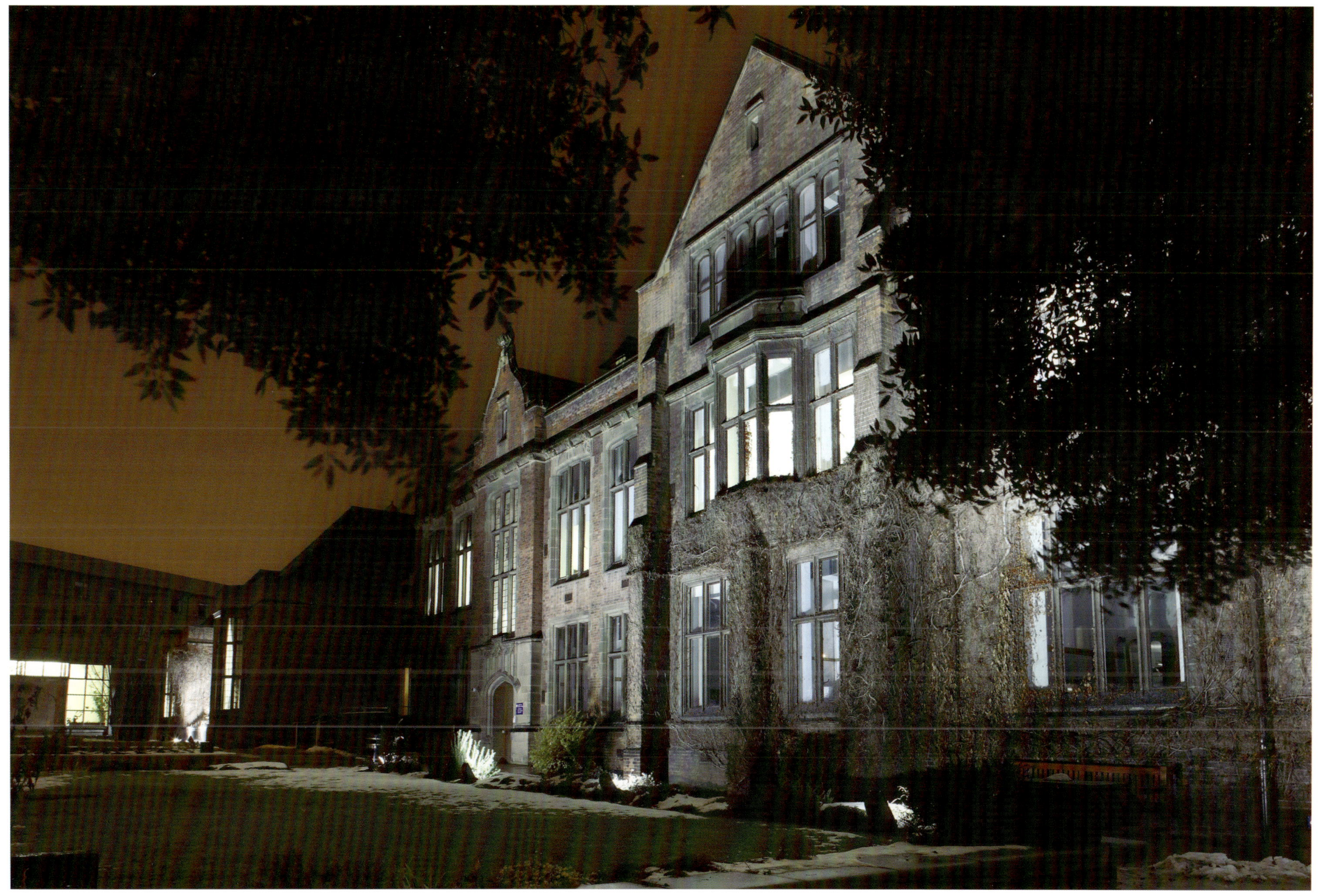

Newcastle University

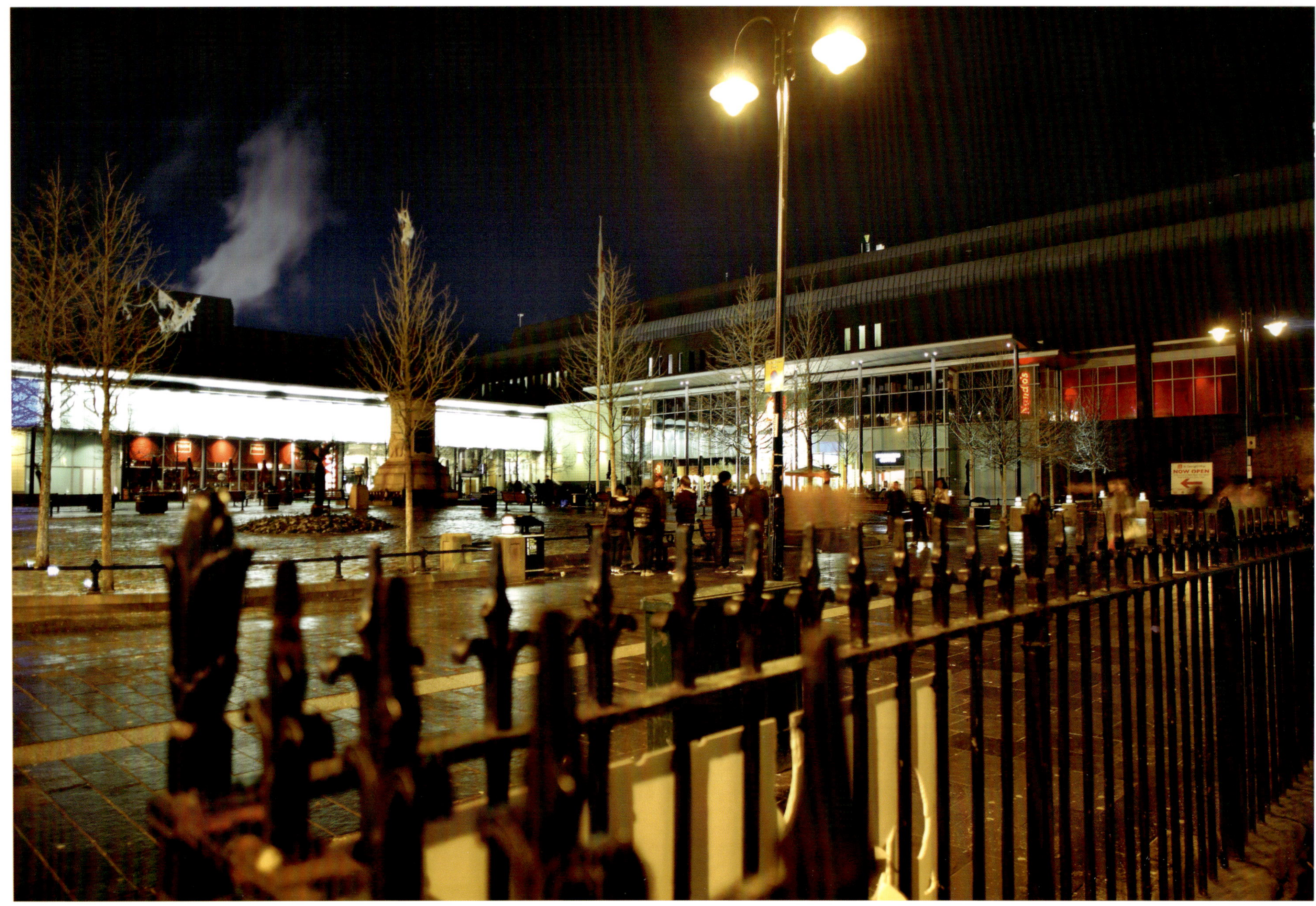

Old Eldon Square

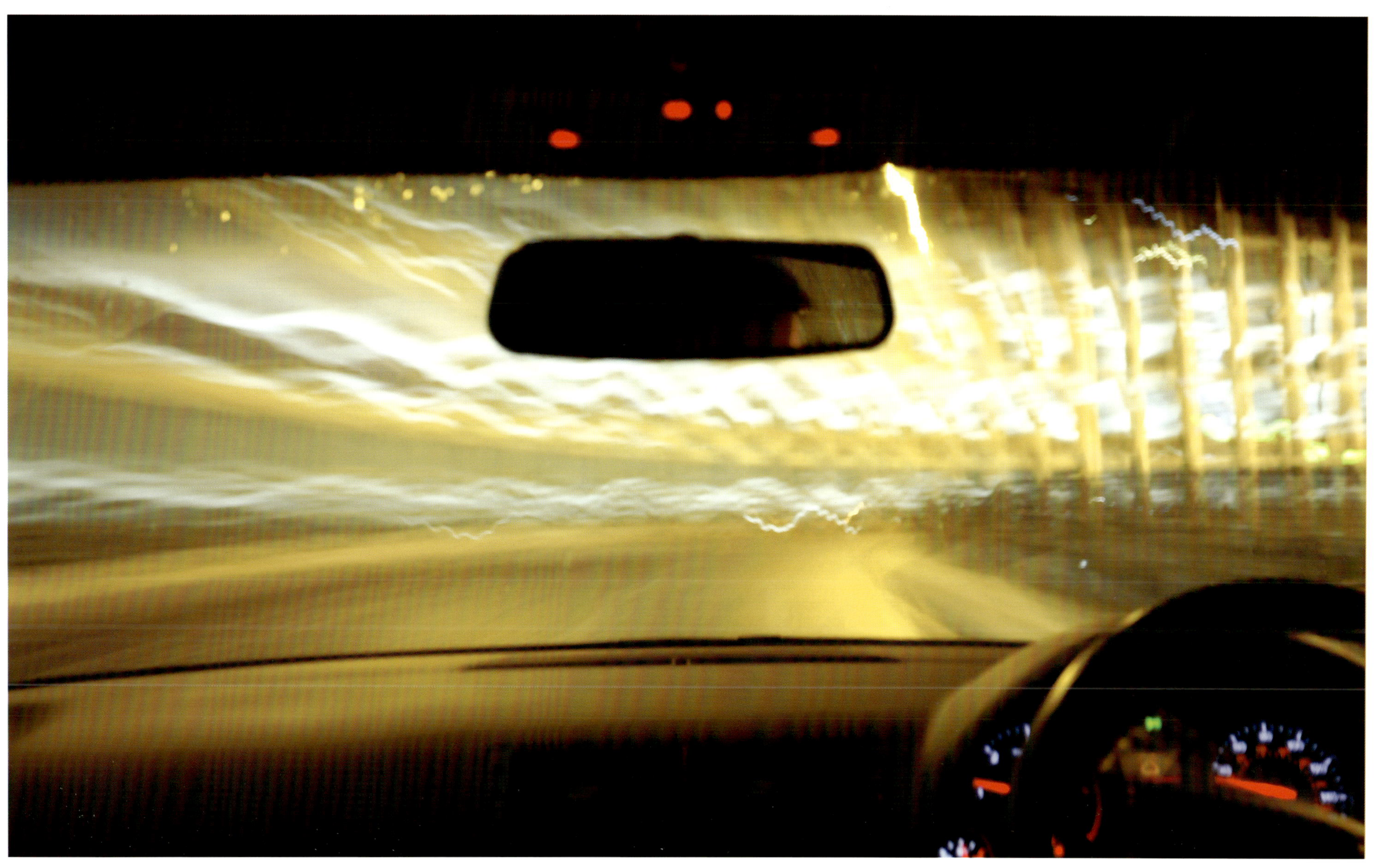

The Journey

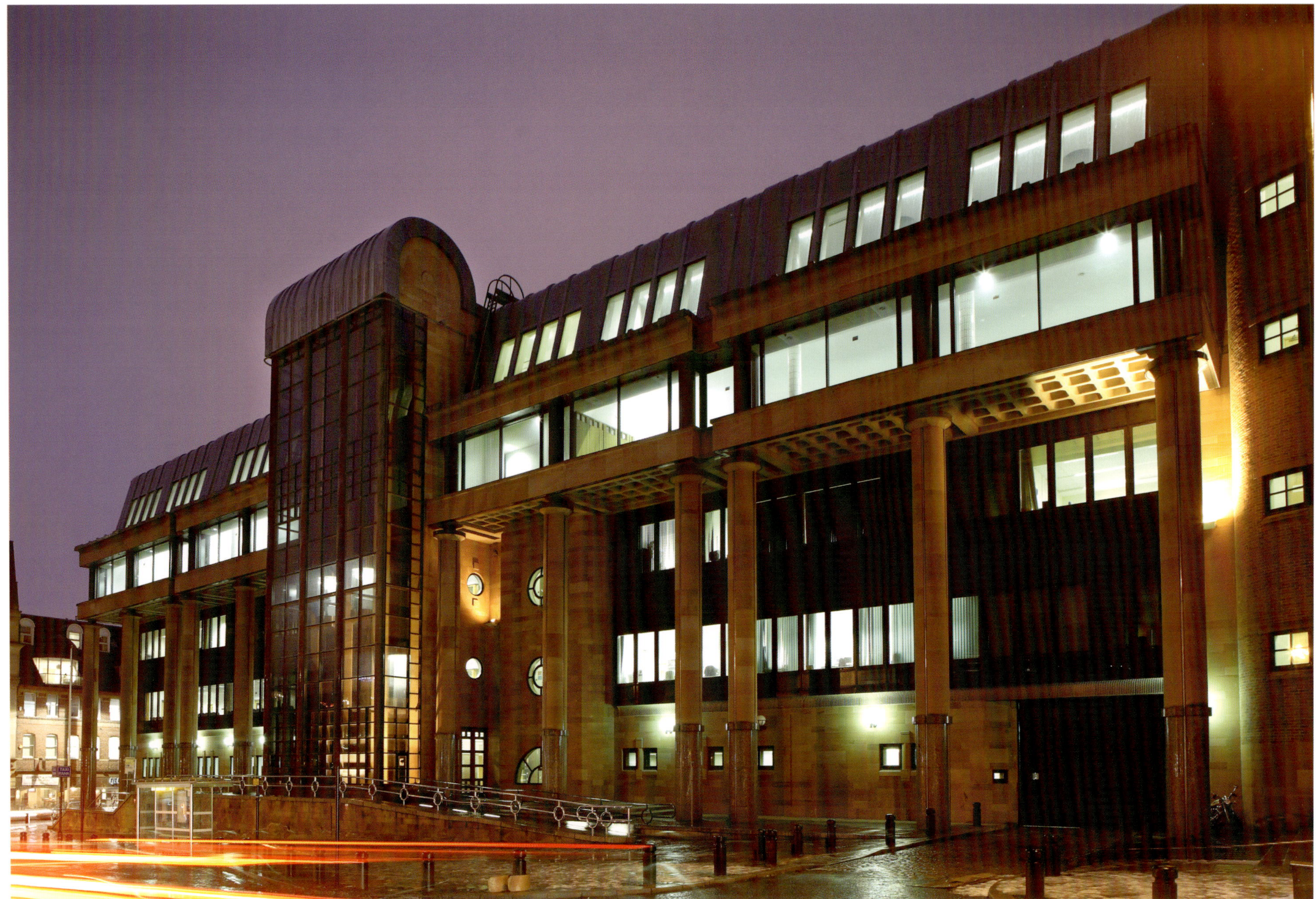

The Law Courts

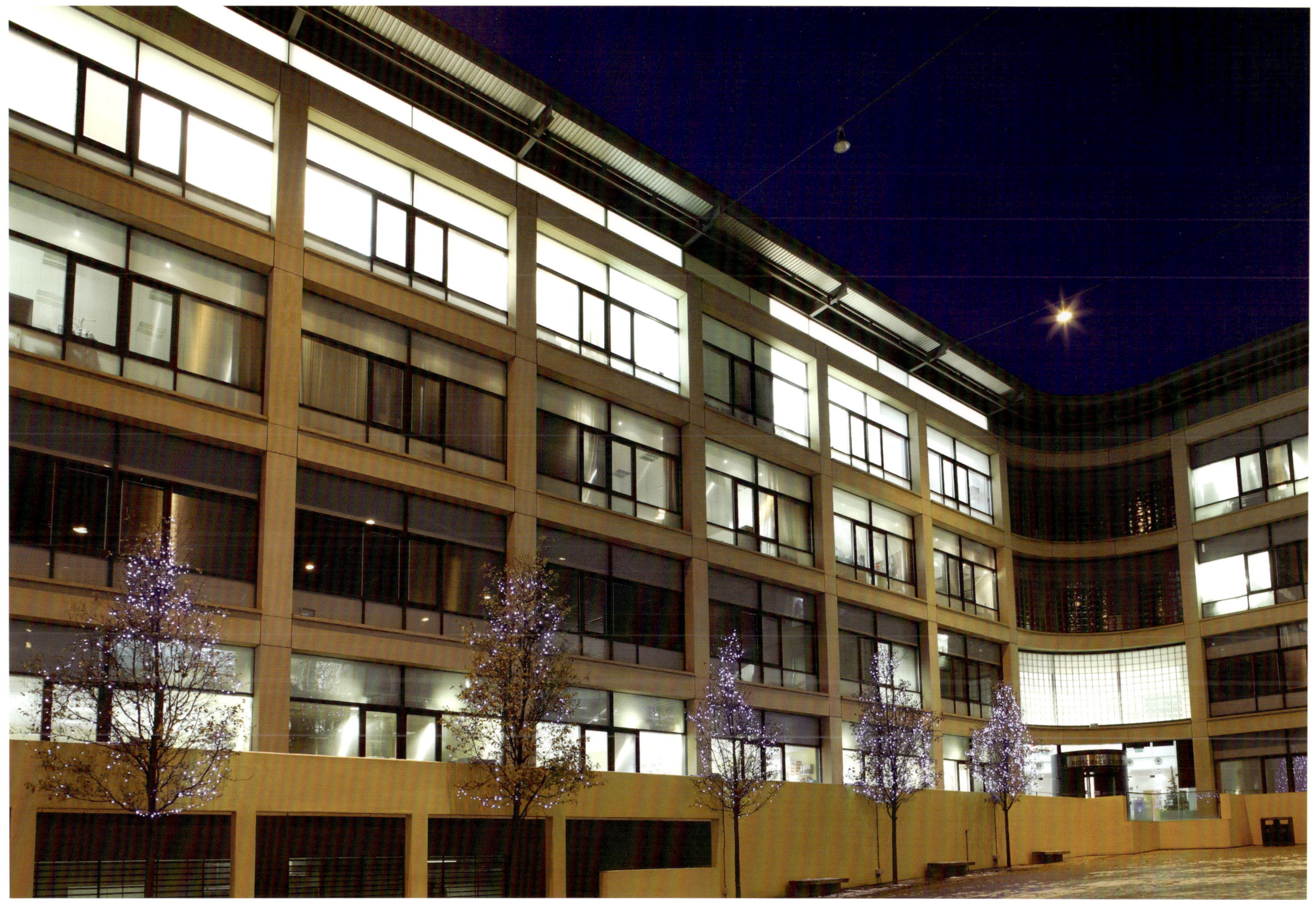

Bioscience Centre

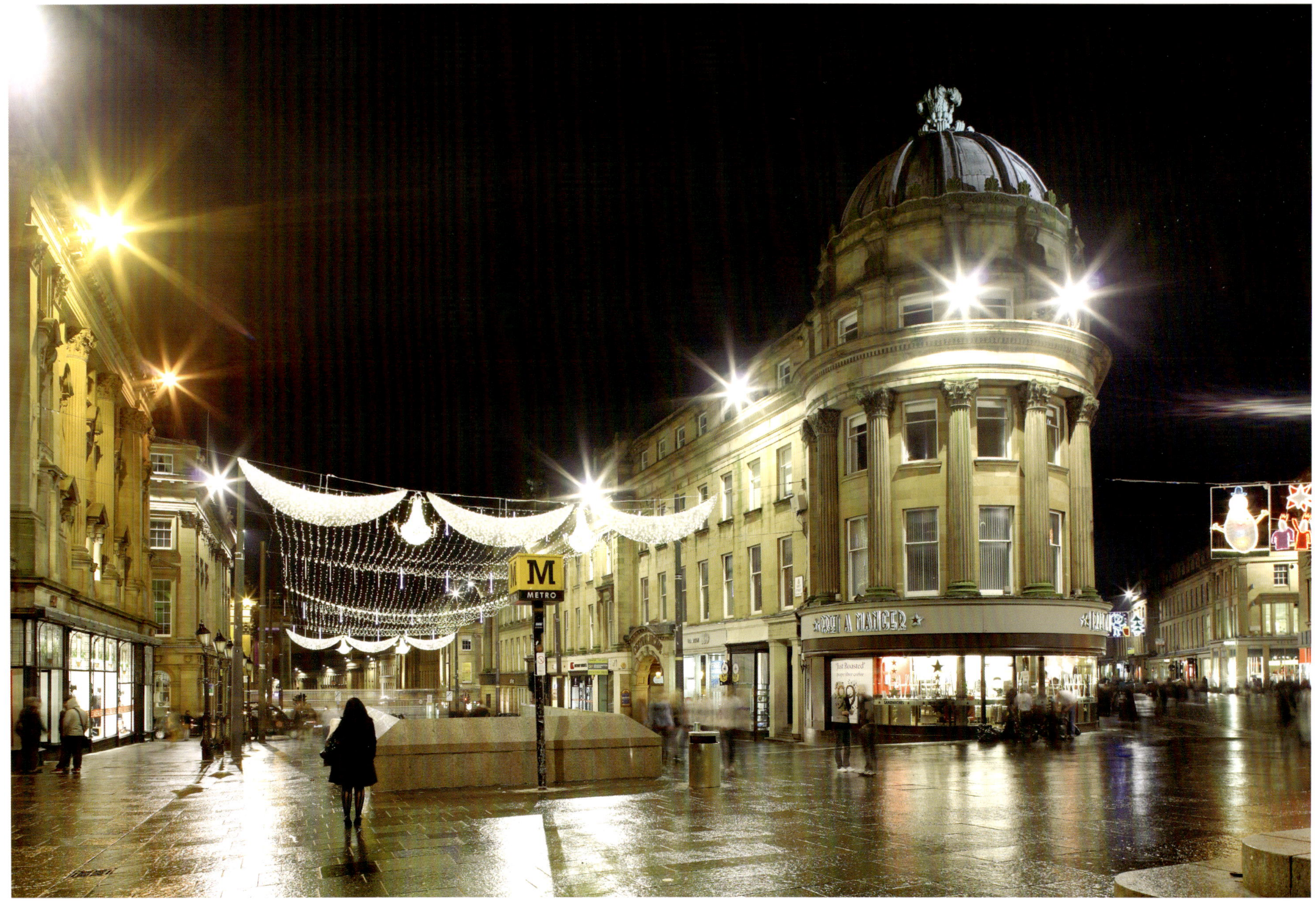

Grey Street

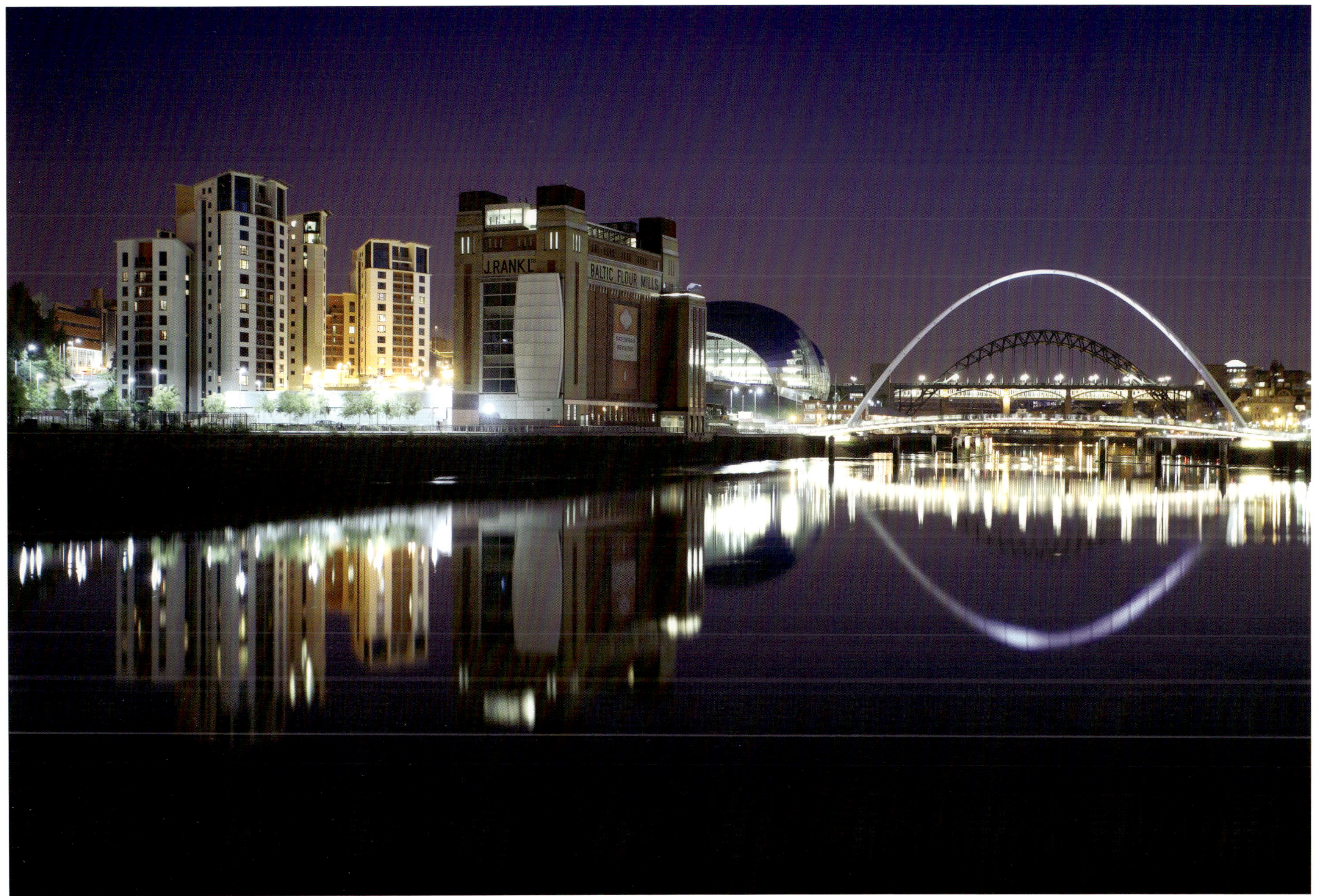

View of the Tyne

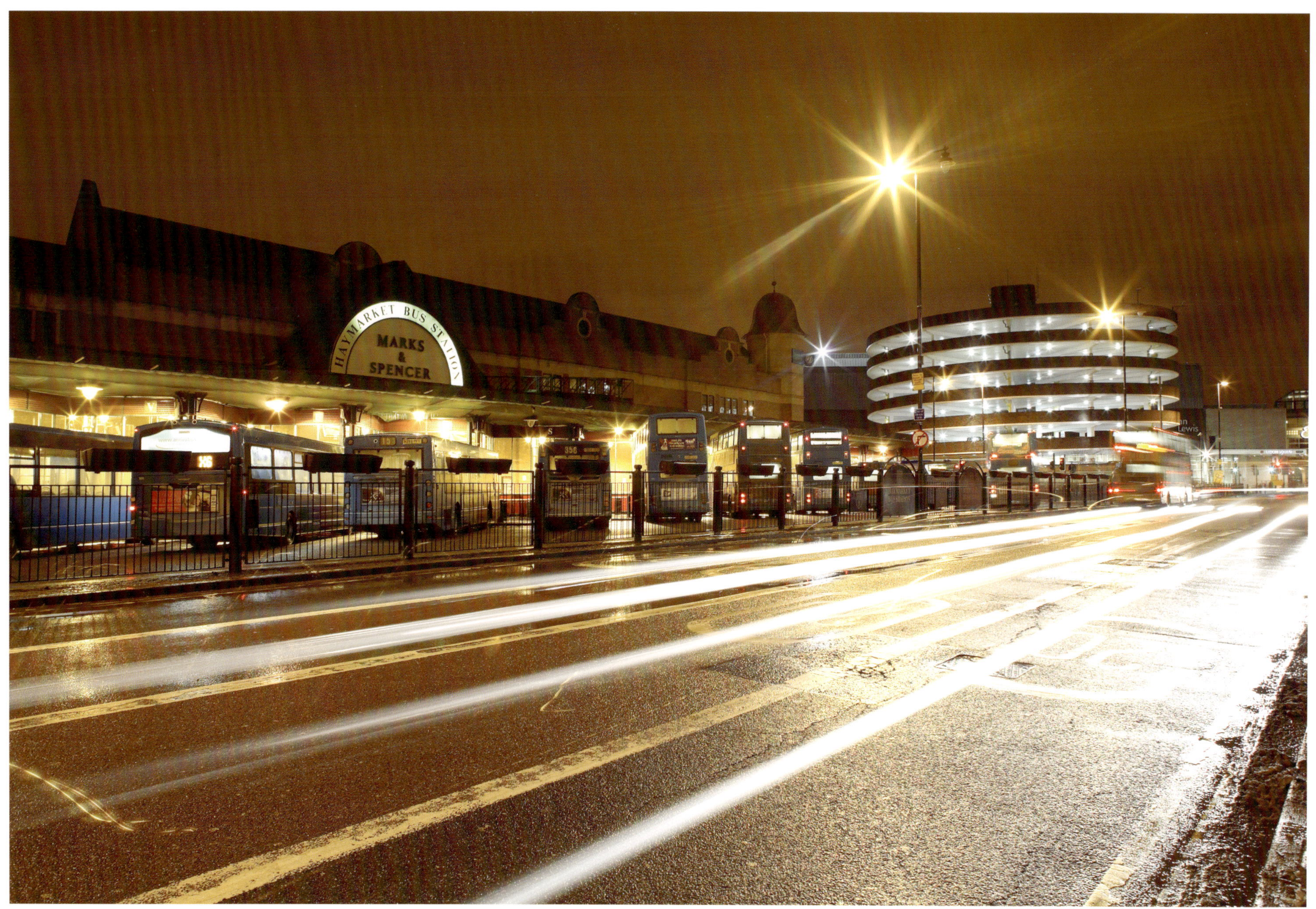

Haymarket Bus Station

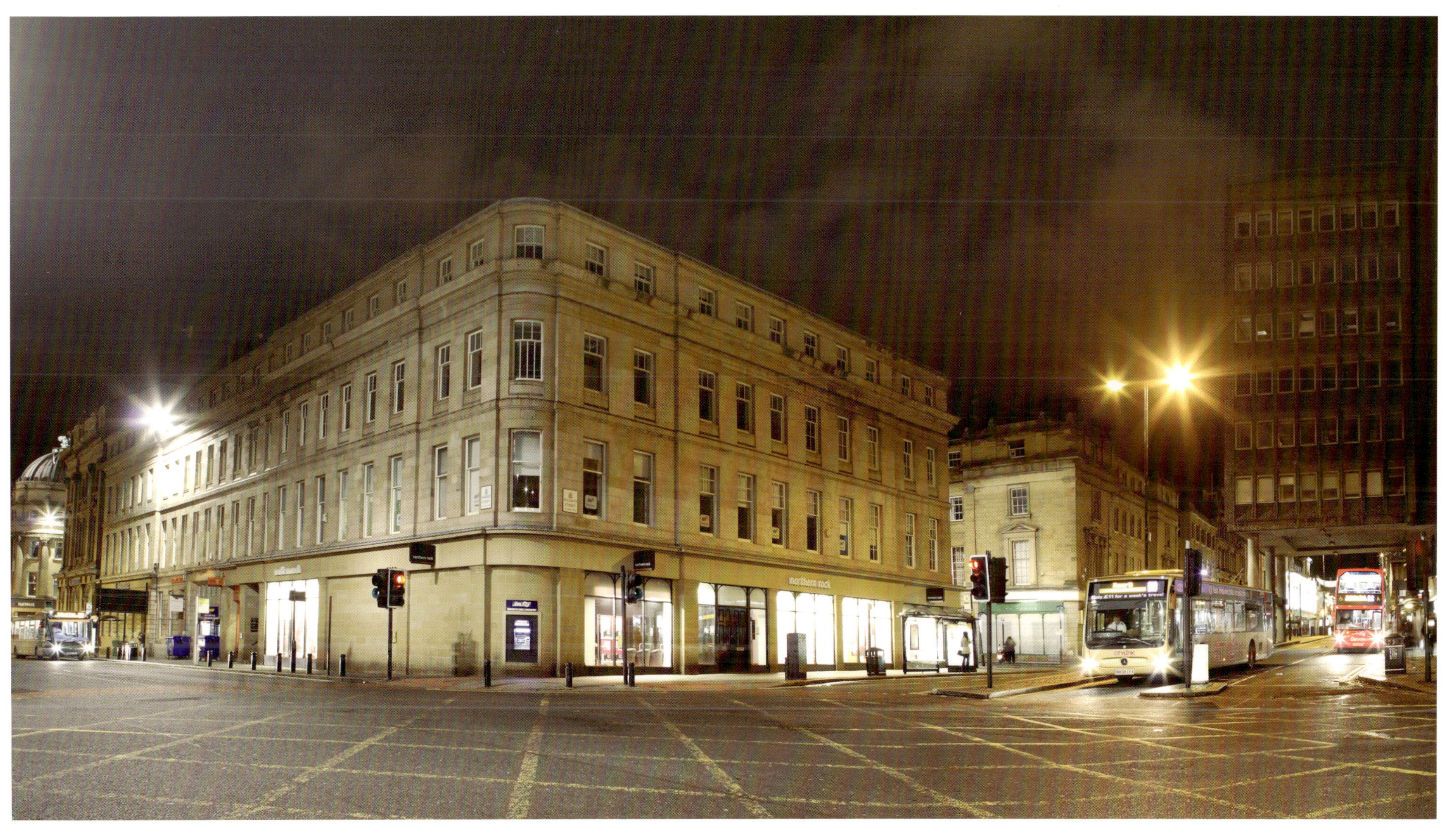

Corner of Pilgrim Street and Market Street

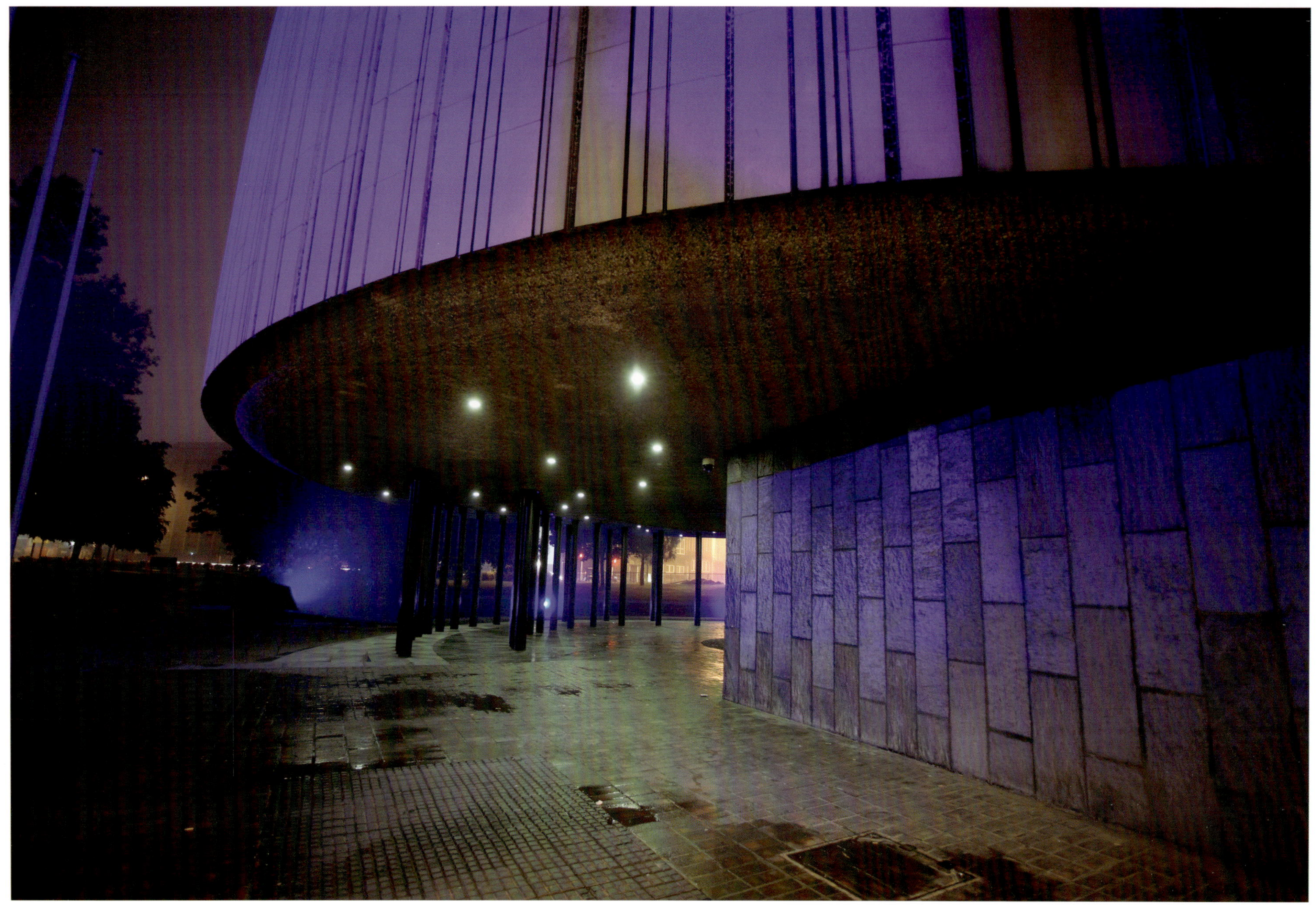

The Civic Centre

The Civic Centre

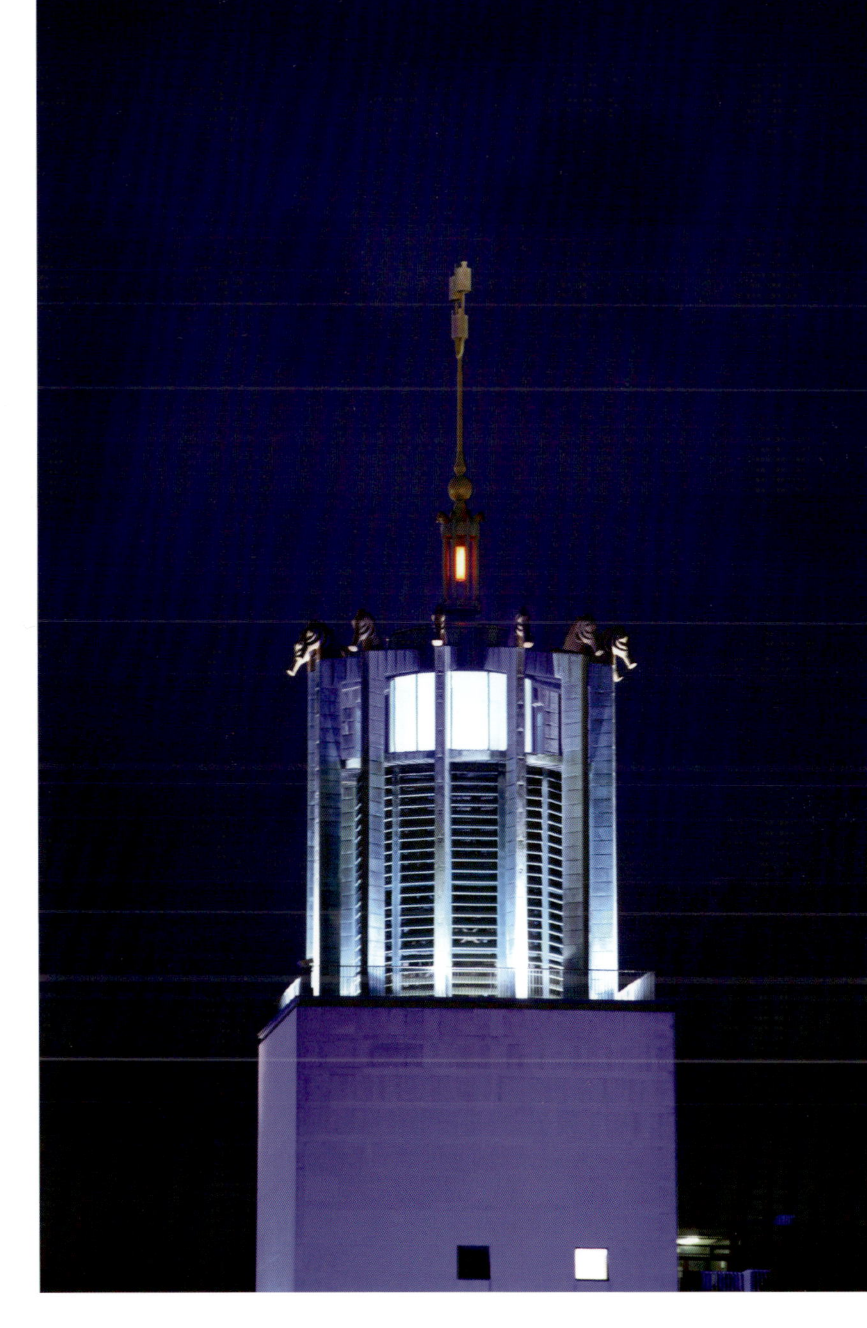

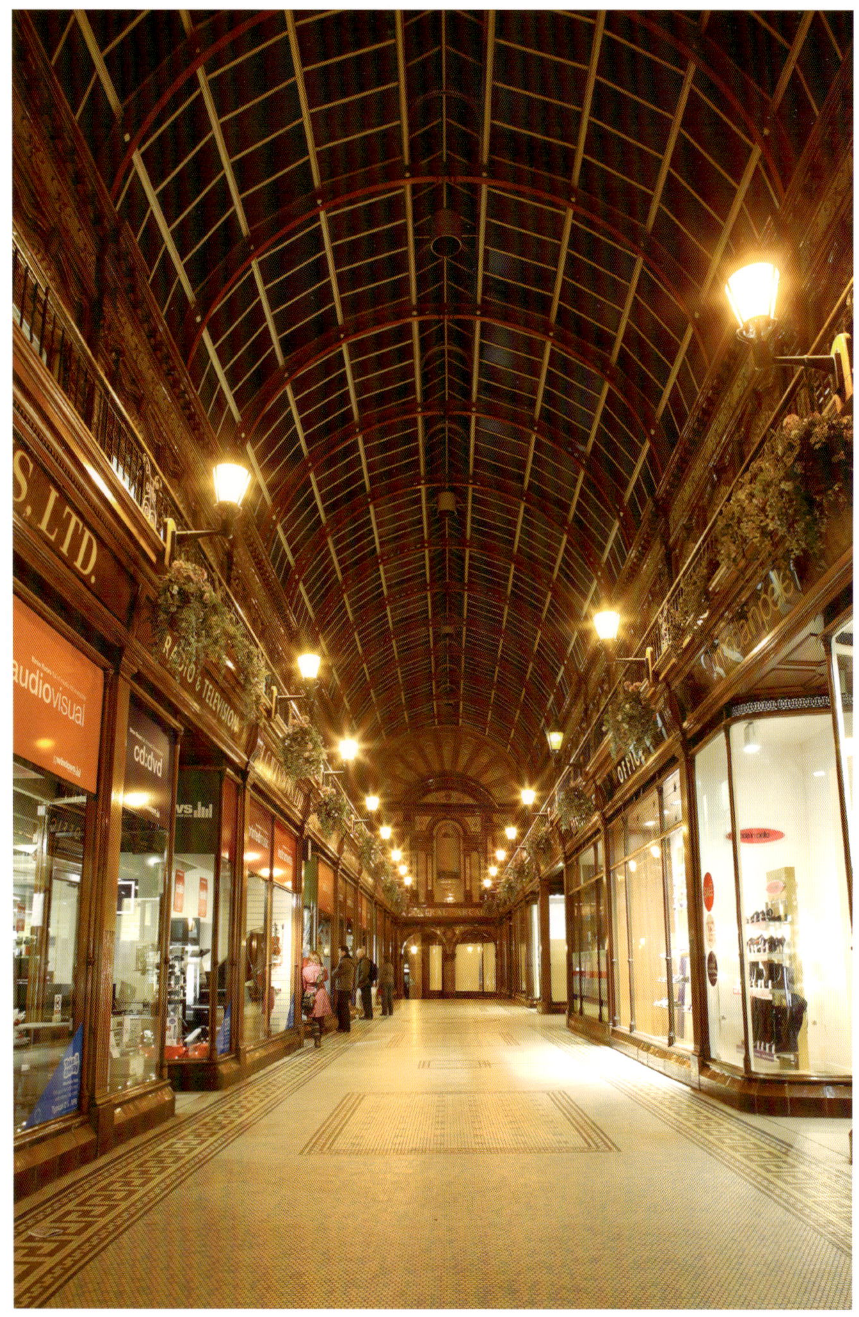

Central Arcade

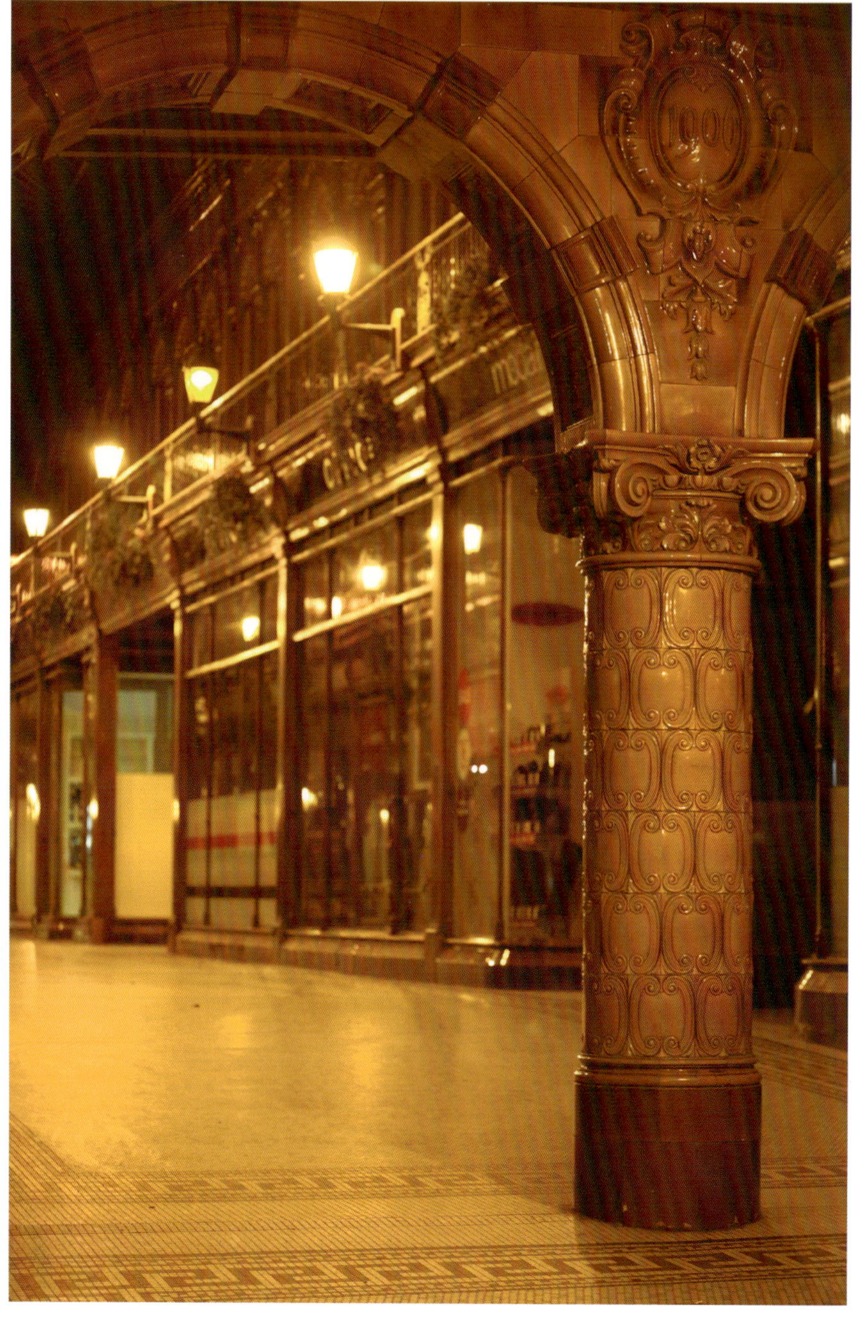

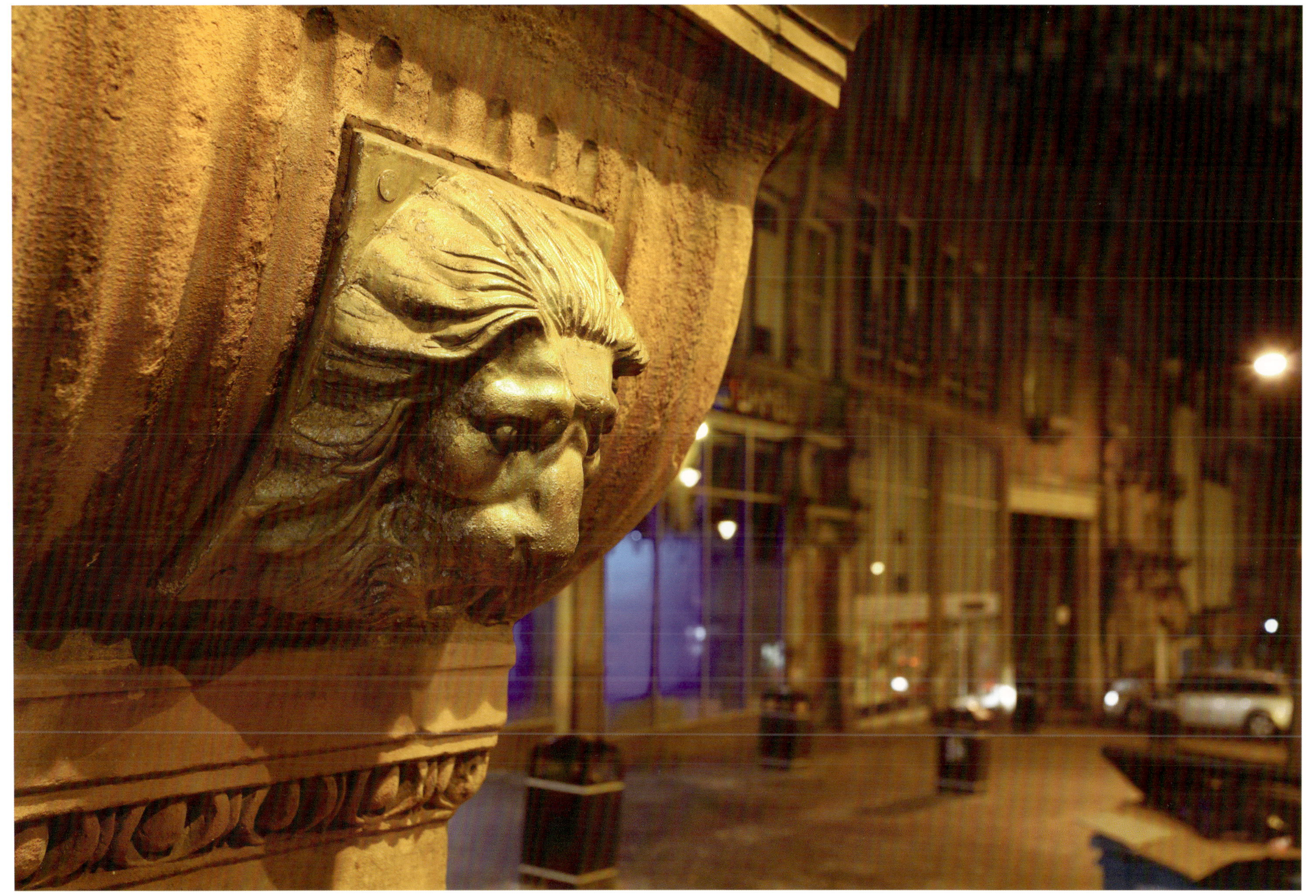

Bigg Market Fountain

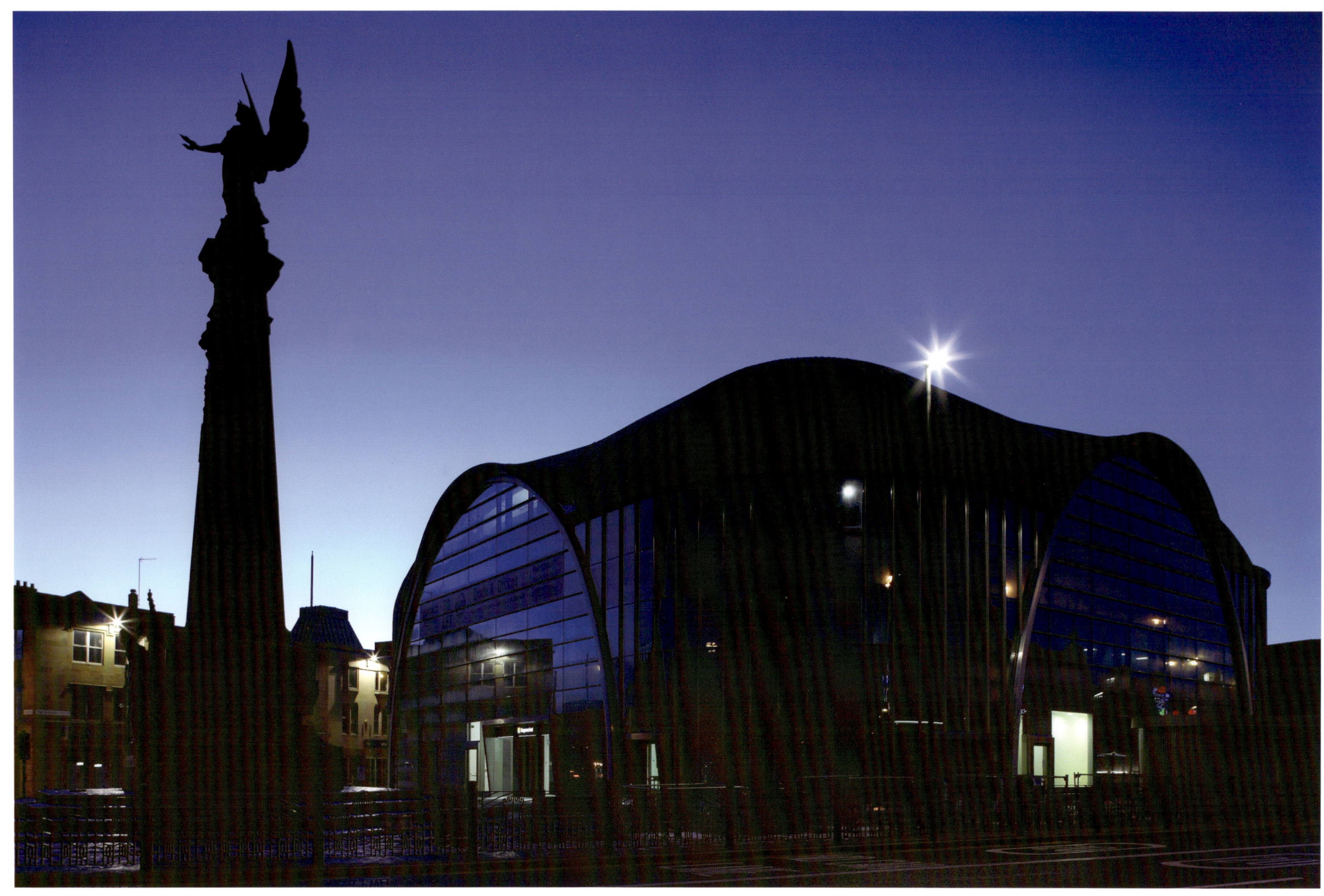

Haymarket and South African War Memorial

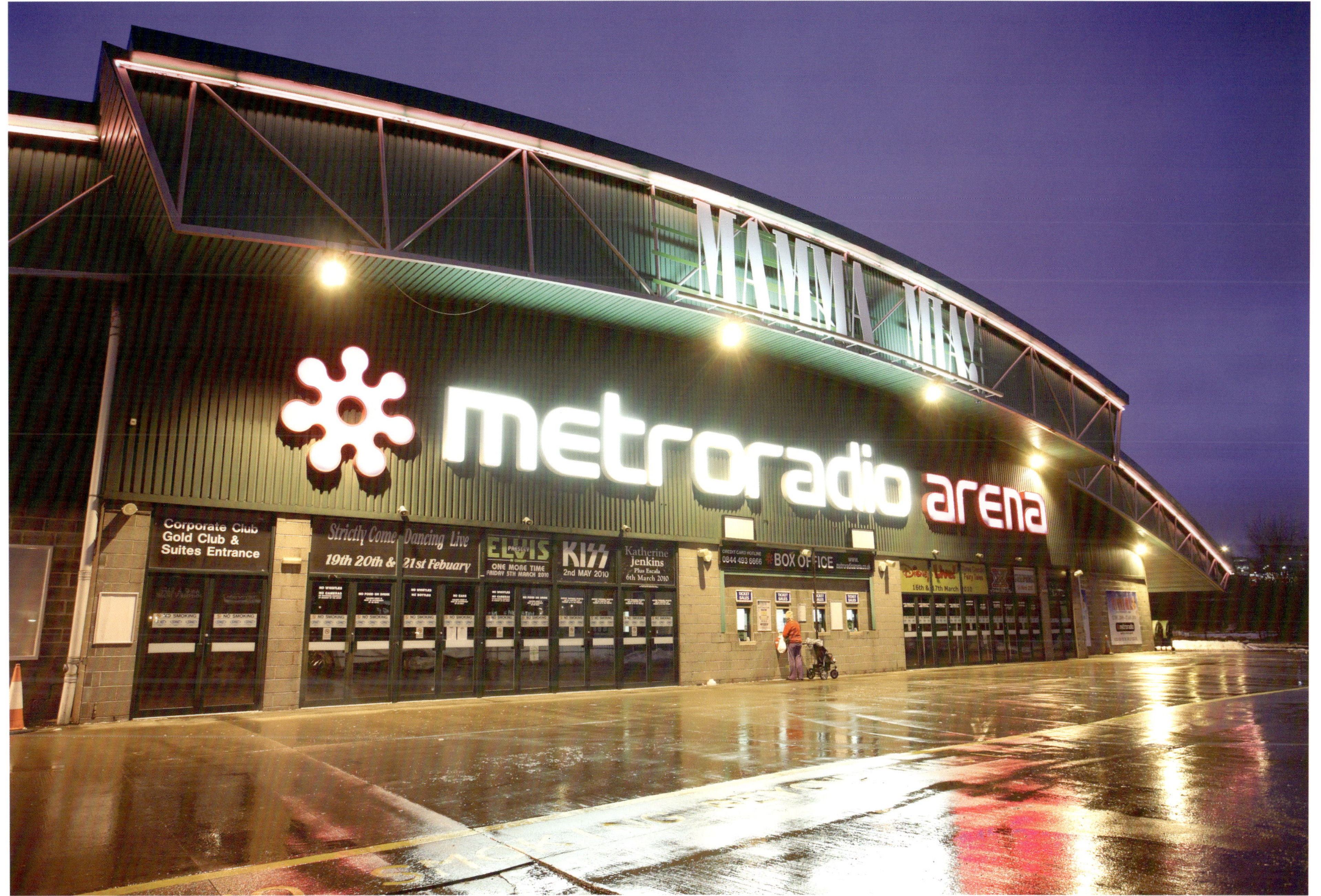

Newcastle Arena

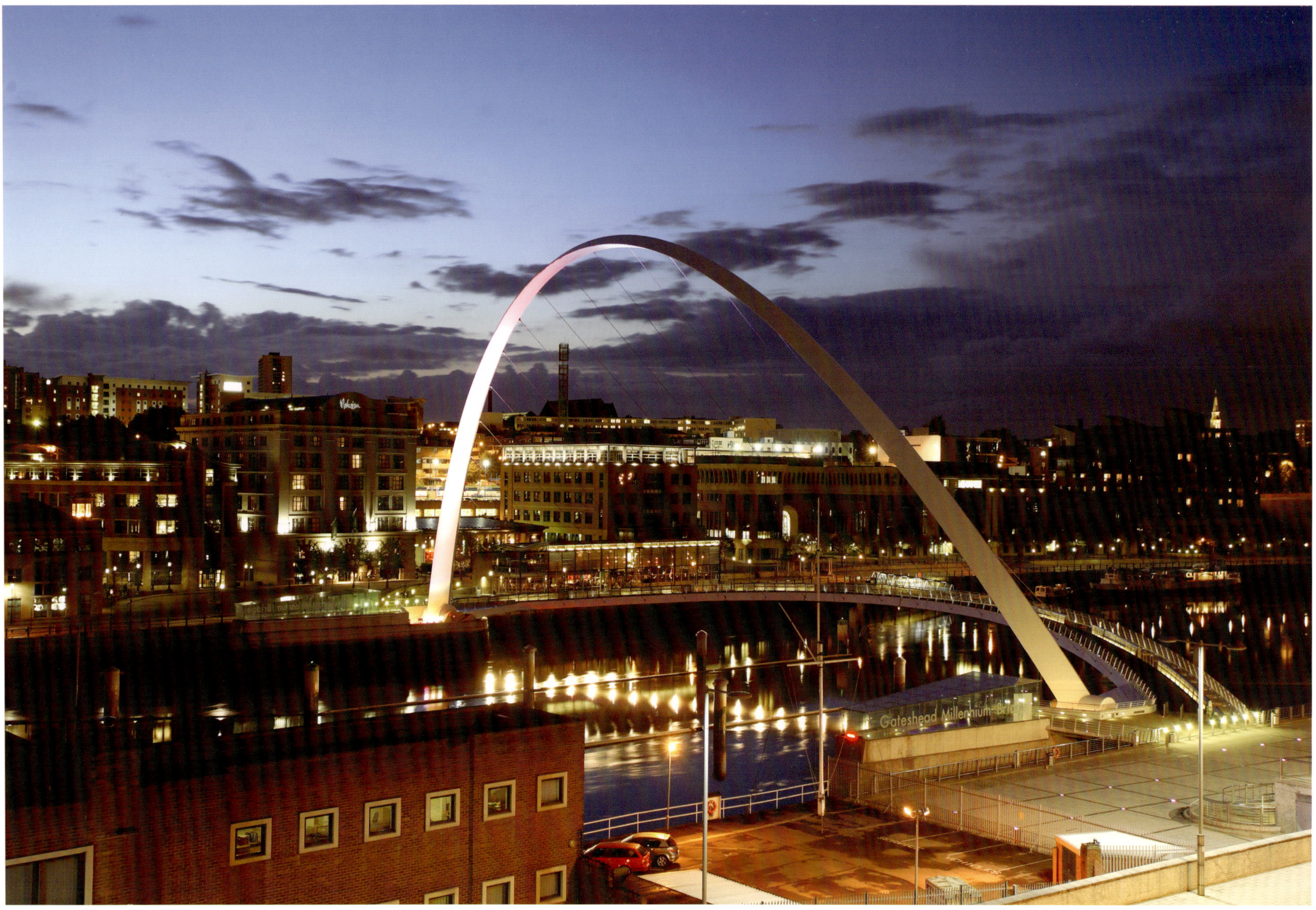

Millenium Bridge

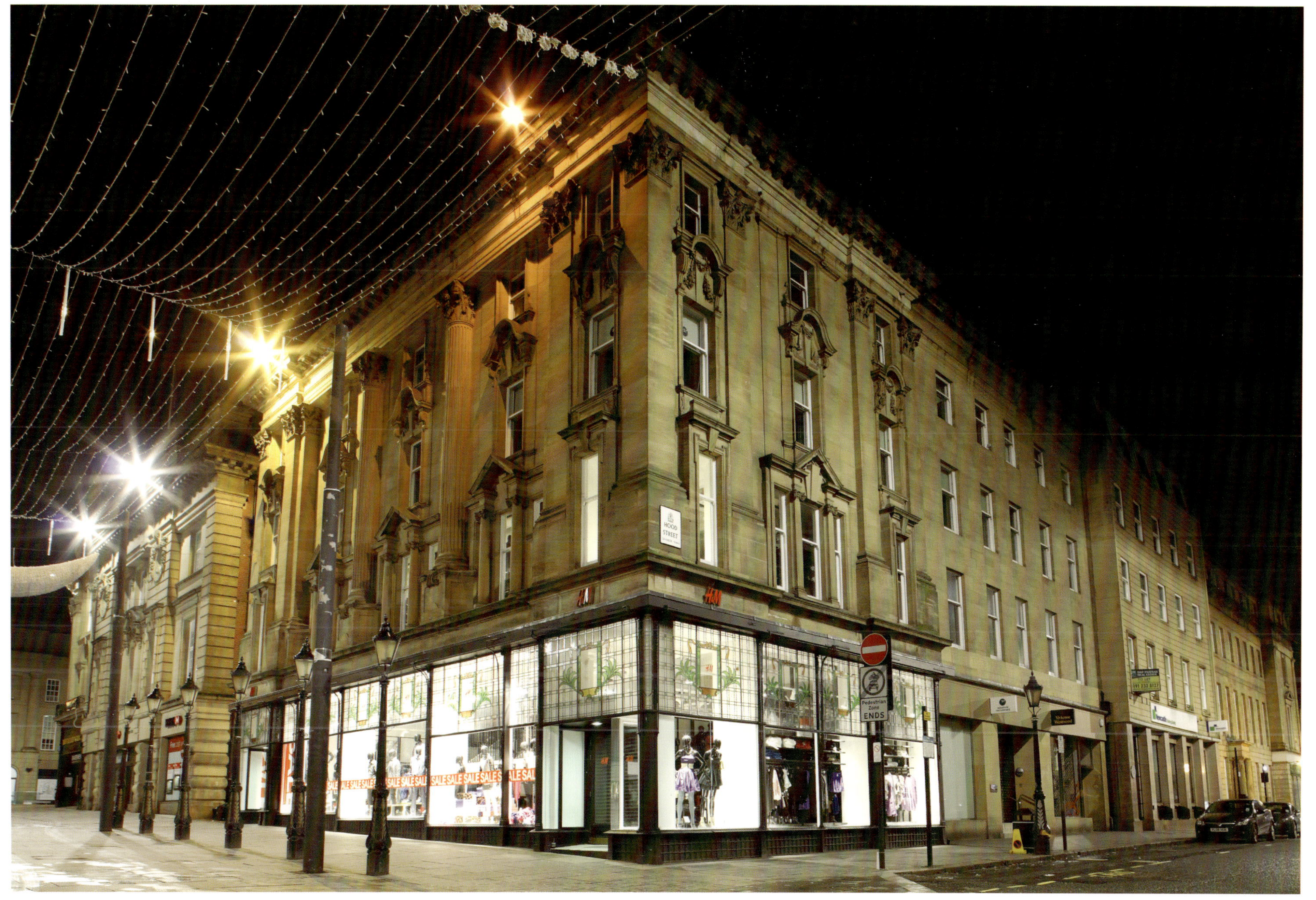

Corner of Hood and Grey Street

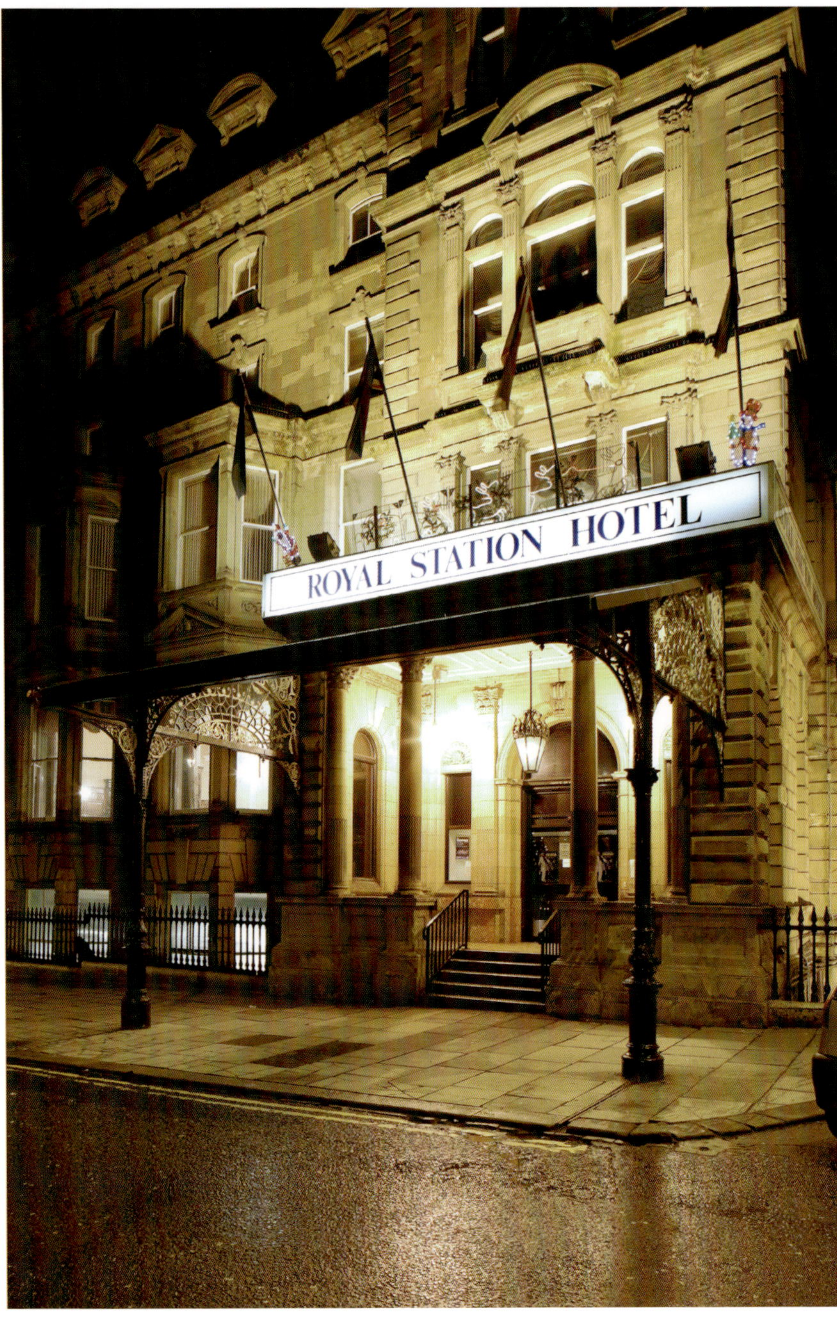

Royal Station Hotel

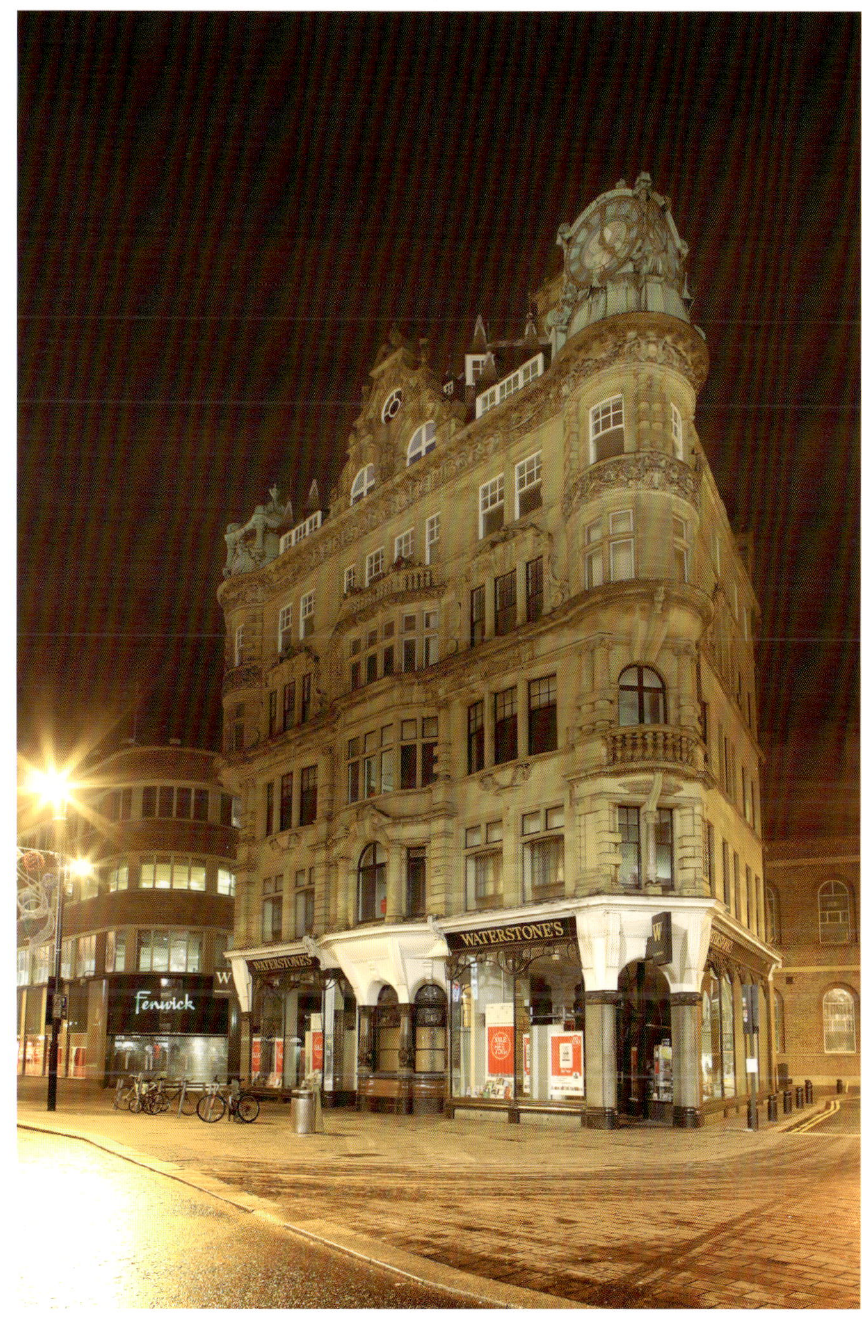

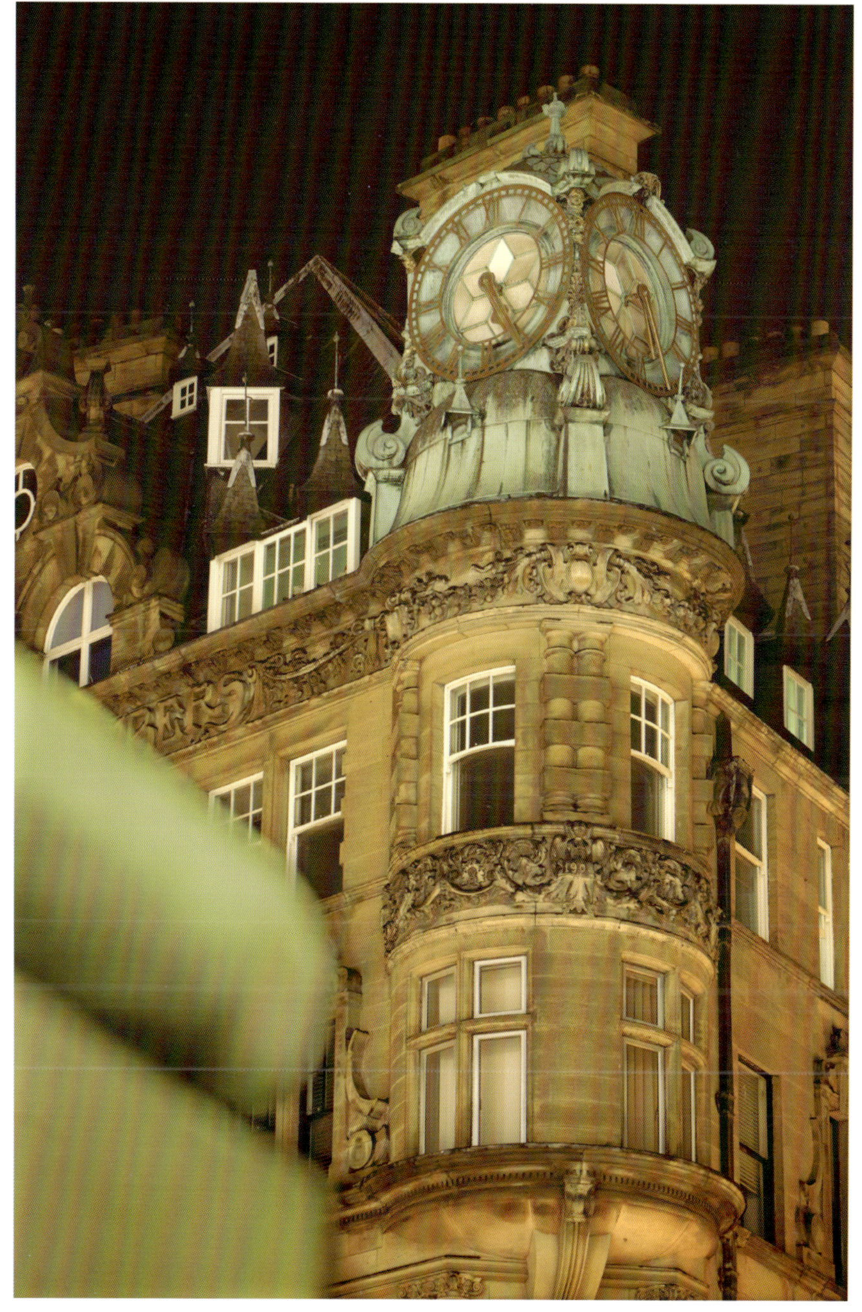

Emerson Chambers - Blackett Street

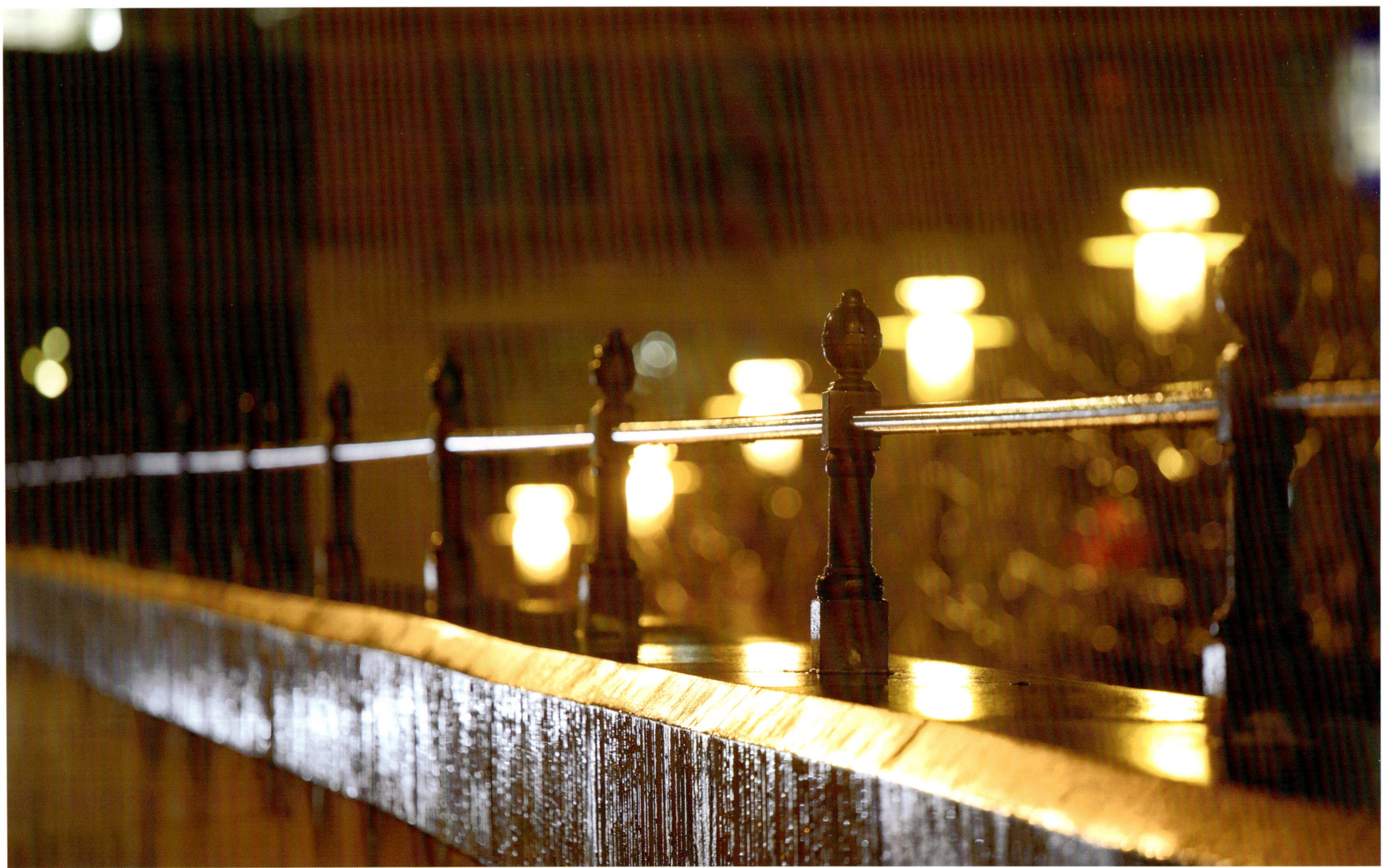

Quayside

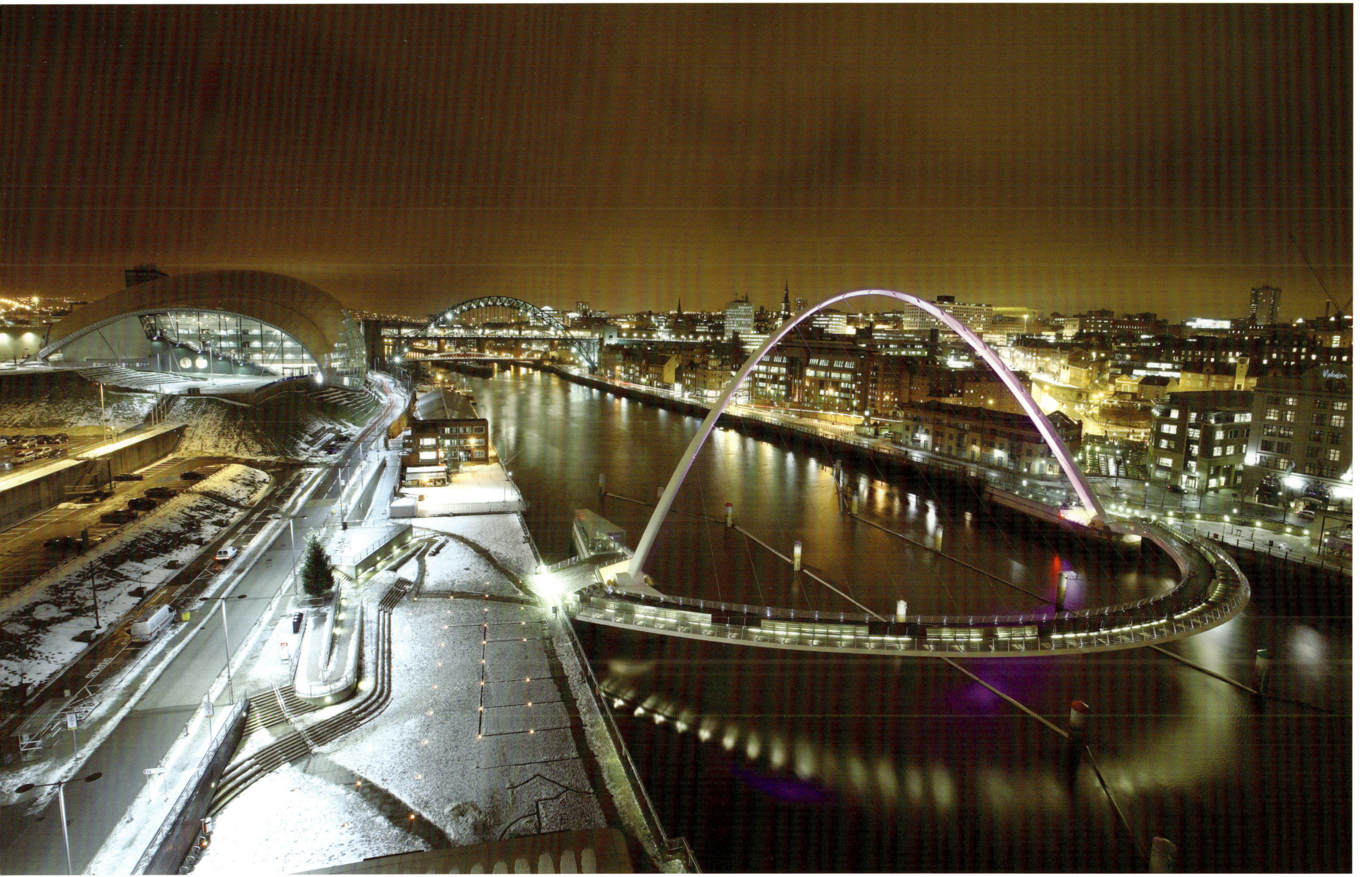

The Tyne

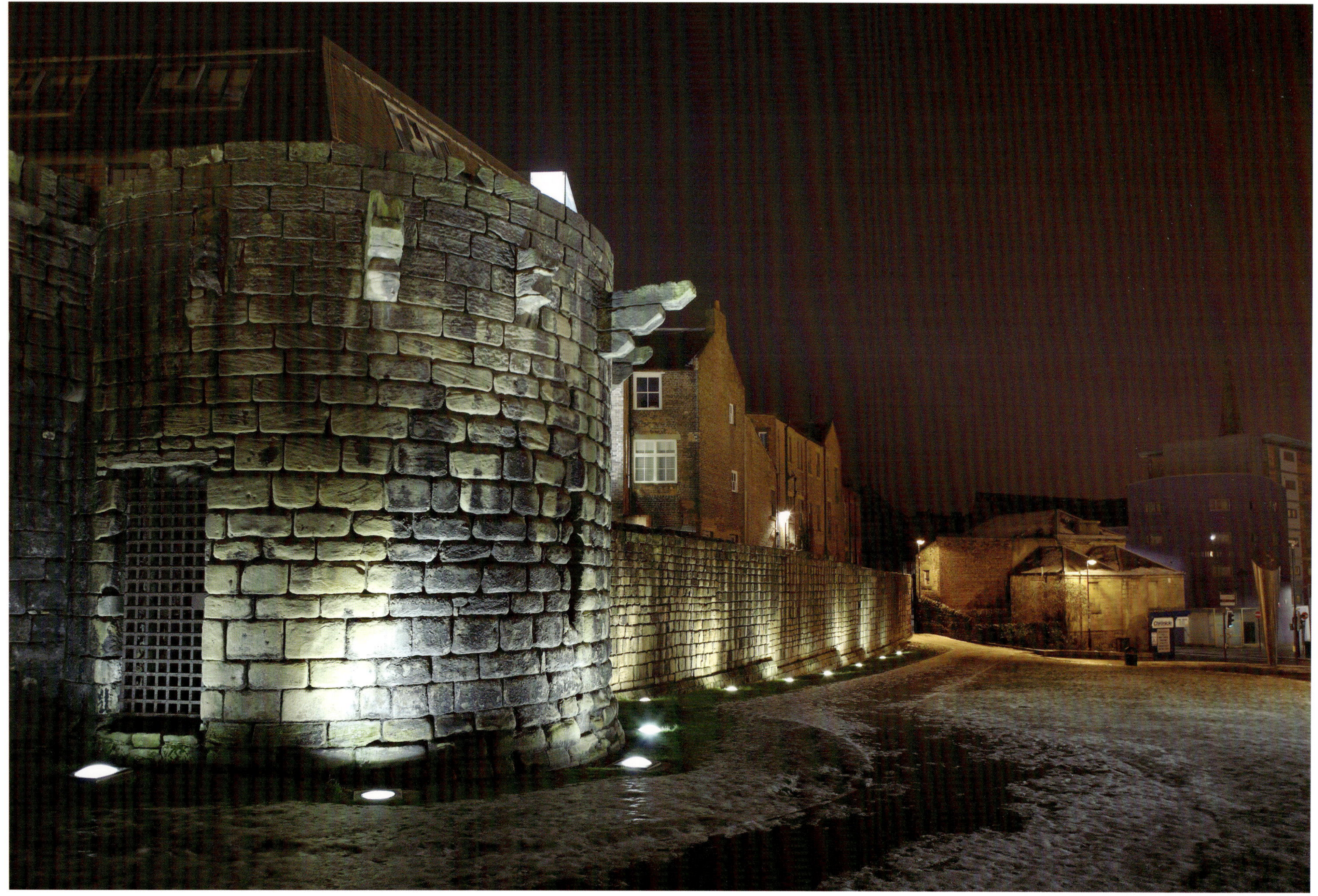

Town Wall

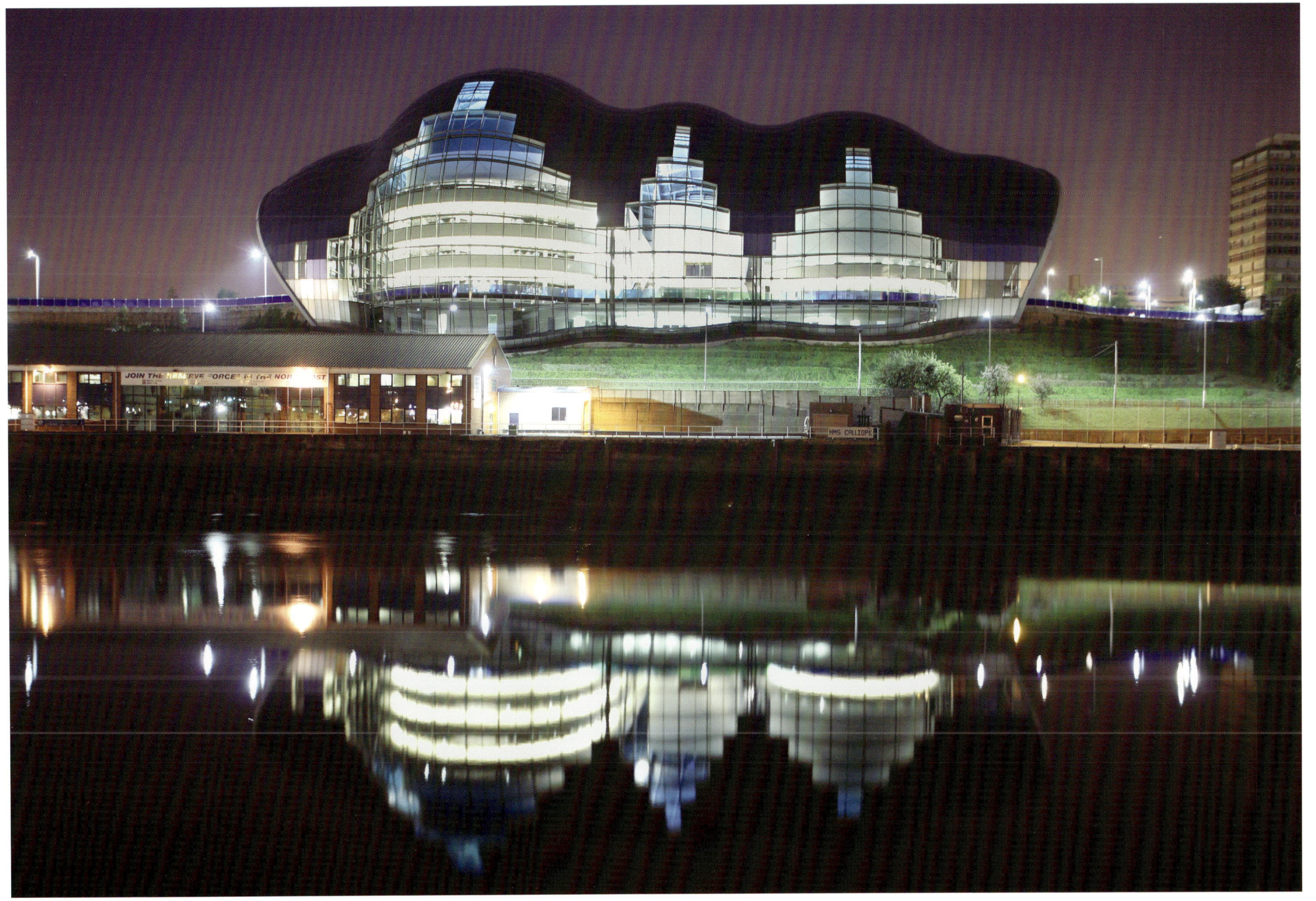

The Sage reflected in the Tyne

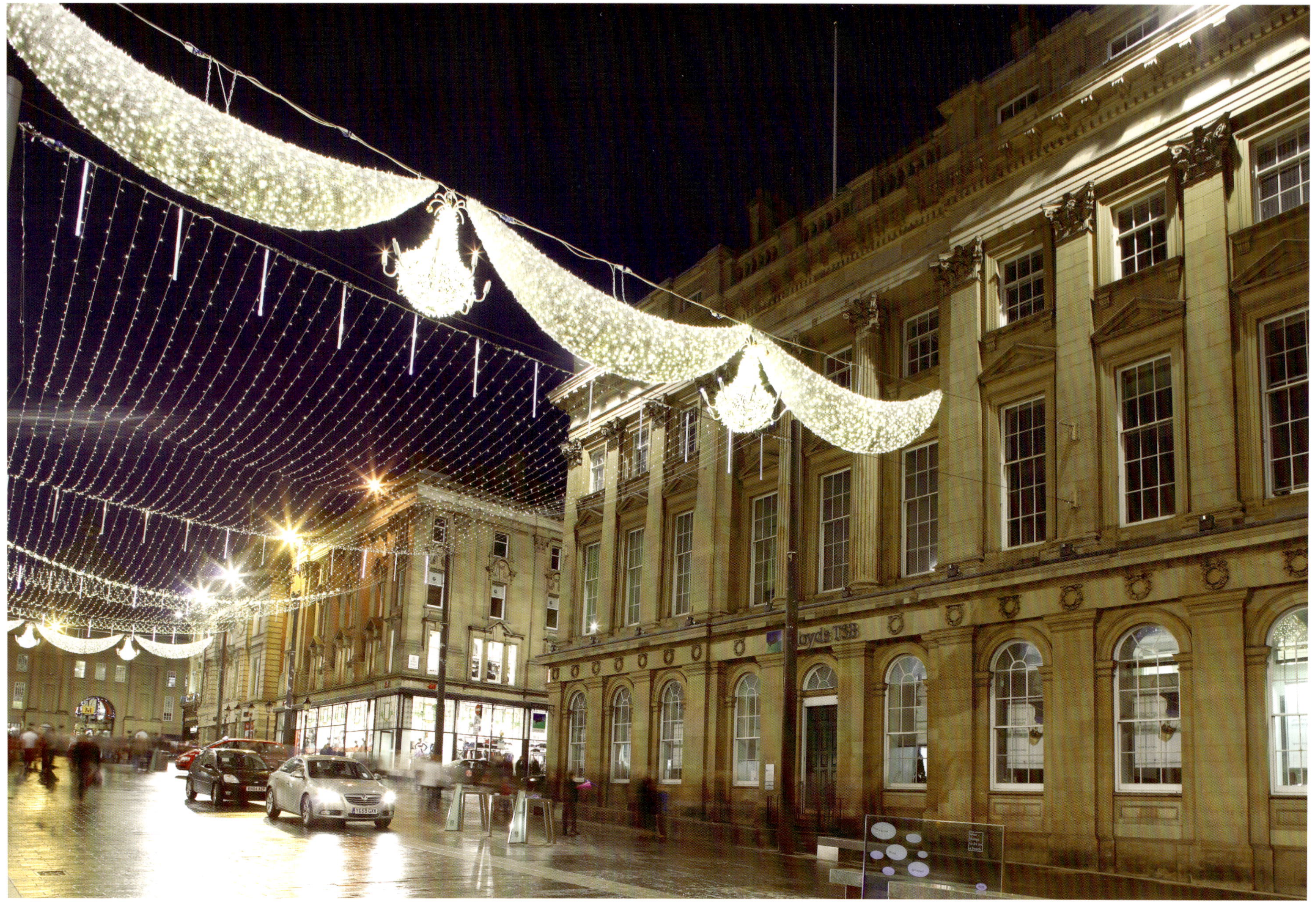

Grey Street

Tyne View

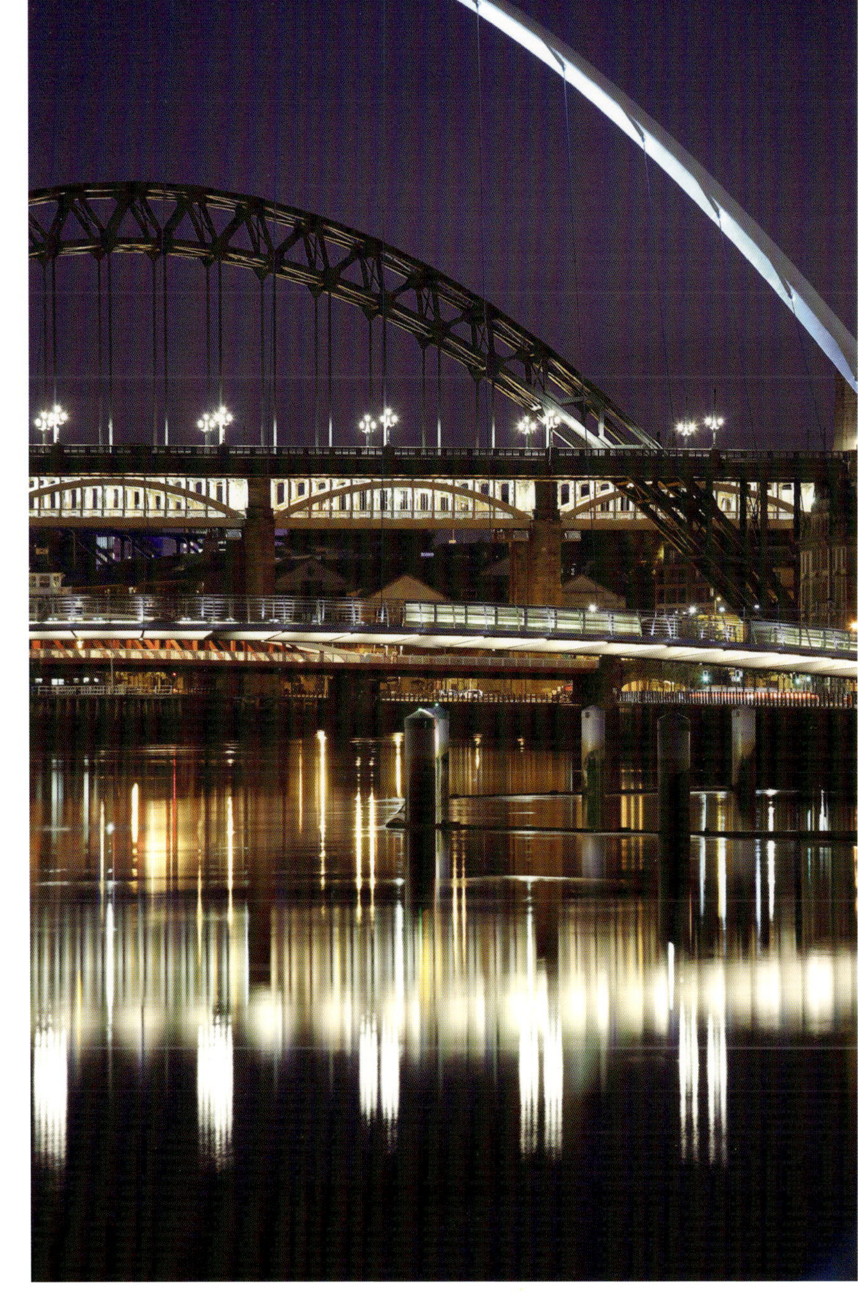

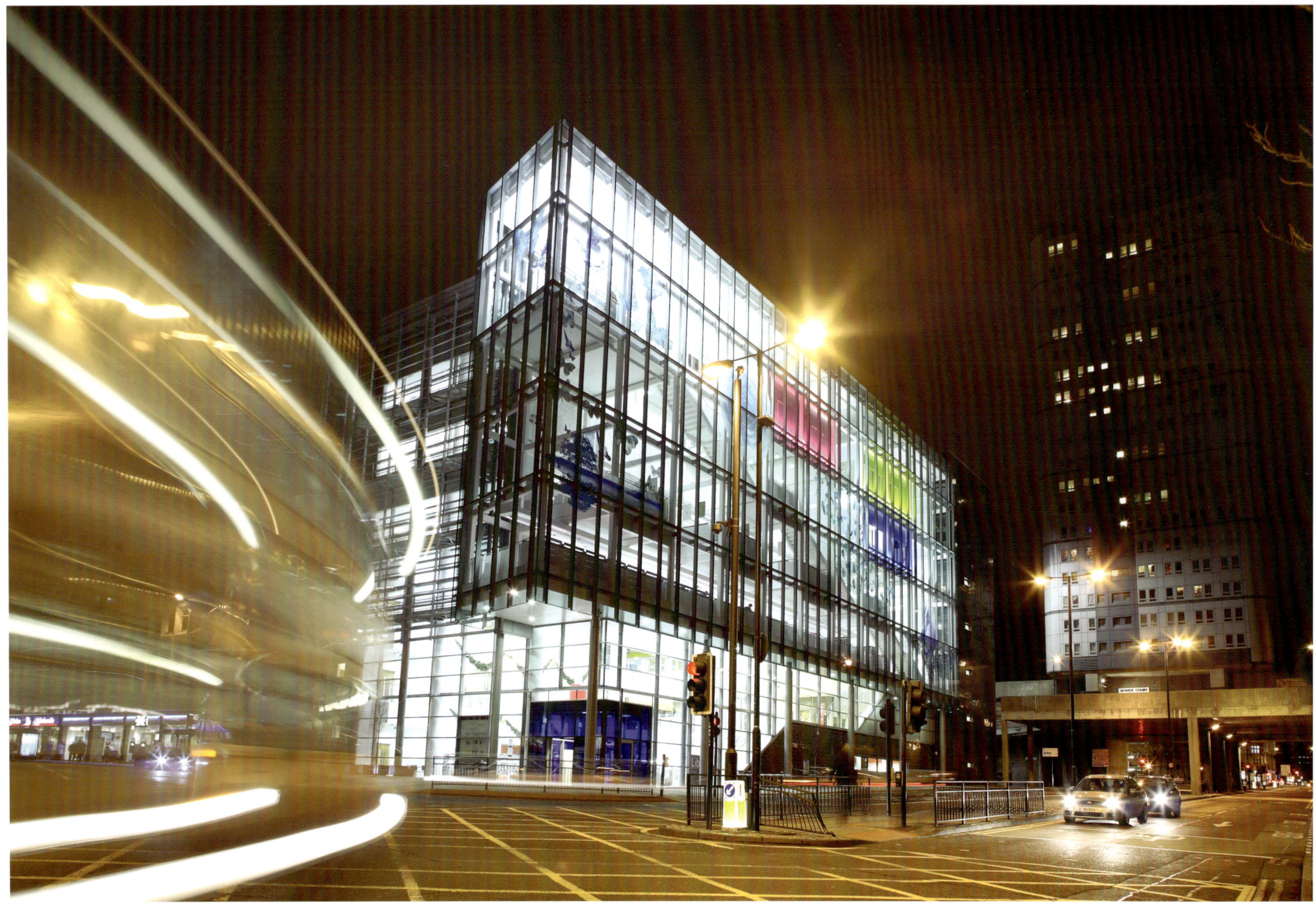

John Dobson Street

All Saints Church

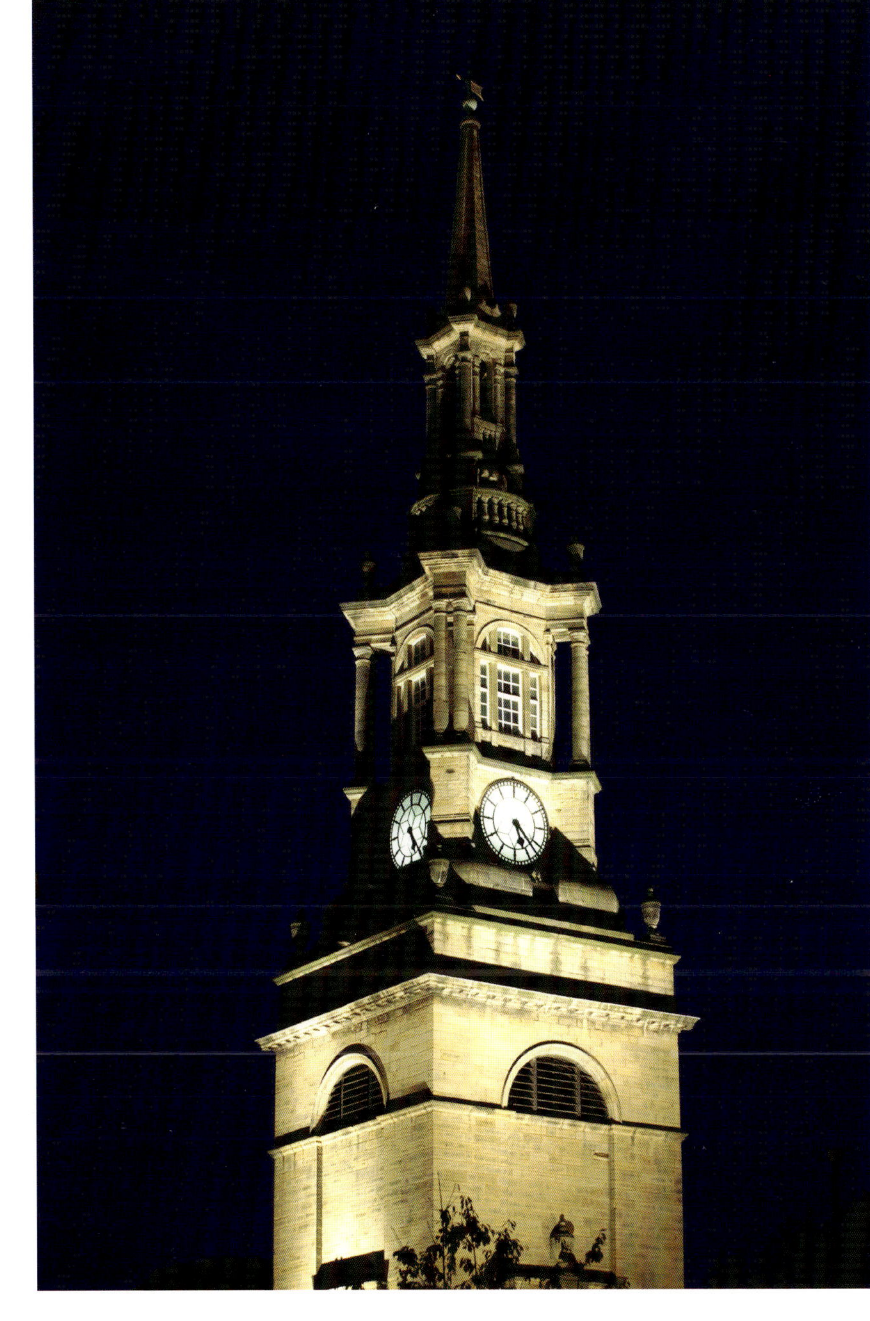

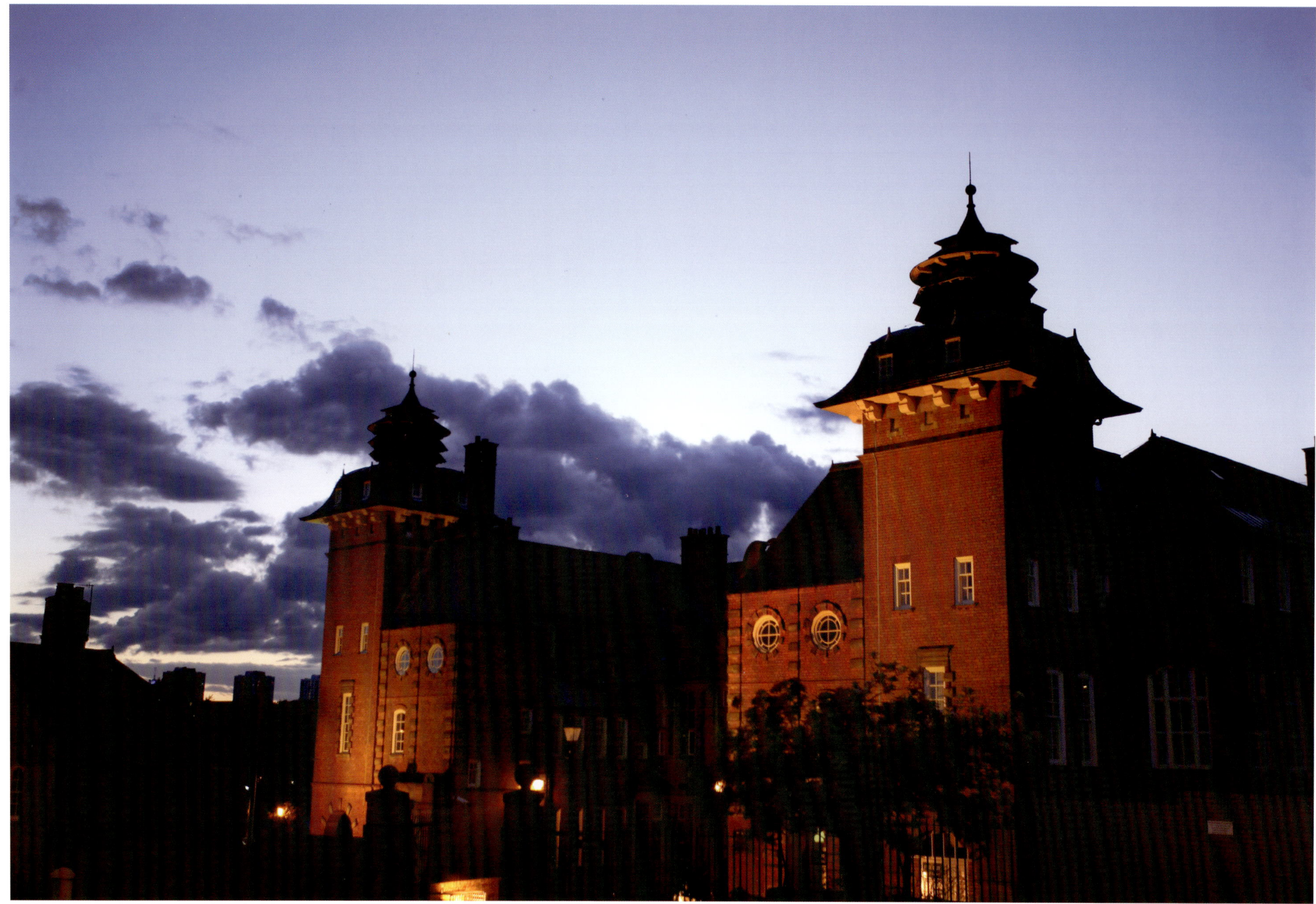

Albion Row

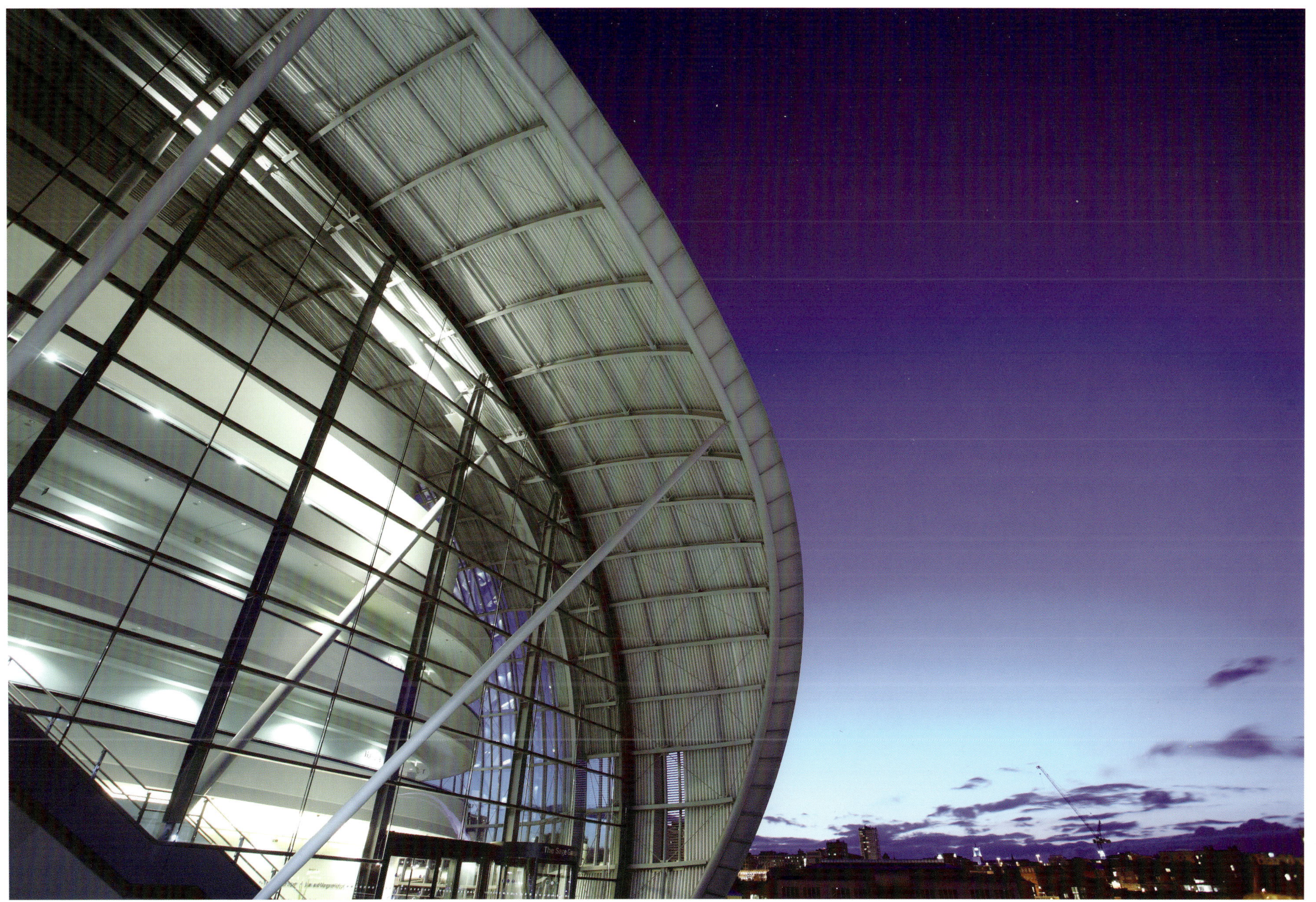

The Sage with Newcastle horizon

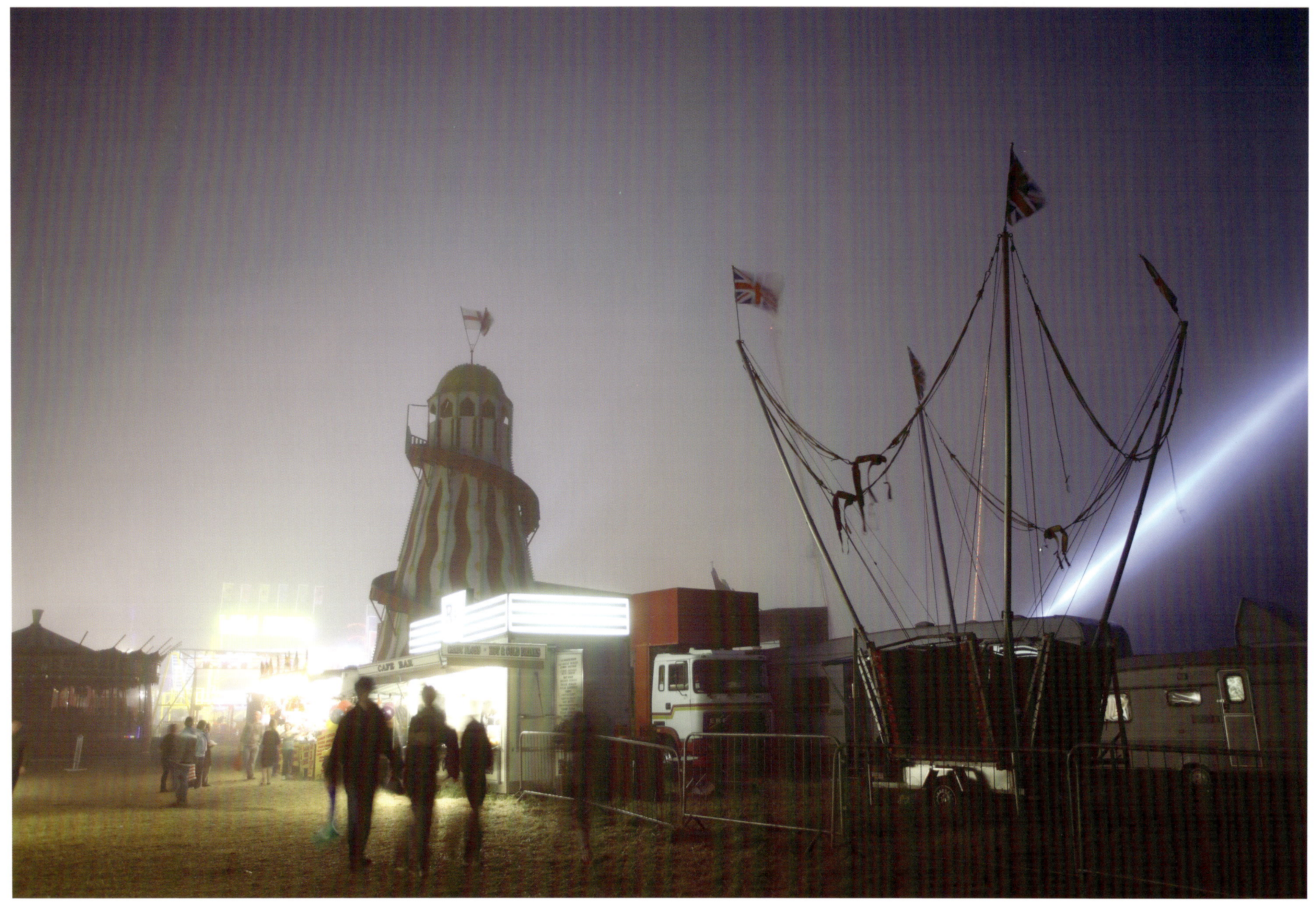

The Hoppings

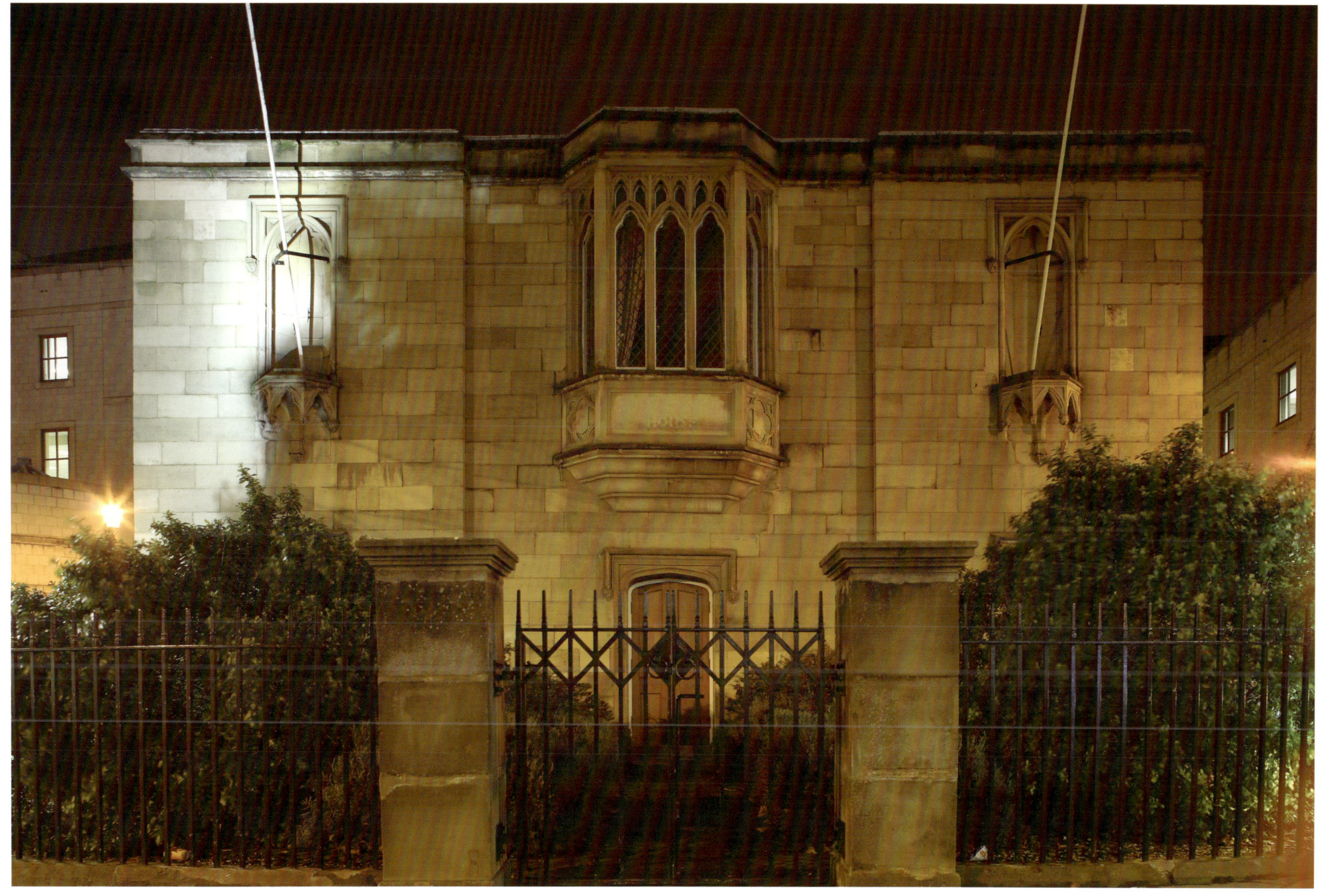

Lying In Hospital

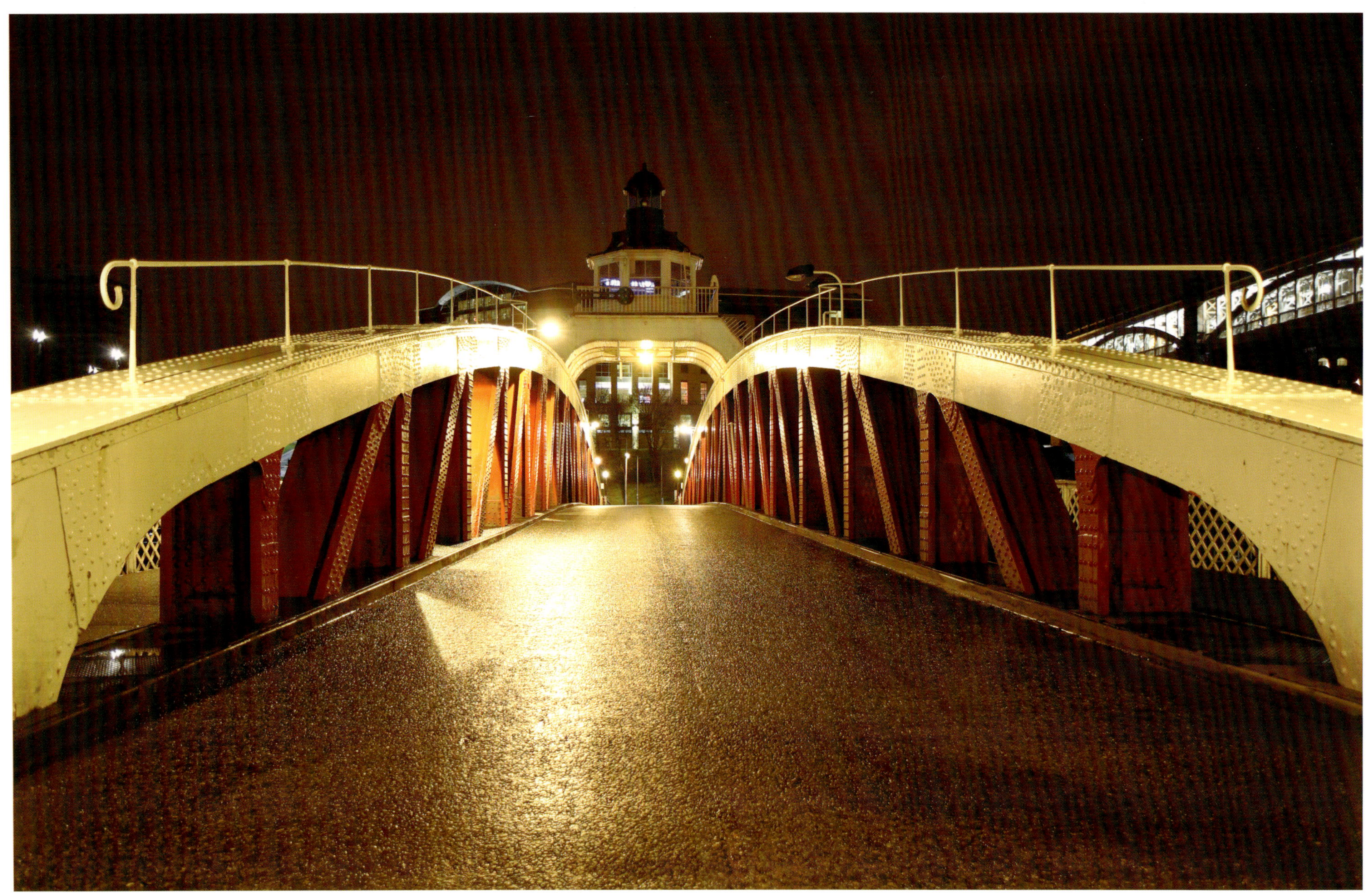

Swing Bridge

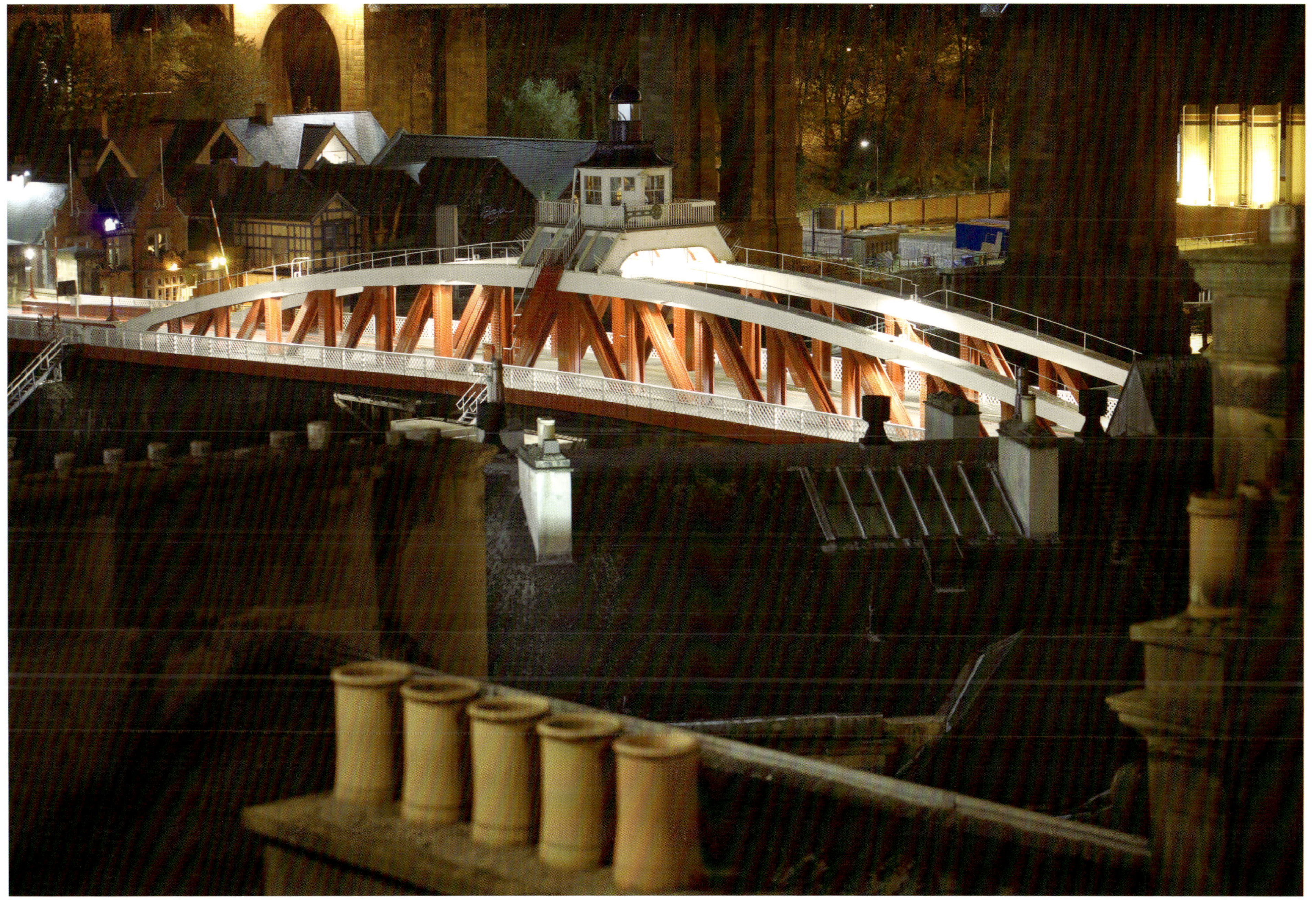

Swing Bridge

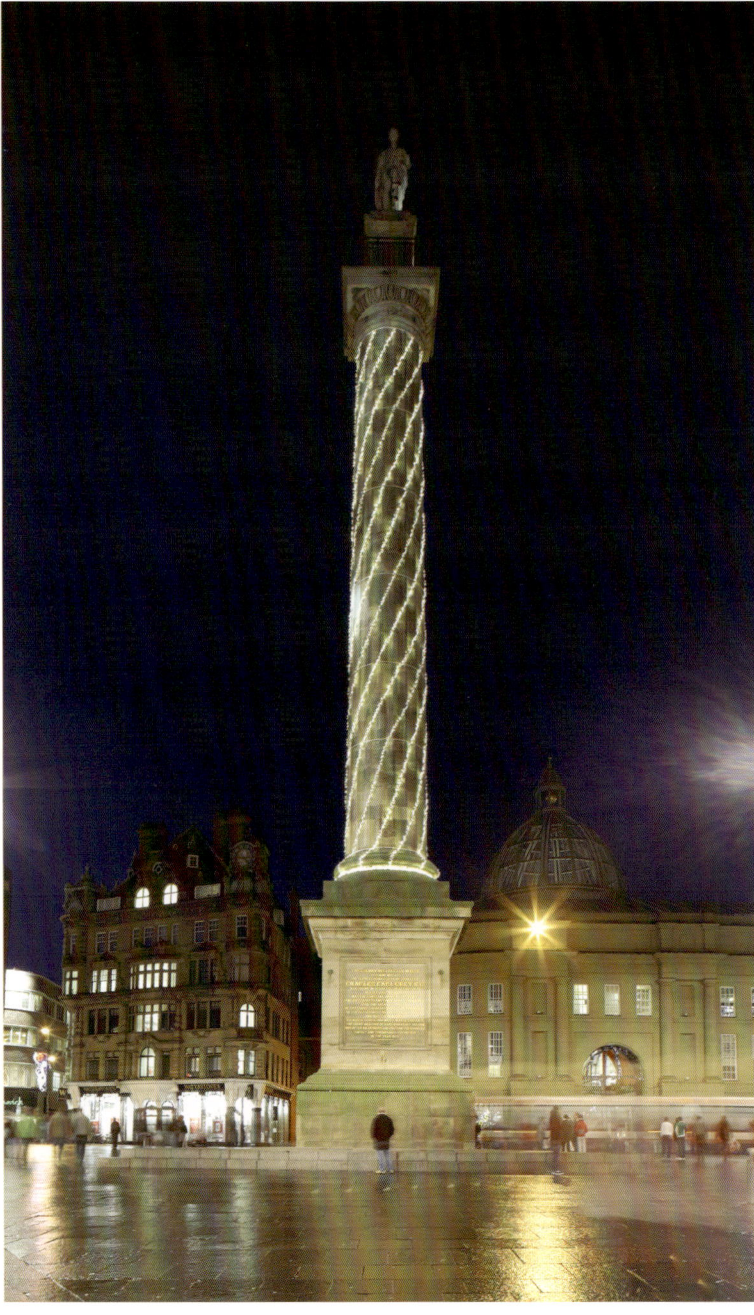

Grey's Monument

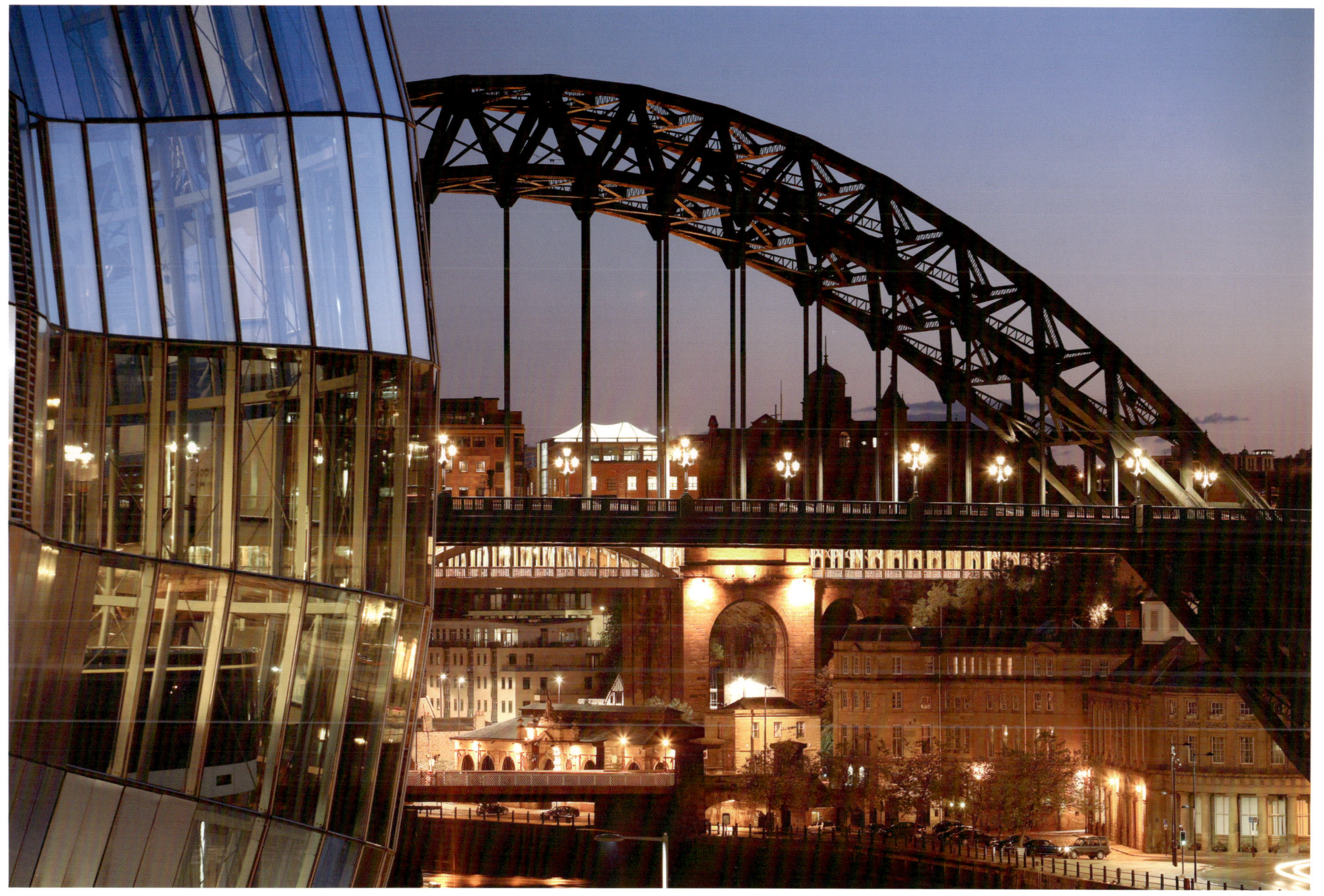

The Sage and The Tyne Bridge

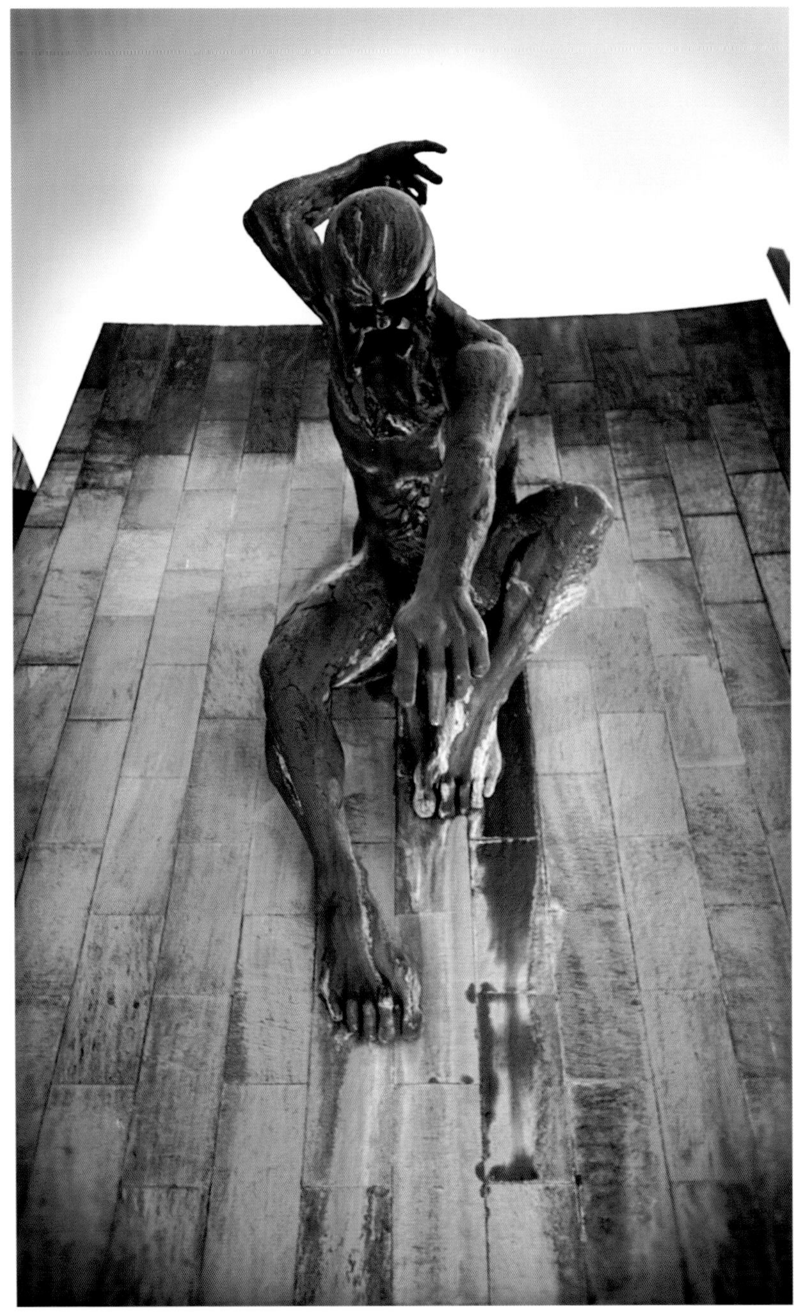

River God Tyne (1968) David Wynne

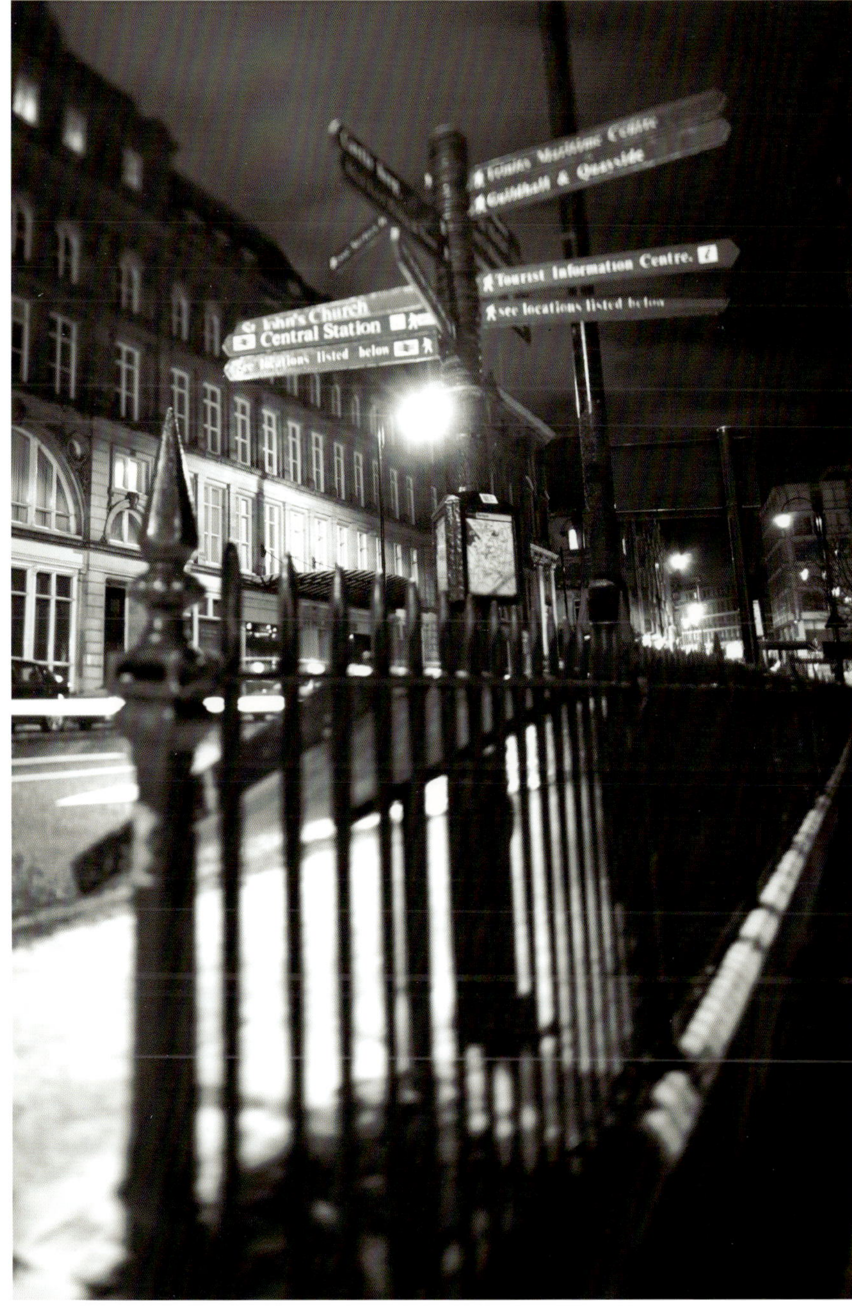

Signpost on St Nicholas Street

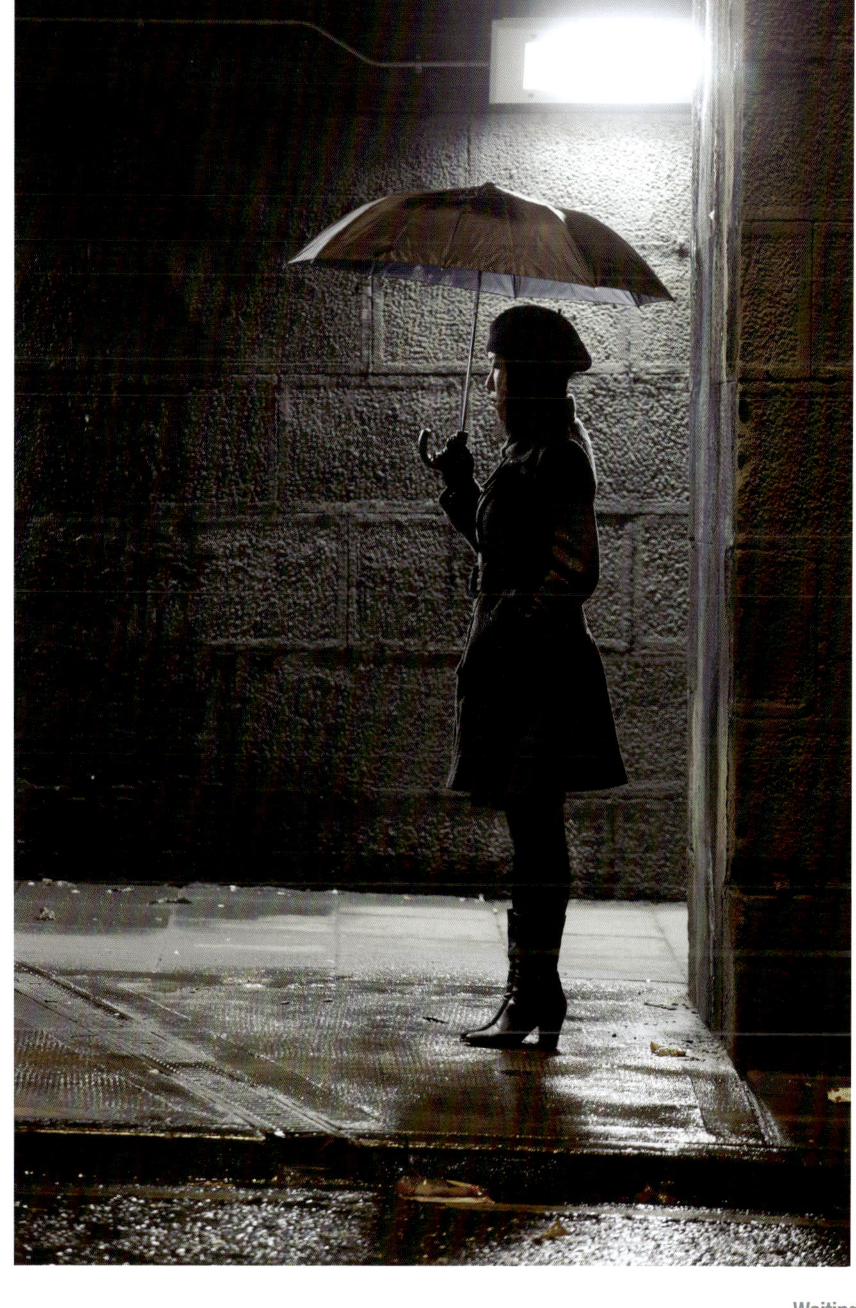

Waiting

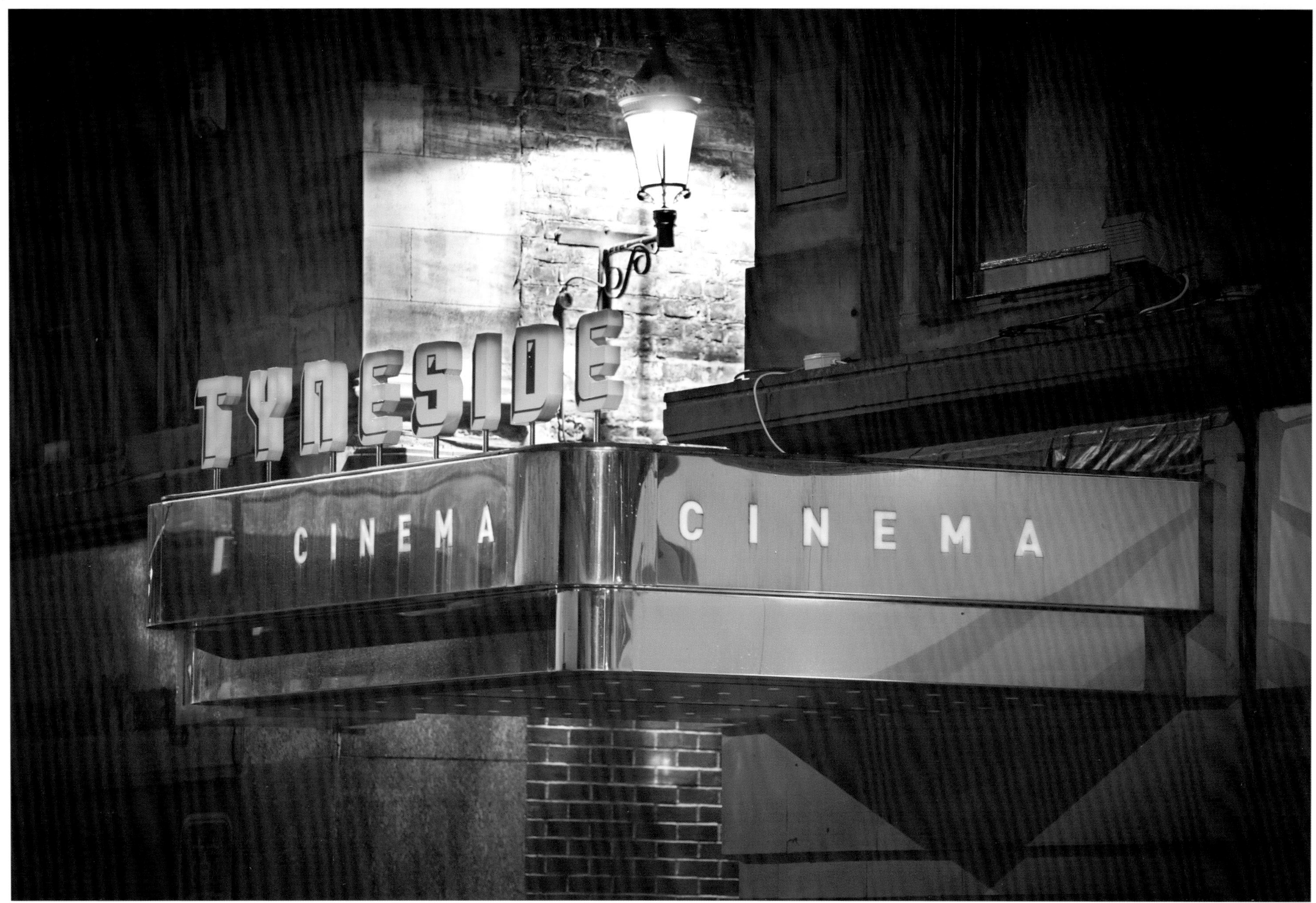

Tyneside Cinema

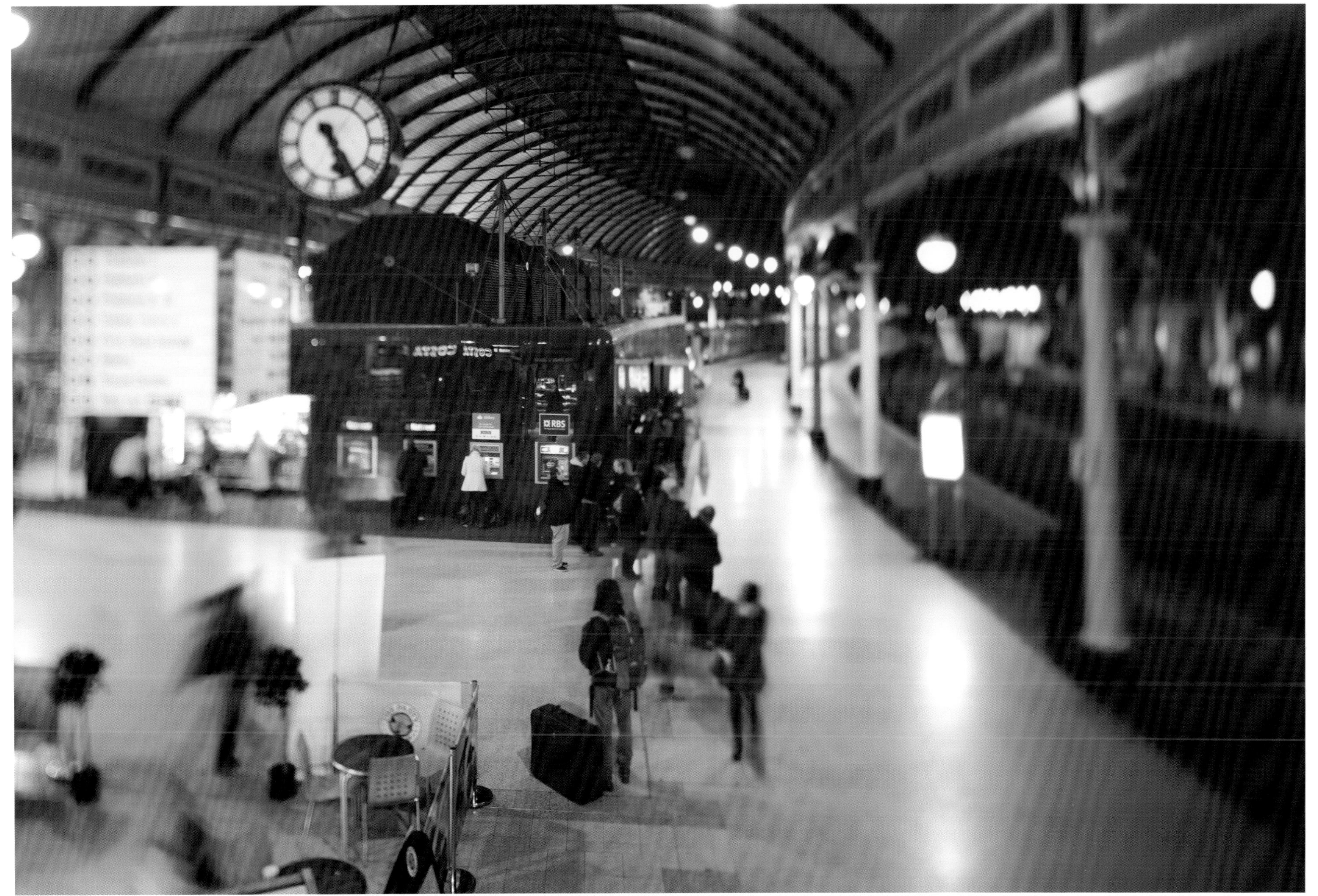

Central Station

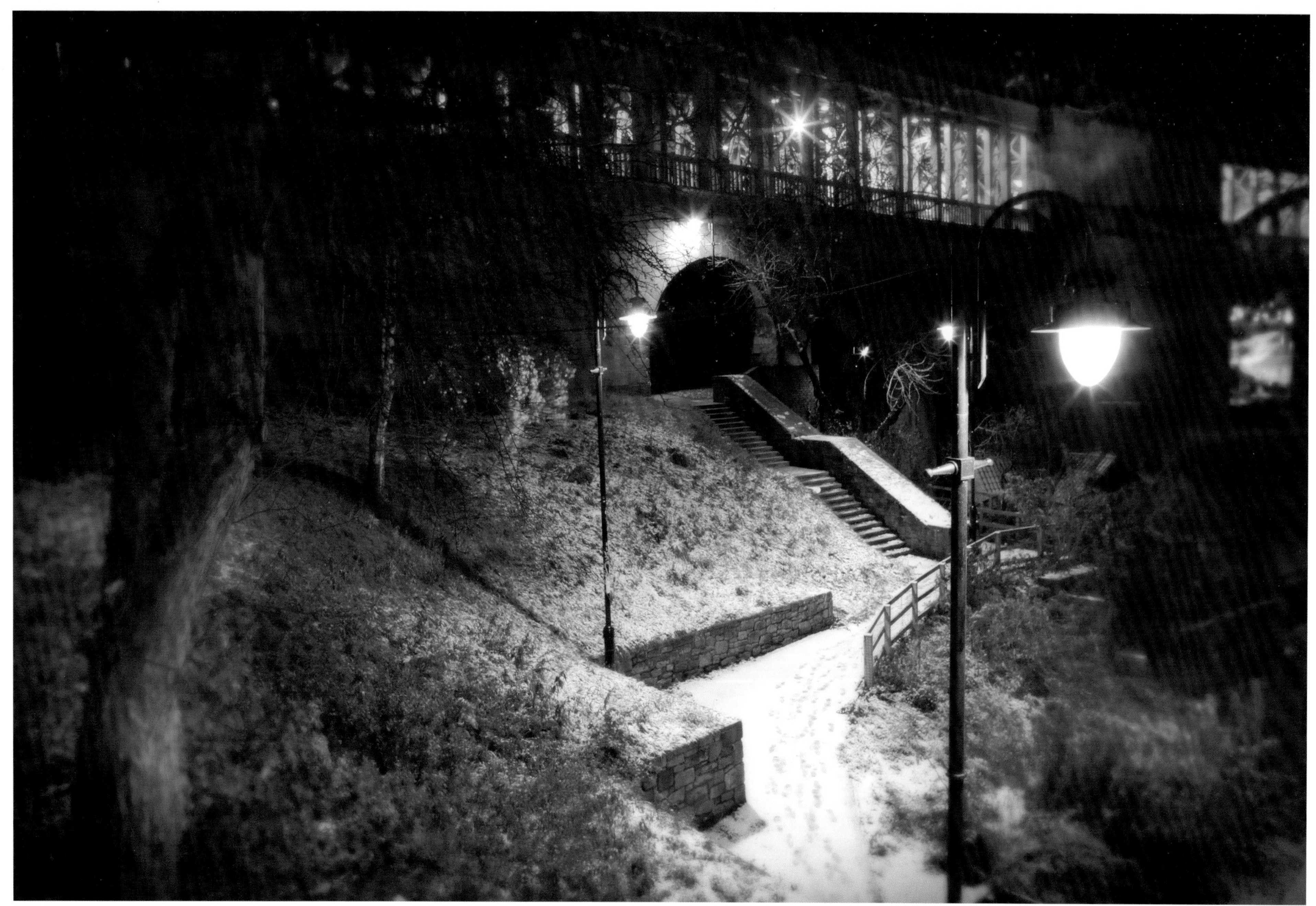

Footpath under High Level Bridge

High Level Bridge

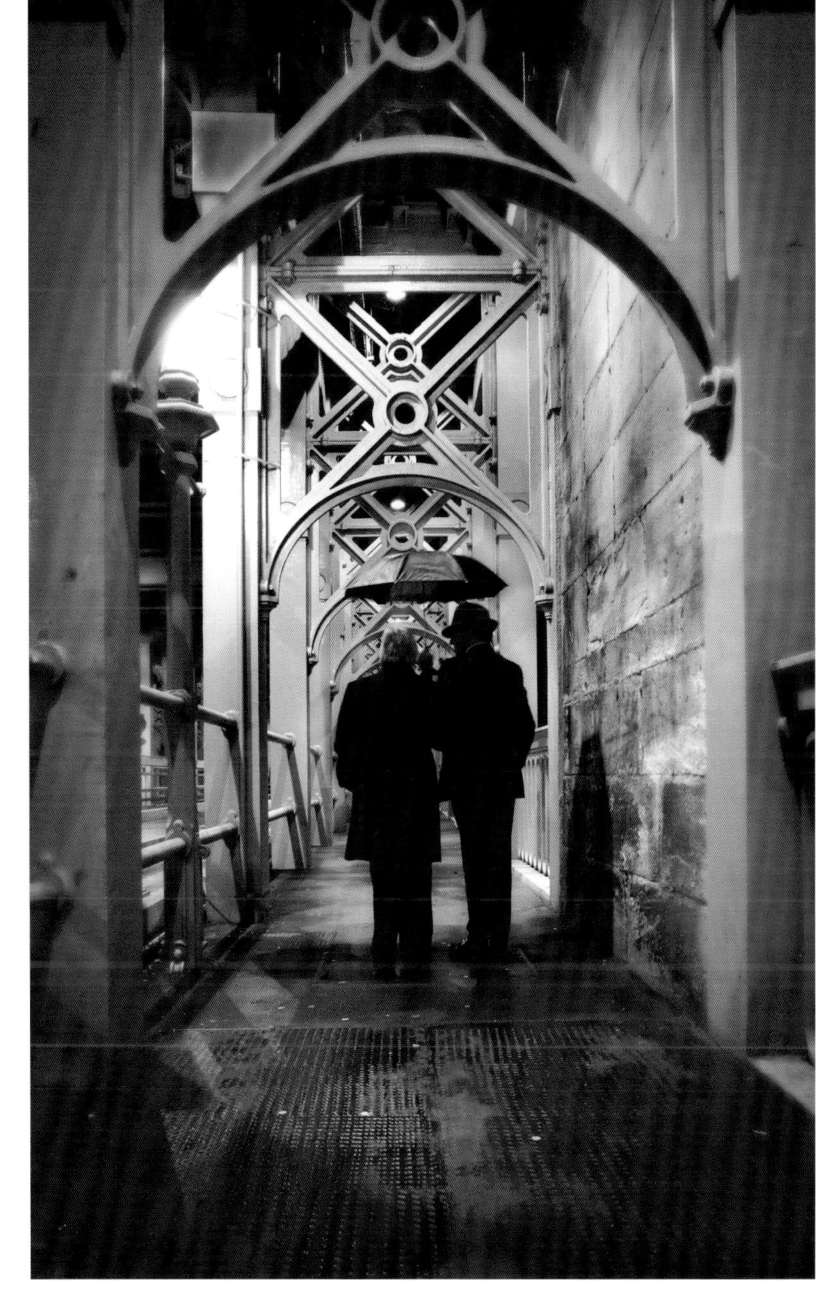

This book is dedicated to my Mam and Dad Jocelyn and Robert

Acknowledgements

A very special thank you to my amazing wife Cristina without whom none of this would have been possible. I would also like to thank my parents and my brother Jonathan for all the advice they have given me with the book. To all my family and friend's who have given me so much support and encouragement over the years, thank you. I would also like to thank all of the amazing Architects of Newcastle past and present for making this book possible.